RECORDED VERSIONS
GUITAR

AUTHENTIC TRANSCRIPTIONS WITH NOTES AND TABLATURE

GUITAR WORLD

50 GREATEST SONGS

50 GREATEST ROCK SONGS OF ALL TIME

ISBN 978-1-4584-1118-1

HAL•LEONARD® CORPORATION

7777 W. BLUEMOUND RD. P.O. BOX 13819 MILWAUKEE, WI 53213

Visit Hal Leonard Online at
www.halleonard.com

Ain't Talkin' 'Bout Love

Words and Music by David Lee Roth, Edward Van Halen, Alex Van Halen and Michael Anthony

*Tune down 1/2 step:
(low to high) Eb-Ab-Db-Gb-Bb-Eb

Intro

Moderate Rock ♩ = 138

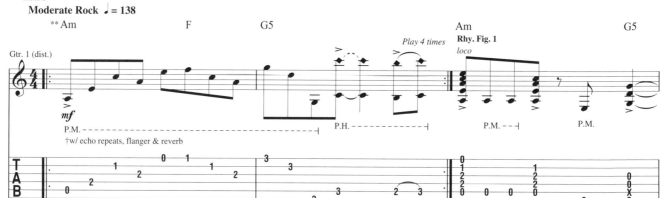

*Recording sounds 1/4 step sharp.
**Chord symbols reflect basic harmony.
†Set echo at approx. 100ms delay.
Set flanger for slow speed w/ regeneration sweep and moderate depth.

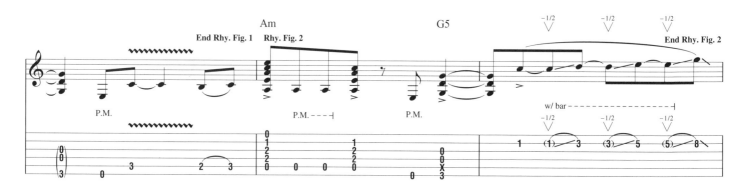

Verse

1. I heard the news, ba-by, all a-bout your dis-ease. ___
   look-in', and on the streets a-gain. ___

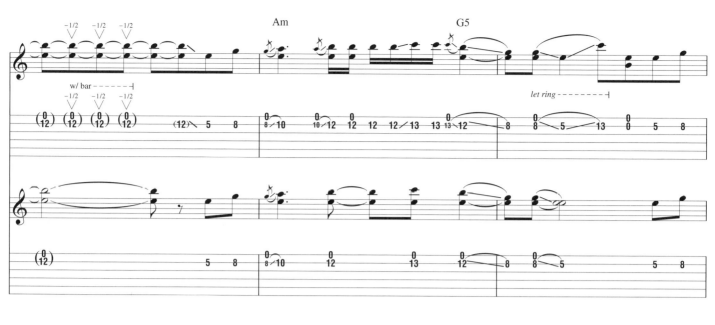

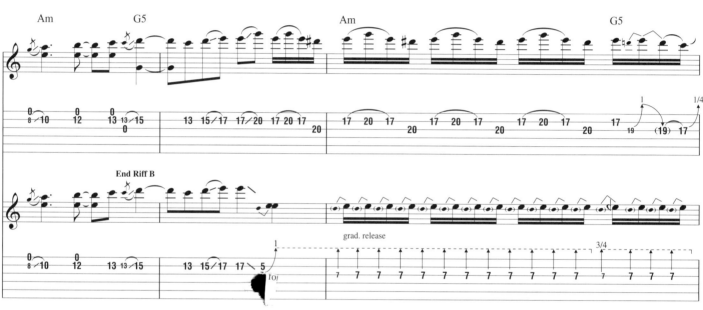

Chorus
Gtr. 1: w/ Rhy. Fig. 1 (3 times)
Gtr. 2 tacet

Ain't talk - in' 'bout love. Babe, it's a rot - ten to the core. __

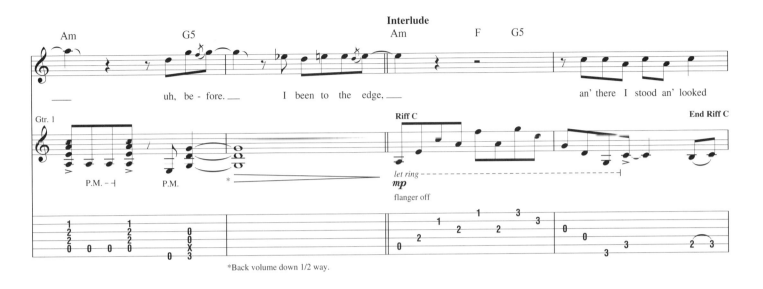

*Back volume down 1/2 way.

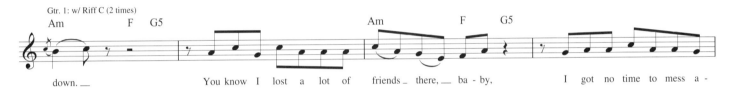

Chorus

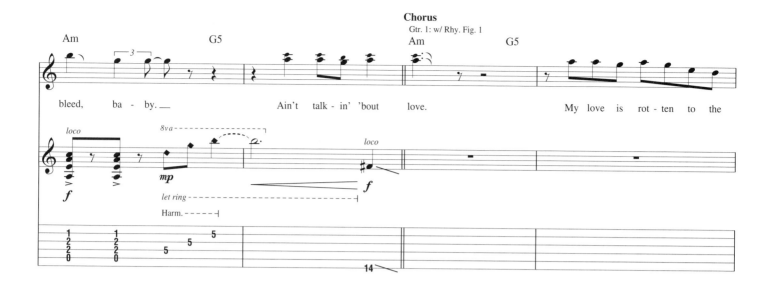

bleed, ba - by.___ Ain't talk - in' 'bout love. My love is rot - ten to the

core. ___ Ain't talk - in' 'bout love. Just like I told you be - fore, ___

___ be - fore, be - fore. ___ Ain't talk - in' 'bout love. Don't wan - na talk a - bout

love. Don't need to talk a - bout love. Ain't gon - na talk a - bout

10

from The Jimi Hendrix Experience - *Electric Ladyland*

All Along the Watchtower

Words and Music by Bob Dylan

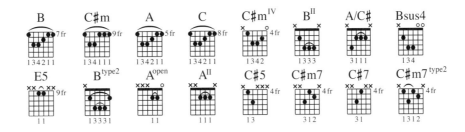

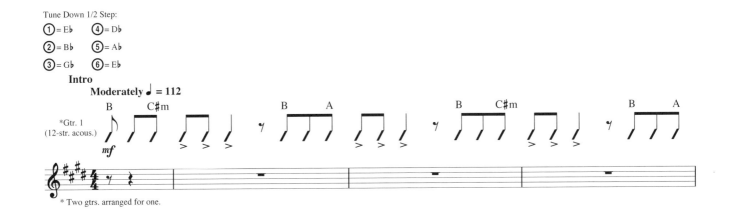

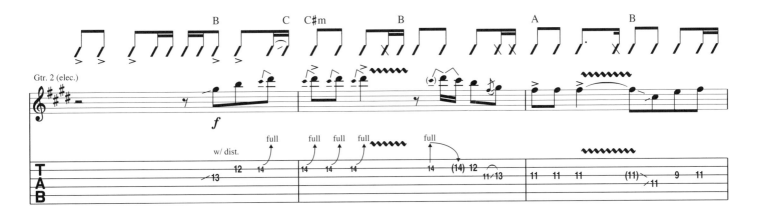

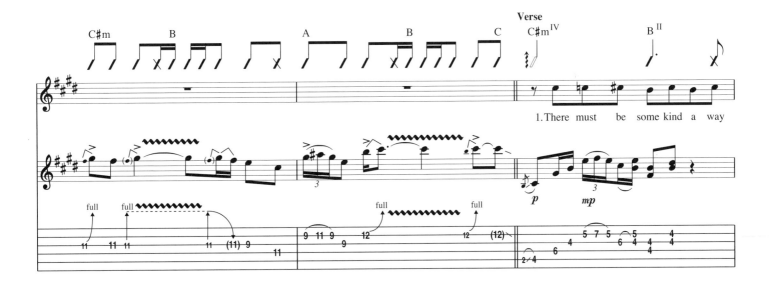

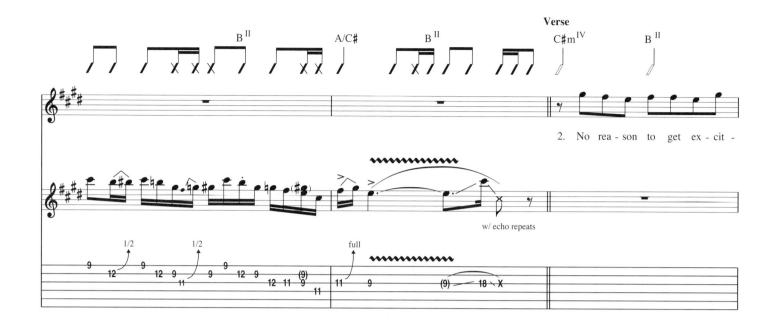

2. No rea-son to get ex-cit-

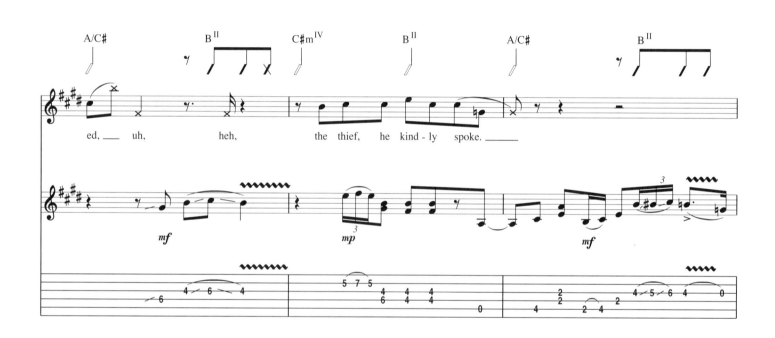

ed, ___ uh, heh, the thief, he kind-ly spoke. _____

There are man-y here a-mong us who feel that life _ is but a joke. _

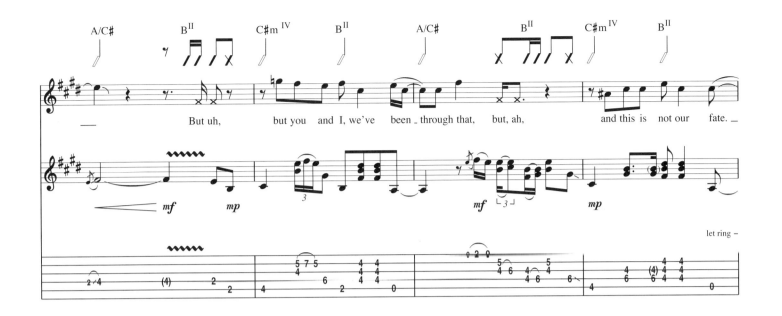

But uh, but you and I, we've been through that, but, ah, and this is not our fate.

So let us not talk false-ly now, the ho-ur's get-tin' late,

* Played ahead of the beat.

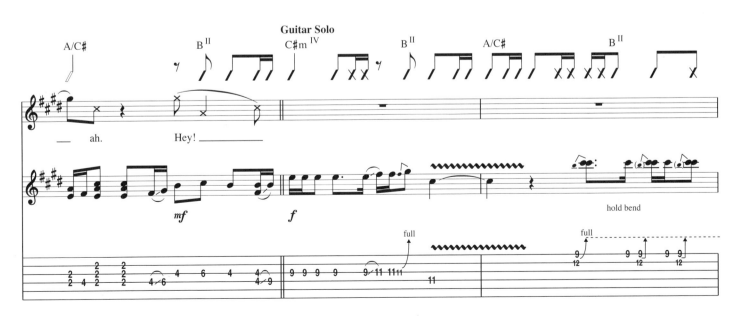

Guitar Solo

ah. Hey!

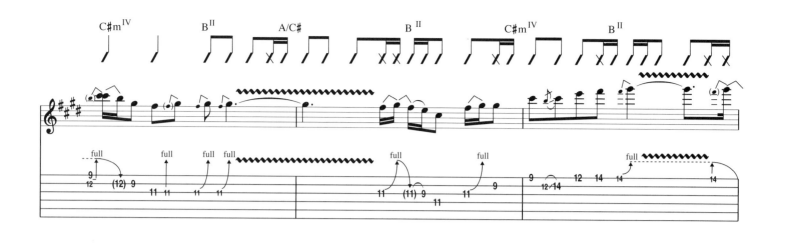

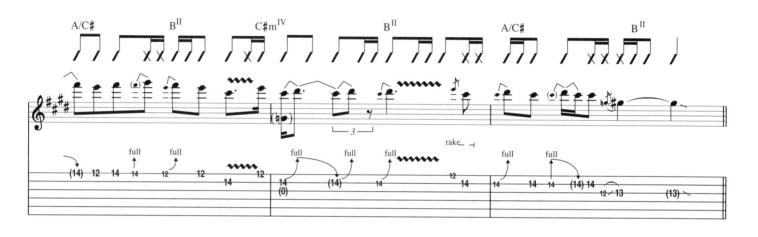

Interlude

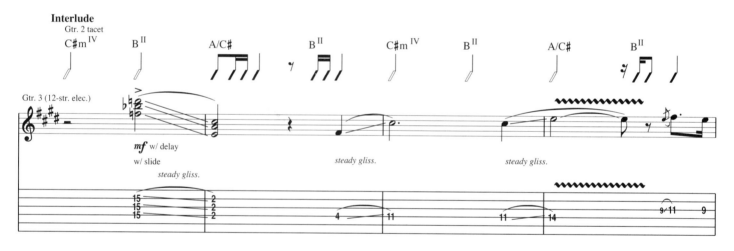

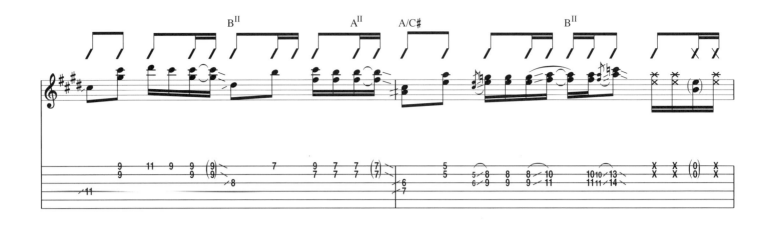

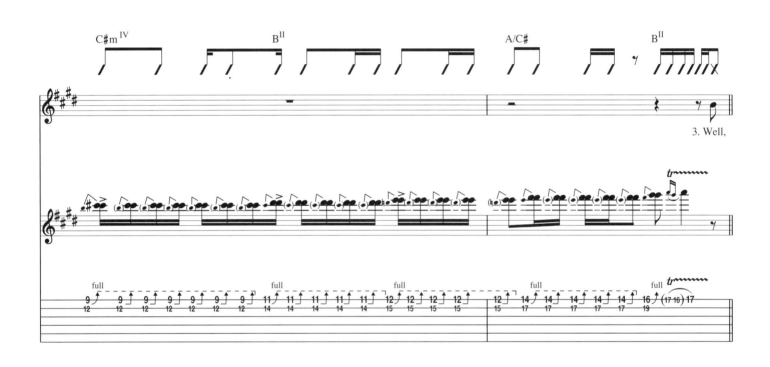

While all the wo-men came ____ and went,   bare feet ser-vants too. ____

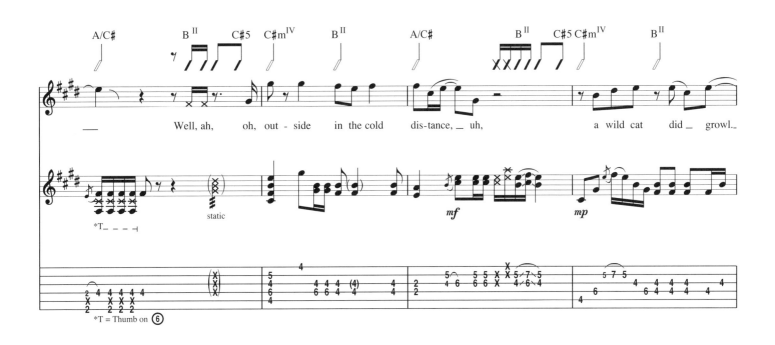

____ Well, ah, oh, out-side in the cold dis-tance, _ uh,   a wild cat did _ growl. ____

*T = Thumb on ⑥

____ ____   Two rid-ers were ap-proach-in' _____   and the

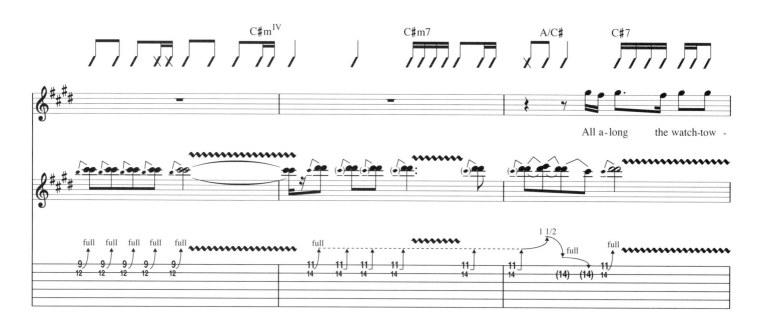

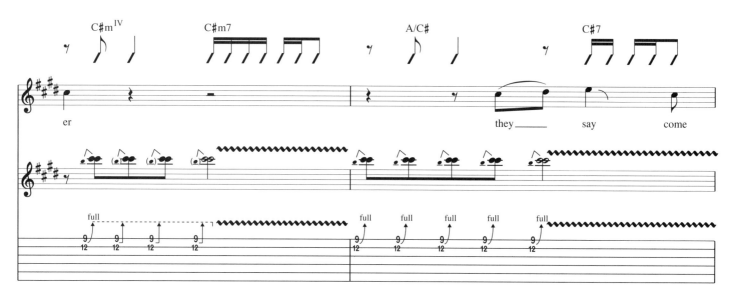

from The Kinks - *The Kinks' Greatest Hits*

All Day and All of the Night

Words and Music by Ray Davies

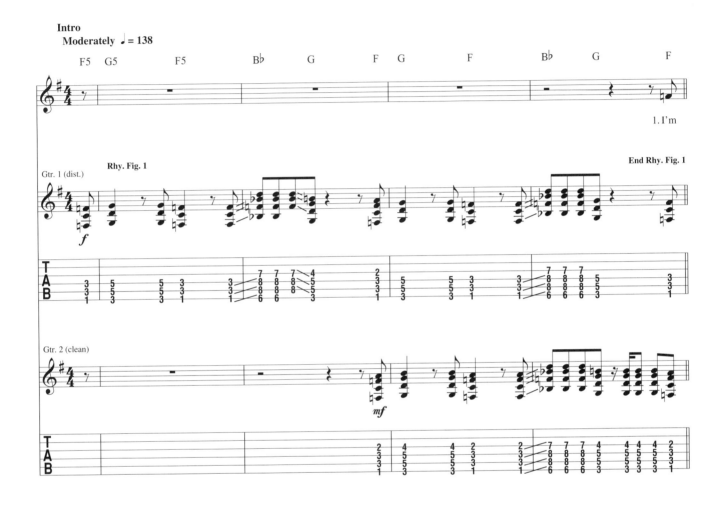

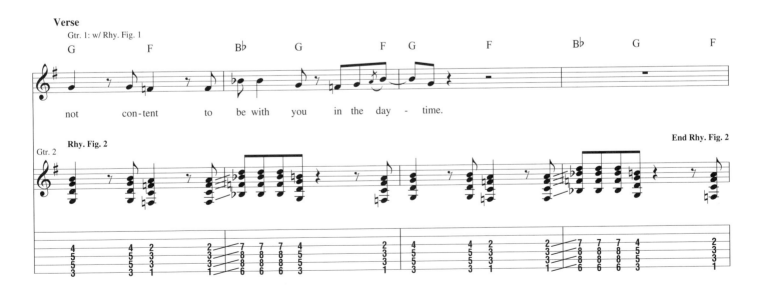

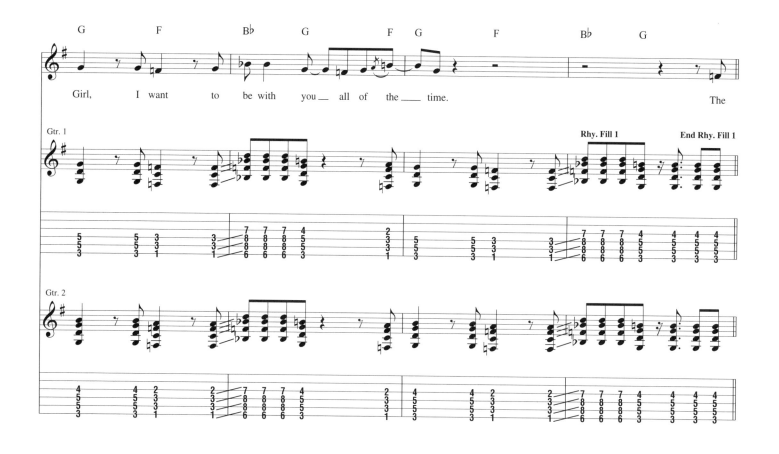

Girl, I want to be with you ___ all of the ___ time.   The

Pre-Chorus

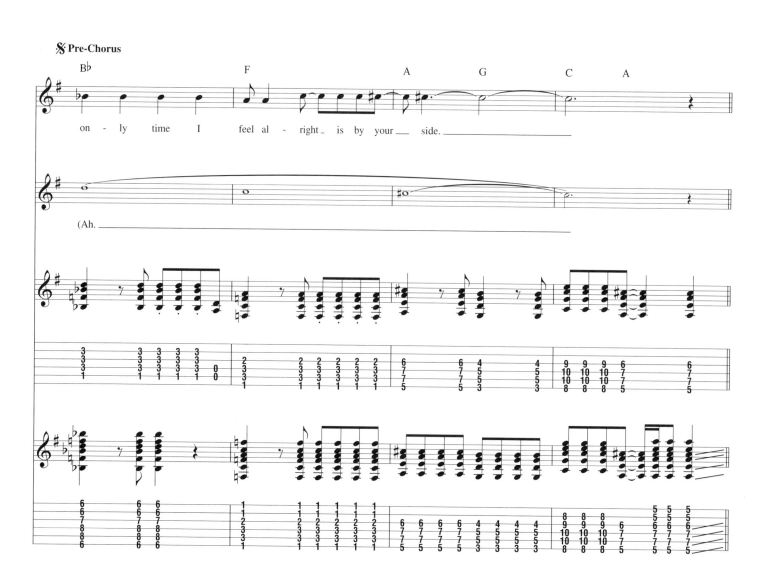

on - ly time I feel al - right ___ is by your ___ side. _____

(Ah. _____

Chorus

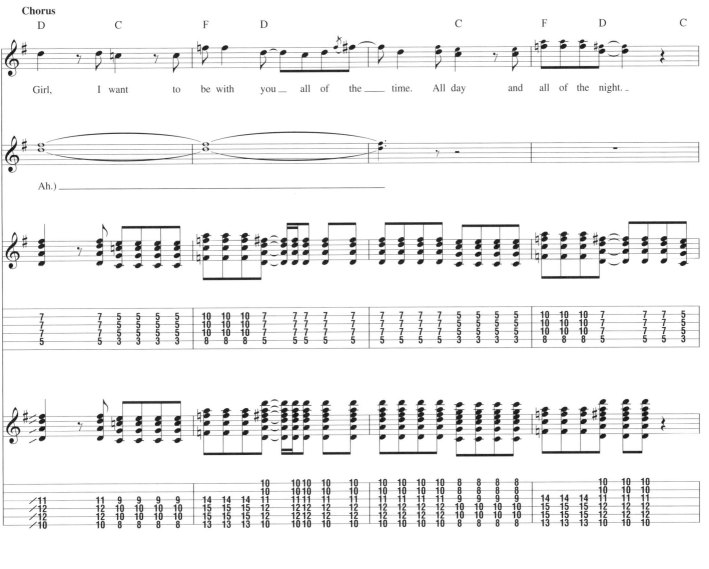

Girl, I want to be with you __ all of the __ time. All day __ and all of the night. __

Ah.) _____

To Coda 1 ⊕   *To Coda 2* ⊕

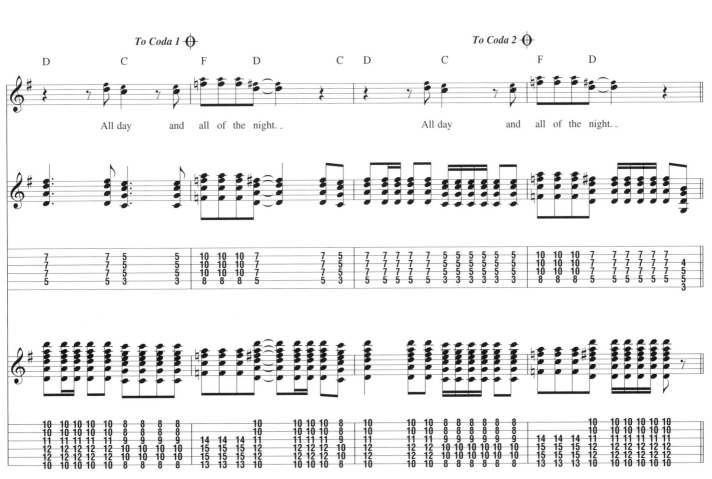

All day __ and all of the night. __   All day __ and all of the night. __

Verse

Gtr. 2: w/ Rhy. Fig. 2 (1 3/4 times)

2. I be - lieve that you and me last for - ev - er. Oh,

D.S. al Coda 1

Gtr. 1: w/ Rhy. Fig. 1 (1st 3 meas.)　　　　　　　　　　　　　　　　　Gtrs. 1 & 2: w/ Rhy. Fill 1

yeah, all day and night I'm yours, leave _ me nev - er. The

Coda 1

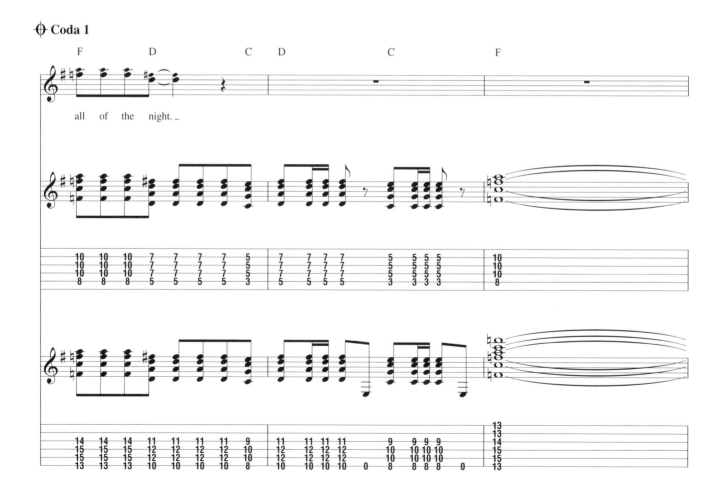

all of the night. _

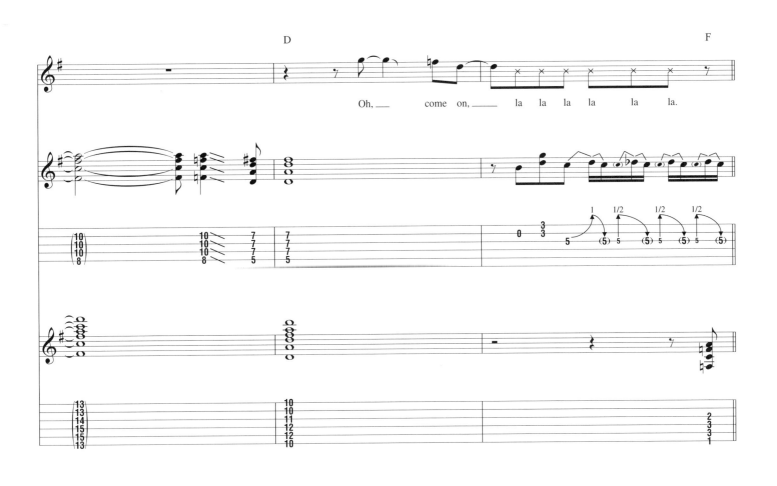

Oh, ___ come on, ___ la la la la la la.

Guitar Solo

Gtr. 2: w/ Rhy. Fig. 2 (2 1/2 times)

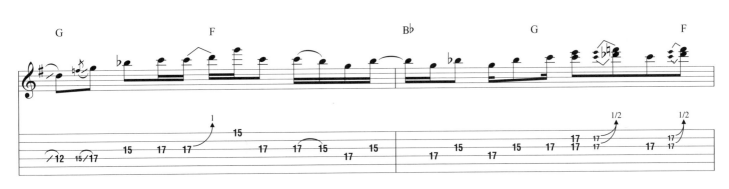

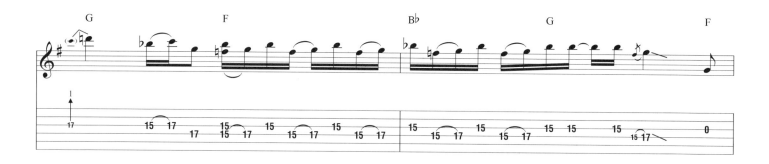

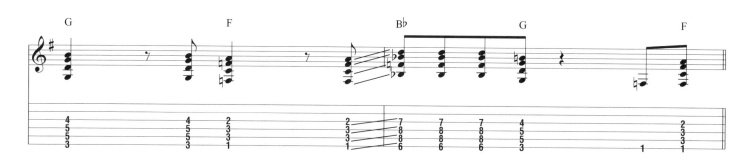

Verse

Gtr. 1: w/ Rhy. Fig. 1 (1 3/4 times)
Gtr. 2: w/ Rhy. Fig. 2 (1 3/4 times)

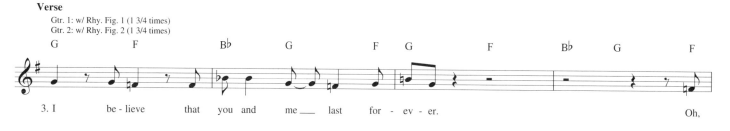

3. I be - lieve that you and me __ last for - ev - er. Oh,

D.S. al Coda 2

Gtrs. 1 & 2: w/ Rhy. Fill 1

yeah, all day and night I'm yours, leave me nev - er. The

Coda 2

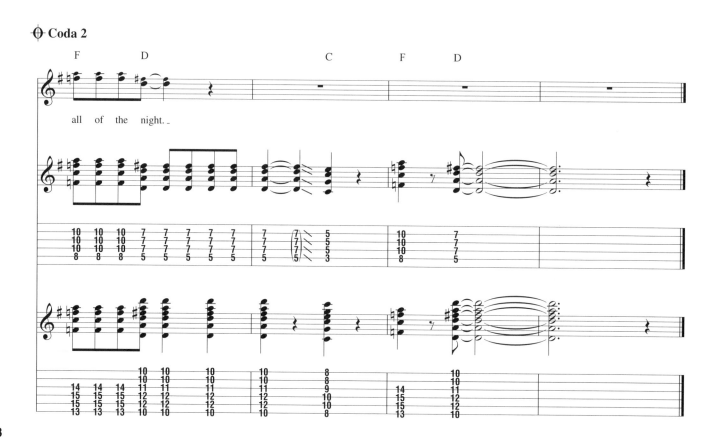

all of the night. __

28

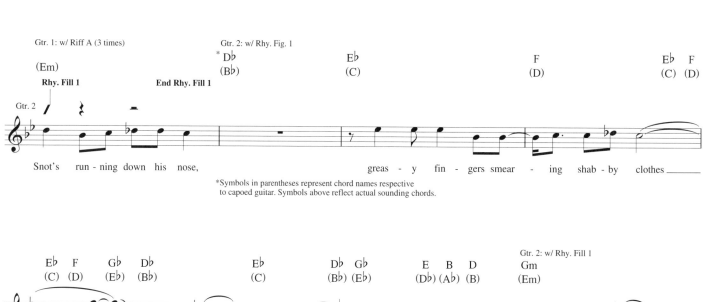

*Symbols in parentheses represent chord names respective
to capoed guitar. Symbols above reflect actual sounding chords.

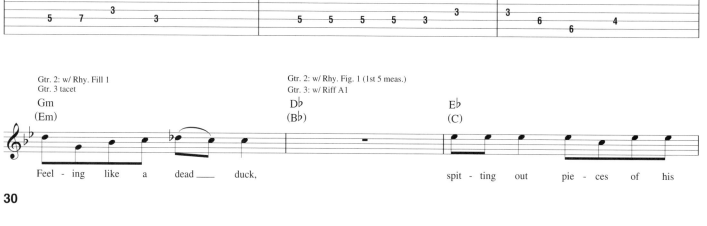

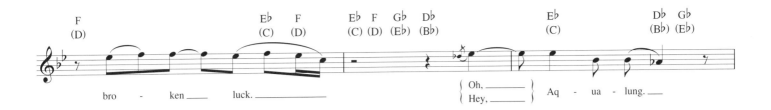

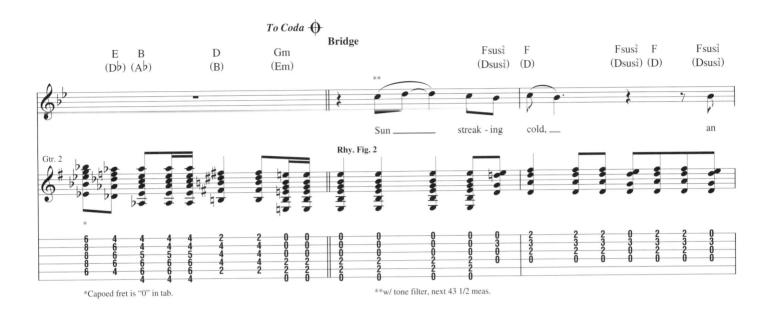

*Capoed fret is "0" in tab.   **w/ tone filter, next 43 1/2 meas.

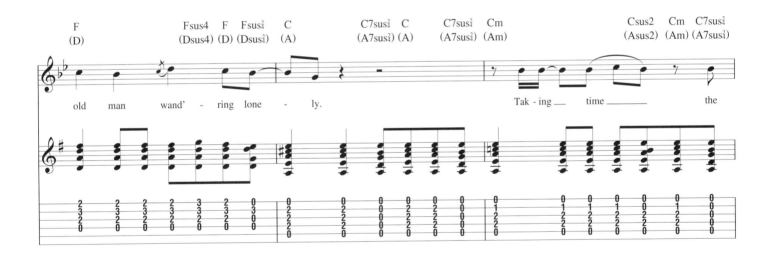

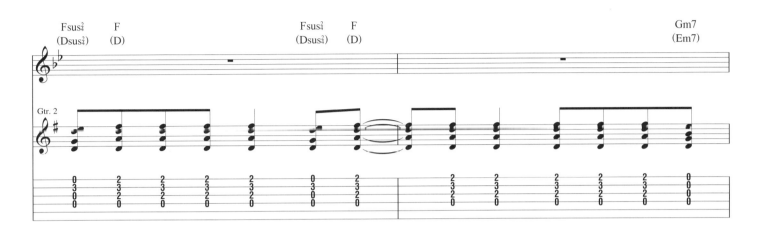

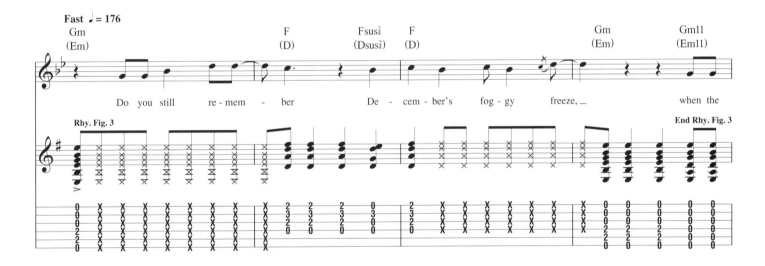

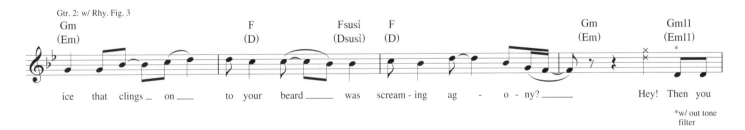

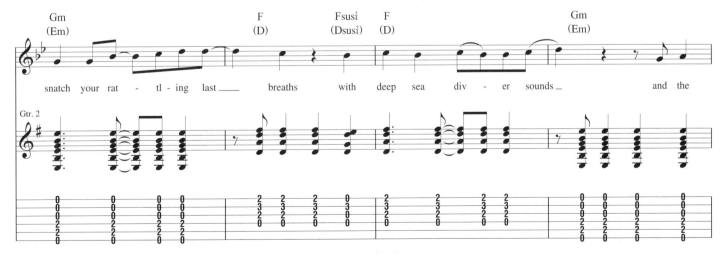

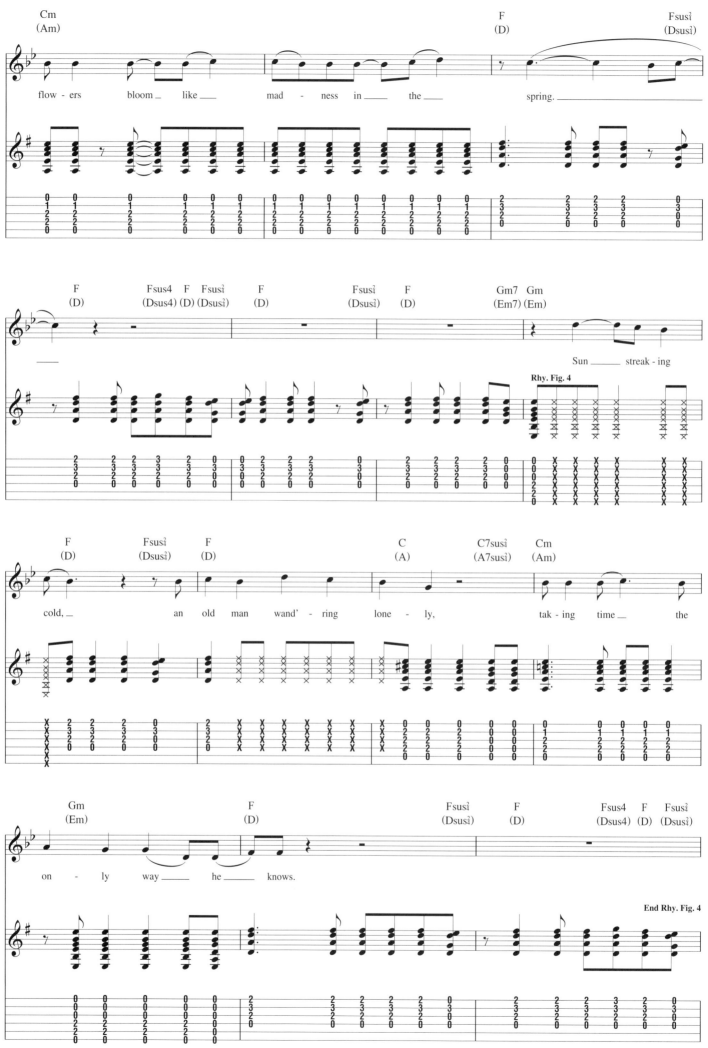

34

Interlude

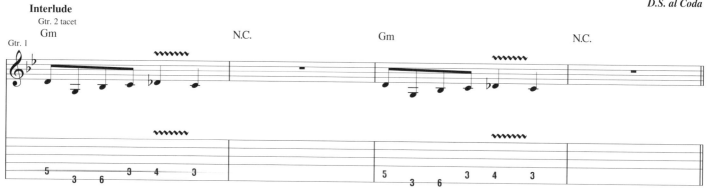

⊕ Coda

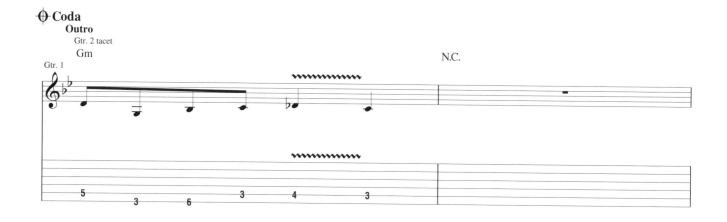

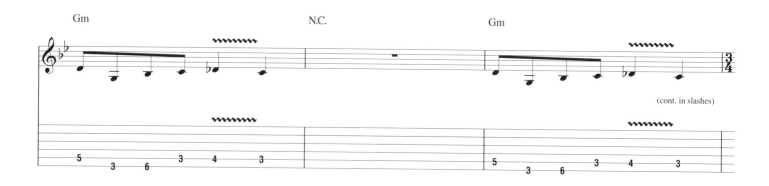

Free time

Whoa, oh,_____ oh, Aq - ua - lung._____

Back in Black

Words and Music by Angus Young, Malcolm Young and Brian Johnson

Guitar Solo

back in— black.—   I wan-na say it.

Gtr. 3 (dist.)

mf
full
f
3/4

Gtrs. 1 & 2

Outro/Guitar Solo

Gtrs. 1 & 2: w/Rhy. Fig. 3, till fade

Gtr. 3

E5   E7   E6   E5

E7   E6   E5   A   E5   A

E5   E7   *Begin Fade*   E6   E5

Barracuda

Words and Music by Nancy Wilson, Ann Wilson, Michael Derosier and Roger Fisher

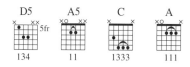

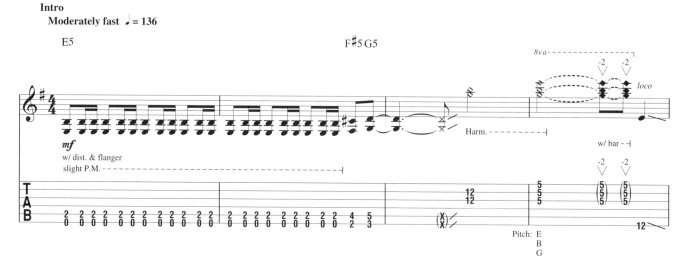

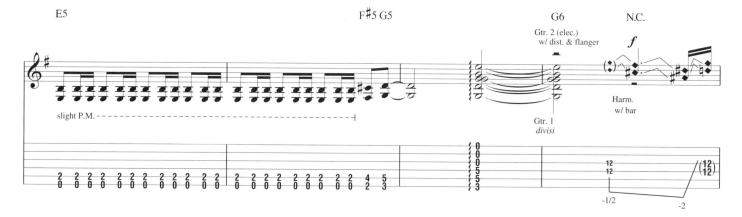

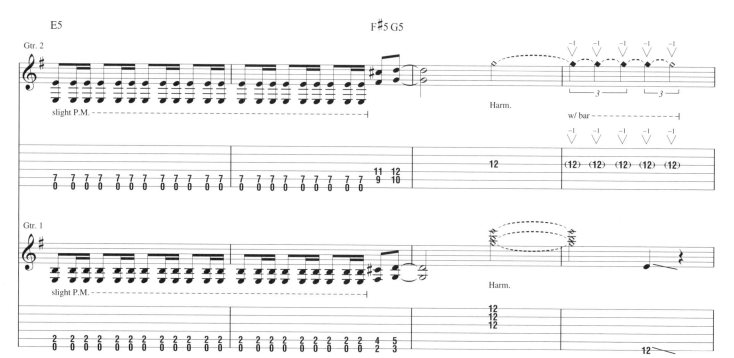

Coda 2

Interlude

Gtrs. 1 & 2: w/ Rhy. Figs. 1 & 1A

Oh, _____ bar - ra, bar -

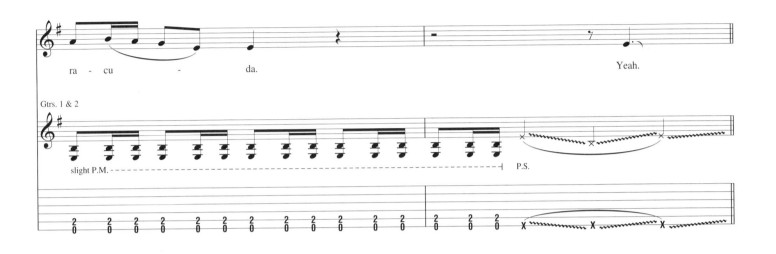

ra - cu - da.   Yeah.

slight P.M. -   P.S.

Outro

Gtr. 4: w/ Fill 1

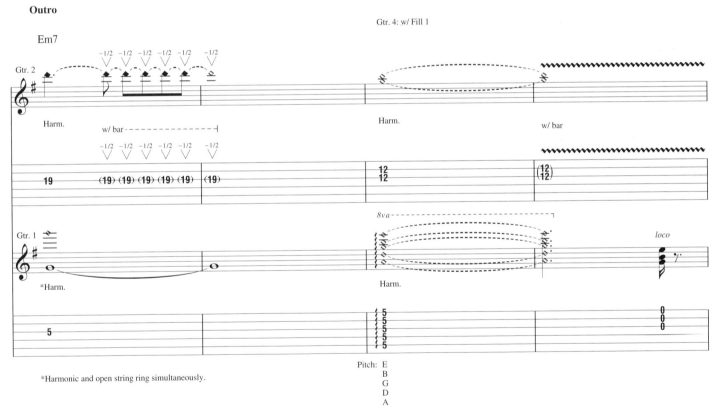

*Harmonic and open string ring simultaneously.

Pitch: E
B
G
D
A

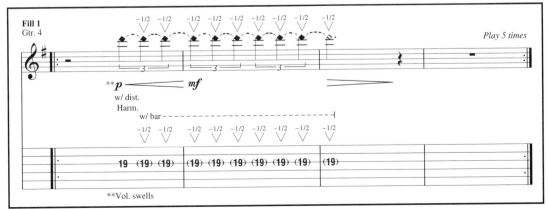

**Vol. swells

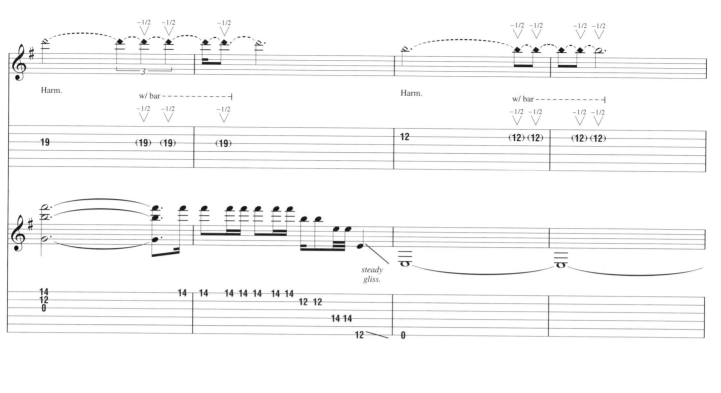

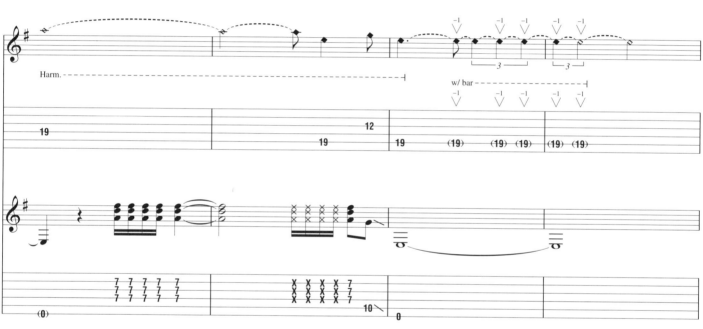

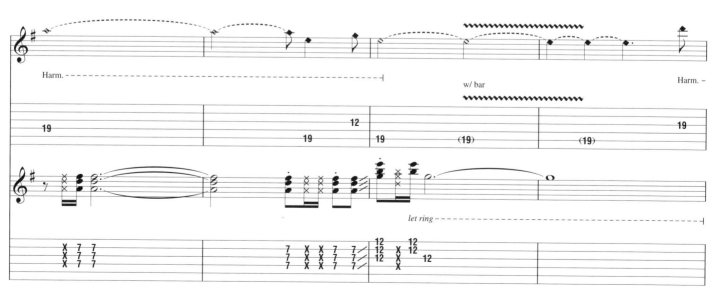

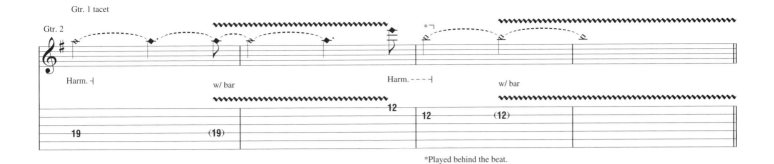

*Played behind the beat.

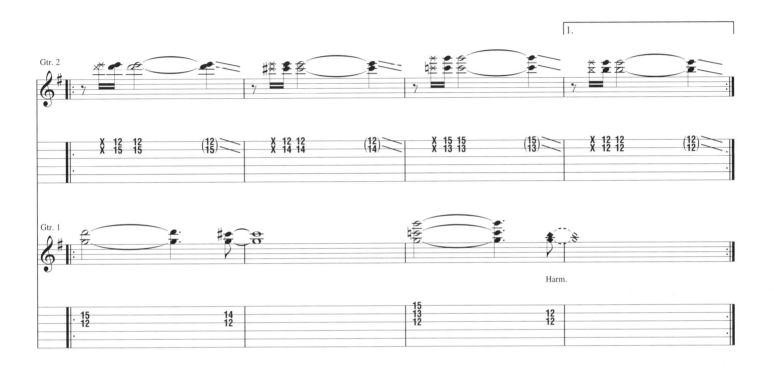

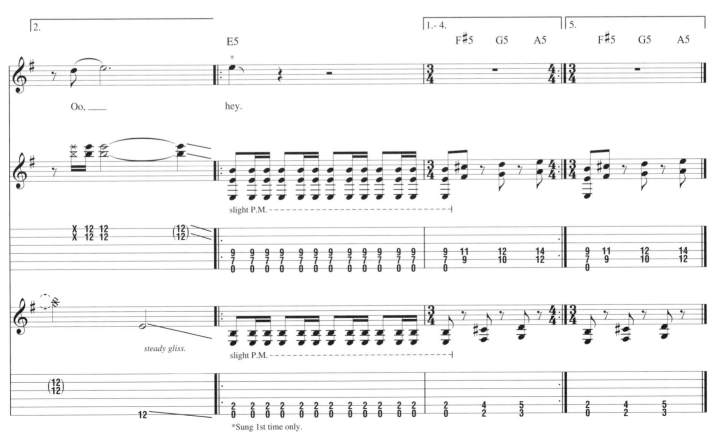

*Sung 1st time only.

Beat It

Words and Music by Michael Jackson

Tune down 1/2 step:
(low to high) E♭-A♭-D♭-G♭-B♭-E♭

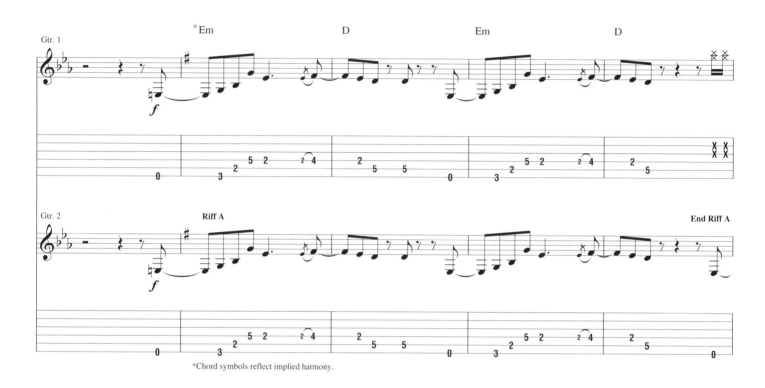

*Chord symbols reflect implied harmony.

wan - na be tough, bet - ter do what you can, so beat it. But you
kick you then they beat you then they'll tell you it's fair, so beat it. But you

𝄋 Chorus

Gtr. 3 tacet
3rd time, Gtr. 4: w/ Fill 1

wan - na be bad. } Just beat it, beat it. No __
wan - na be bad. } (Beat it, beat it.)

Gtr. 1

Gtr. 3

Gtr. 2
divisi

P.M.

Gtrs. 1 & 2: w/ Riff A (last 2 meas.)

1st time, Gtrs. 1 & 2: w/ Riff A (2 times)
2nd & 3rd times, Gtrs. 1 & 2: w/ Riff A (3 times)

__ one wants to be de - feat - ed, show - in' how funk - y strong __

__ is your fight. It does - n't mat - ter who's __ wrong or right. Just

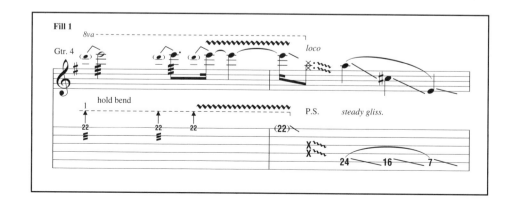

Fill 1

Gtr. 4

hold bend

P.S. steady gliss.

60

61

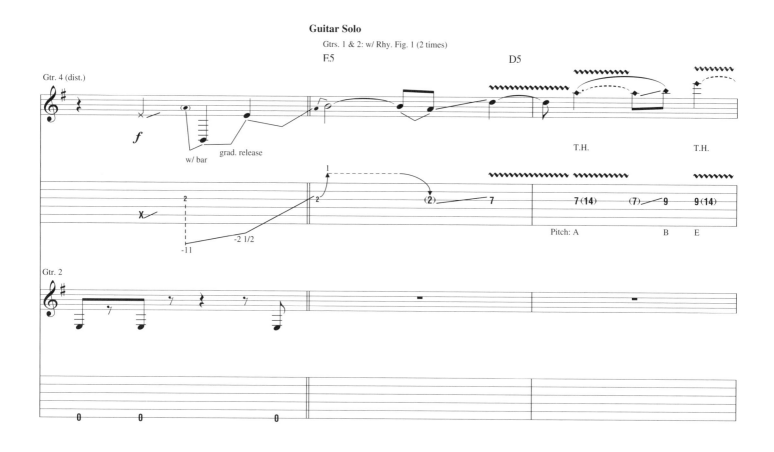

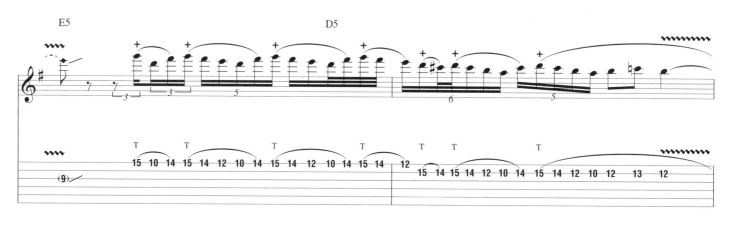

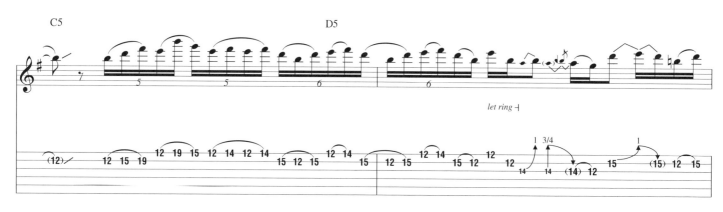

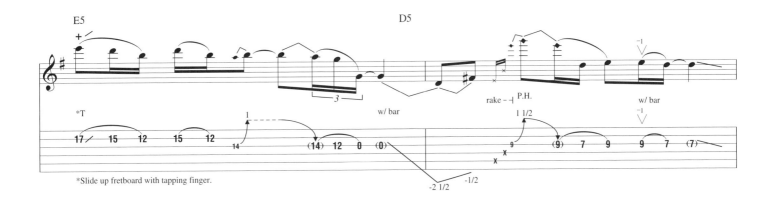

1.
Em D Em D
beat it. Just beat it. Just beat it. Just beat it. Oh!
(Beat it. Beat it. Beat it. Beat it. Oh!)
2.
2nd time, w/ ad lib voc. (till fade)
2nd time, Gtrs. 1 & 2: w/ Riff A
Em D Em D
beat it, beat it. No one wants to be de - feat - ed, show -
(Beat it, beat it.)
To Coda
Em D Em D
- in' how funk - y strong is your fight. It does - n't mat - ter who's wrong or right. Just
Bridge
E5 D5
beat it. Beat it.
Gtr. 2
Riff C
End Riff C
*w/ echo set for quarter-note regeneration w/ 3 repeats, next 12 meas.
Gtr. 2: w/ Riff C (2 3/4 times)
E5 D5
Beat it. Beat it.
E5
Gtr. 1
Riff D
End Riff D

*Slide up fretboard with tapping finger.

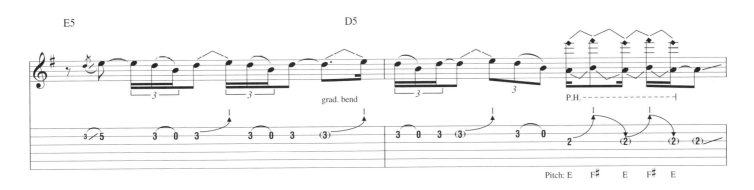

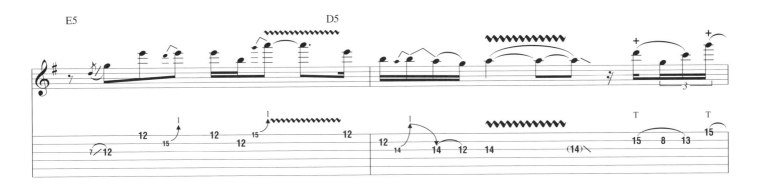

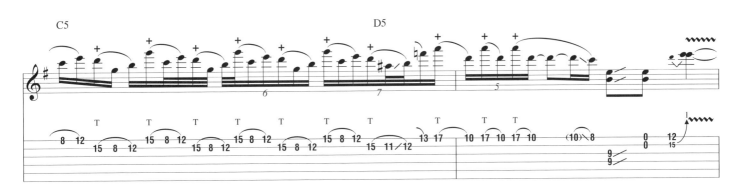

D.S. al Coda
(take 2nd ending)

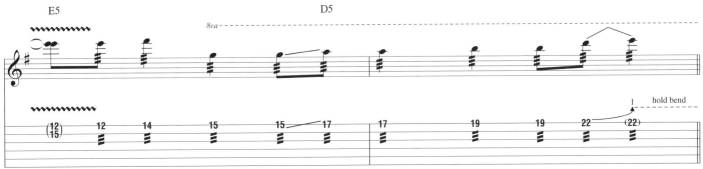

Coda

Outro-Chorus

beat it, beat it. No ___

(Beat it, beat it.)

Gtrs. 1 & 2

2nd time, Begin fade

___ one wants to be de - feat - ed, show - in' how funk - y strong ___

___ is your fight. It does - n't mat - ter who's ___ wrong or right. Just

Gtrs. 1 & 2: w/ Riff A (1st 3 meas.)

Fade out

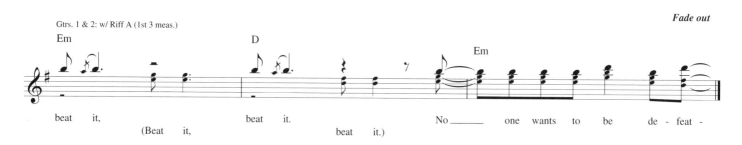

beat it, beat it. No ___ one wants to be de - feat -

(Beat it, beat it.)

from Ramones - *Ramones*

Blitzkrieg Bop

Words and Music by Jeffrey Hyman, John Cummings, Douglas Colvin and Thomas Erdelyi

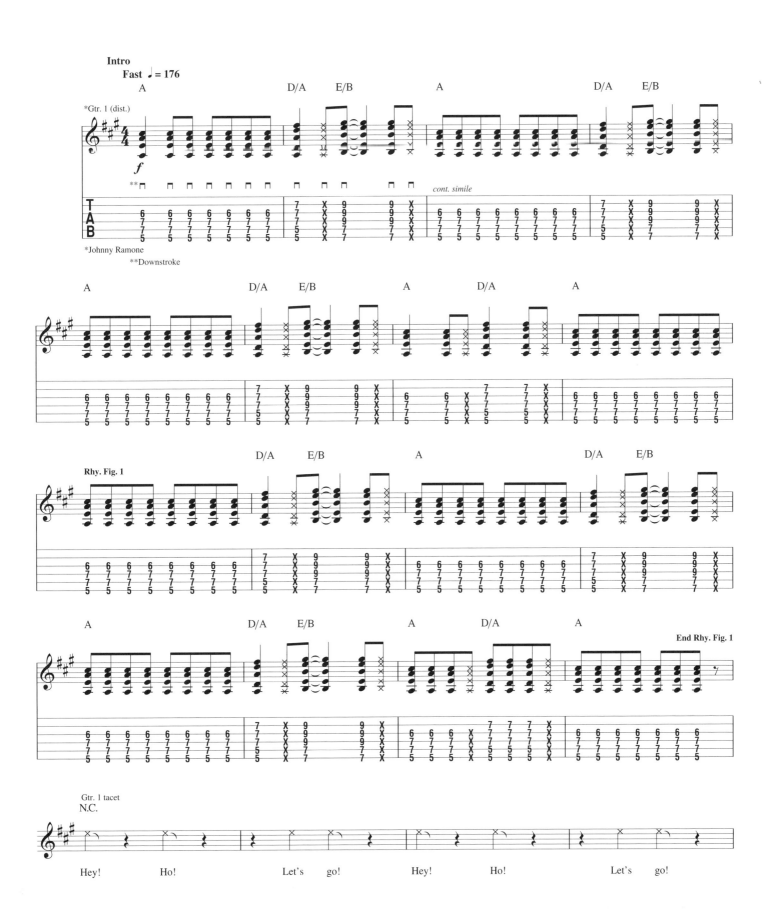

Hey!   Ho!   Let's   go!   Hey!   Ho!   Let's   go!

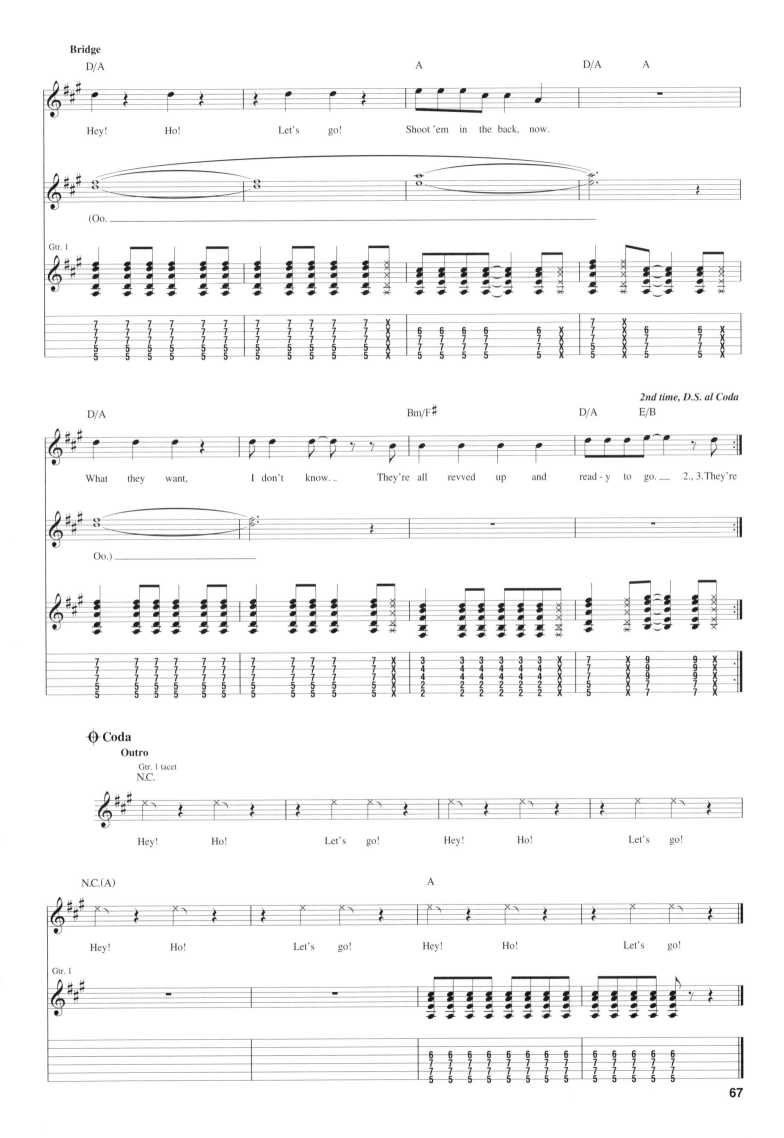

Bohemian Rhapsody

Words and Music by Freddie Mercury

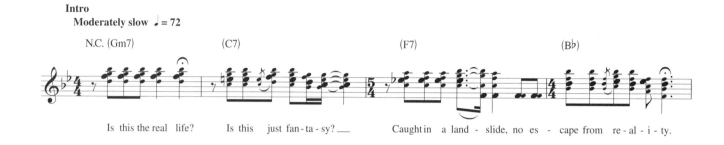

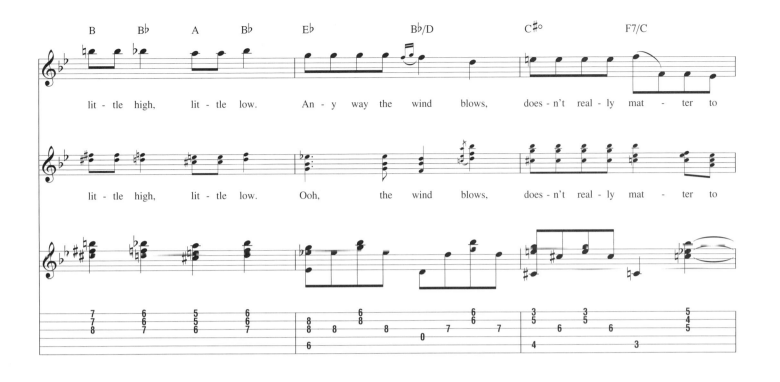

Verse

Gtr. 1: w/ Rhy. Fig. 1

2.Too late, _____ my time has come, _____ sent shiv-ers down _ my spine, _ bod-y's

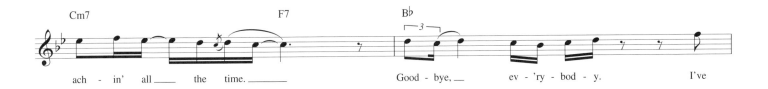

ach - in' all _____ the time. _____ Good - bye, _ ev-'ry-bod-y. I've

got to go, _____ got - ta leave you all be - hind _____ and face _____

_____ the truth. _____ Ma - ma, _____ ooh, _____ I don't want to die. _____ I

(Ooh. _____) Ooh. _____

(An - y way the wind blows.)

*Gtr. 2 (dist.)

*Two gtrs. arr. for one.

some - times wish I'd nev - er been born at all. ____

Ooh, ____ ooh, ____ ooh, ____ ooh. ____ Ooh. ____

(Ooh, ooh, ____ ooh. ____ Ooh. ____

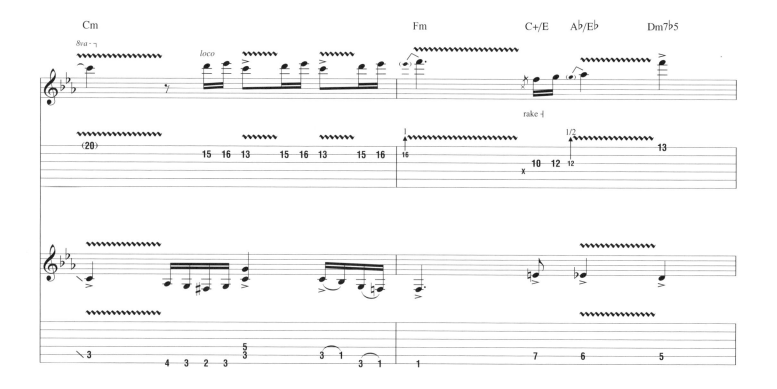

Interlude

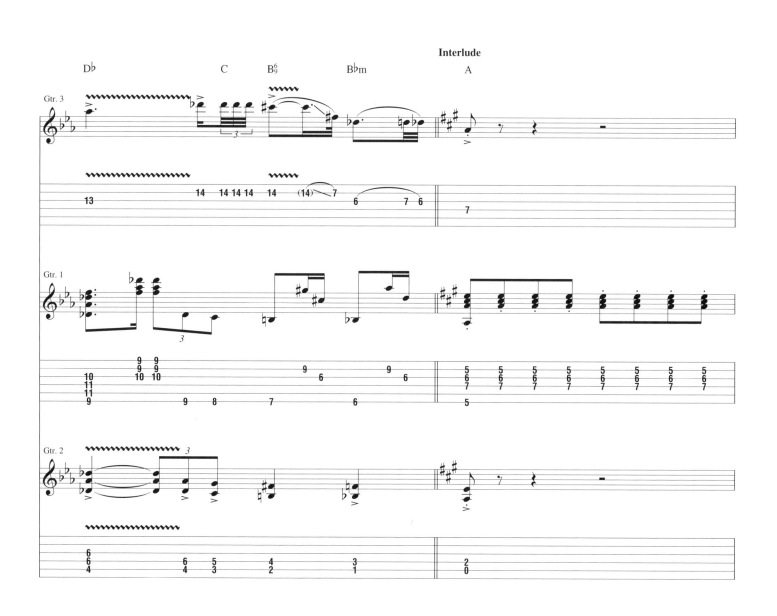

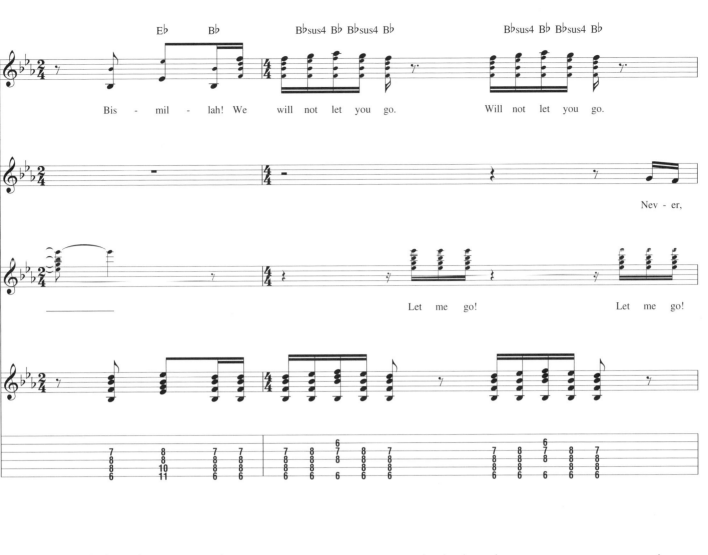

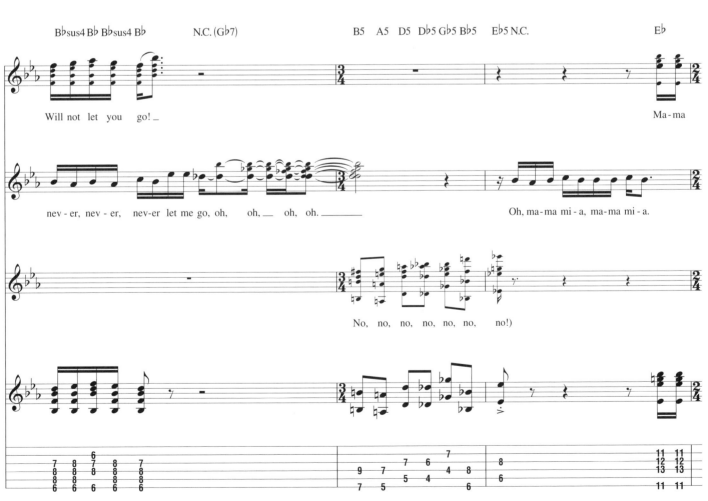

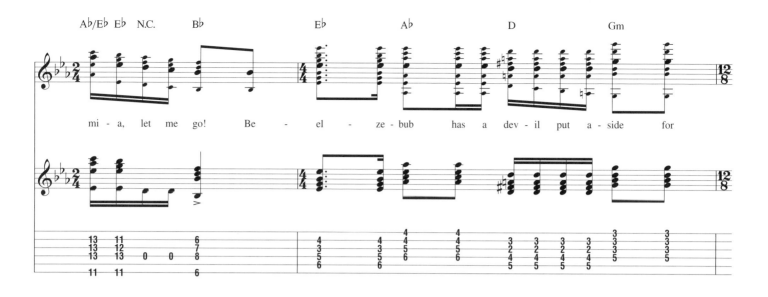

mi - a, let me go! Be - el - ze - bub has a dev - il put a - side for

me, _____ for me, _____ for me!

me, for me, for me!

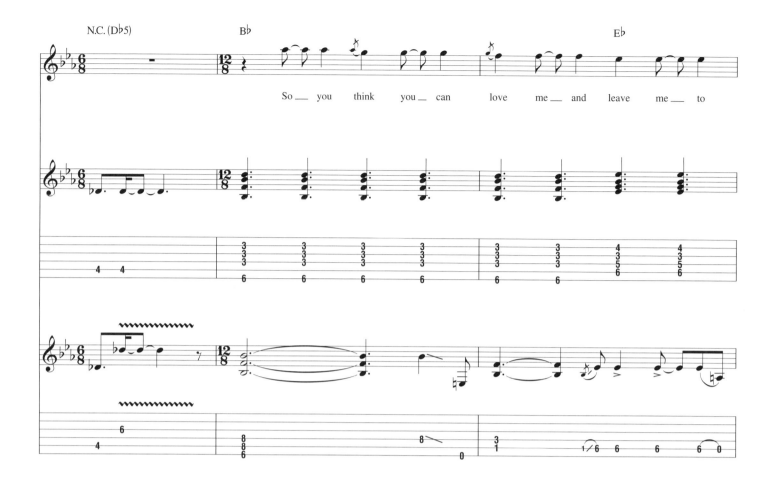

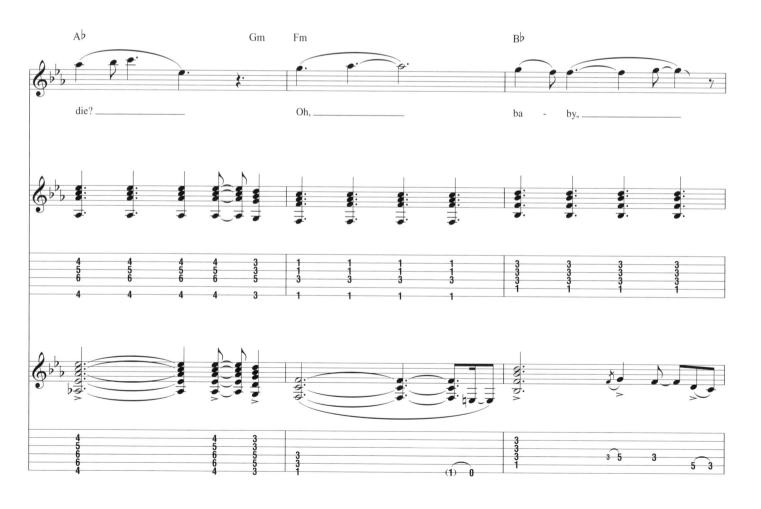

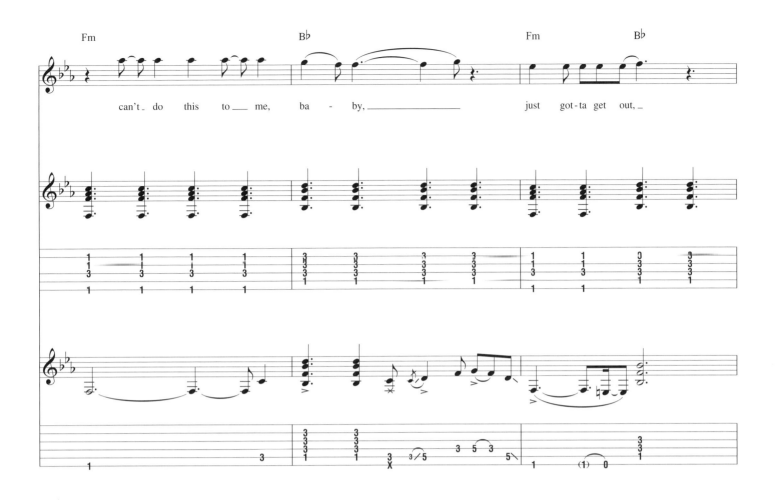

can't do this to me, ba - by, just got - ta get out,

just got - ta get right out - a here.

Nothing really matters, _____

Born to Be Wild

Words and Music by Mars Bonfire

*Chord symbols reflect basic harmony.

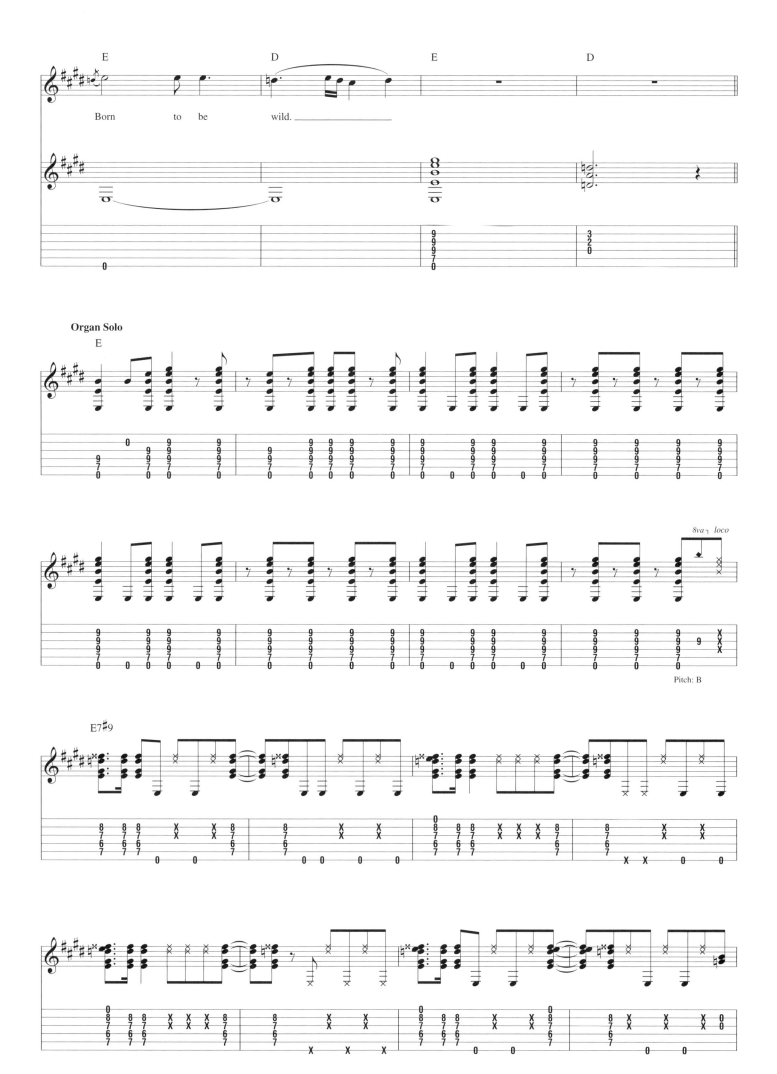

Born to be wild. _____

Organic Solo

Pitch: B

E

Gtr. 2
(clean)

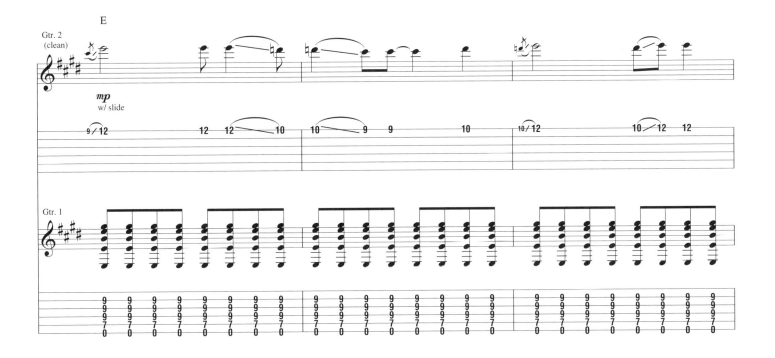

mp
w/ slide

D.S. al Coda

Gtr. 2 tacet

N.C.

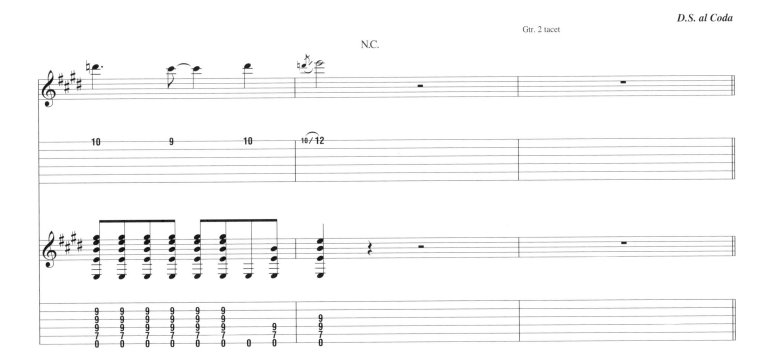

Gtr. 1

Coda

Pre-Chorus

G   A   E   G   A

Yeah,   dar - lin', go   make __ it hap - pen,   take the world   in a

let ring - - - -| let ring - - - - - - - - - - - -|

91

from Thin Lizzy - *Jailbreak*

The Boys Are Back in Town

Words and Music by Philip Parris Lynott

Tune down 1/2 step:
(low to high) E♭-A♭-D♭-G♭-B♭-E♭

Intro
Moderately fast ♩ = 162

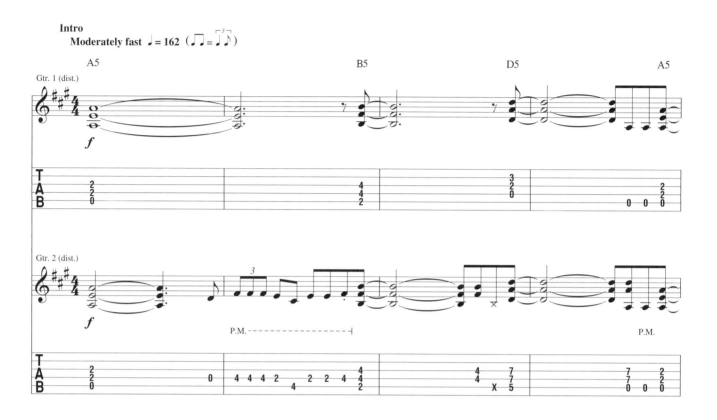

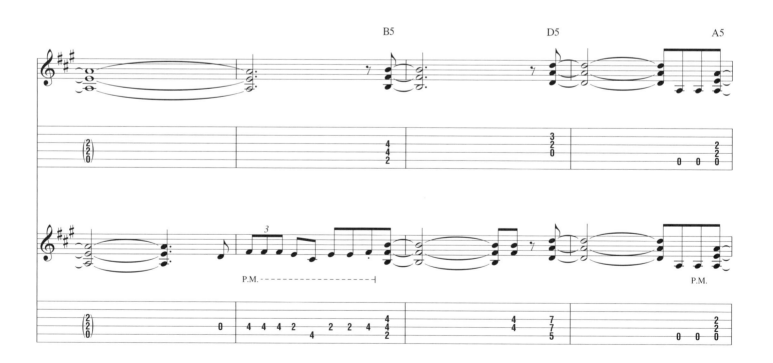

Verse

1. Guess who just got back to - day.
2. You know that chick that used to dance a lot?

Them wild - eyed boys
Ev - 'ry night she'd be on the

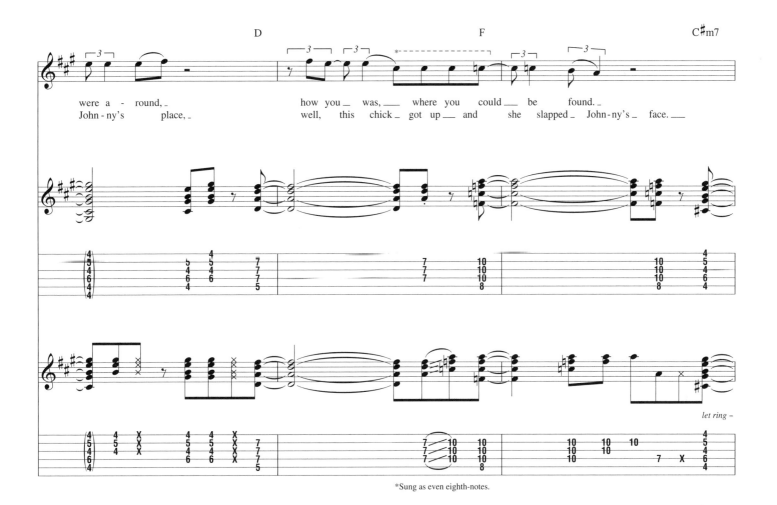

*Sung as even eighth-notes.

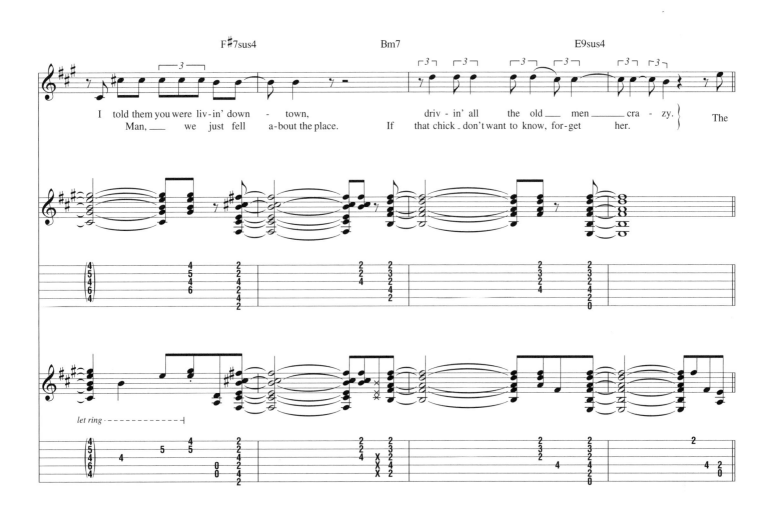

𝄋 Chorus

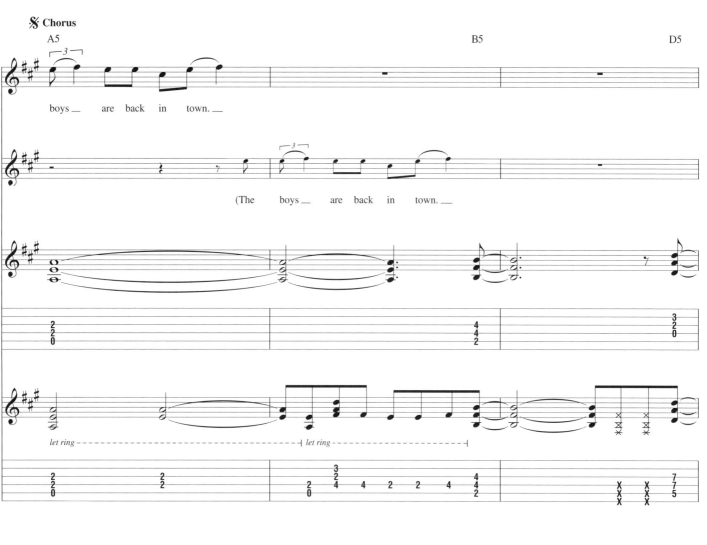

boys __ are back in town. __

(The boys __ are back in town. __

I said, the boys __ are back in town. __

The

To Coda

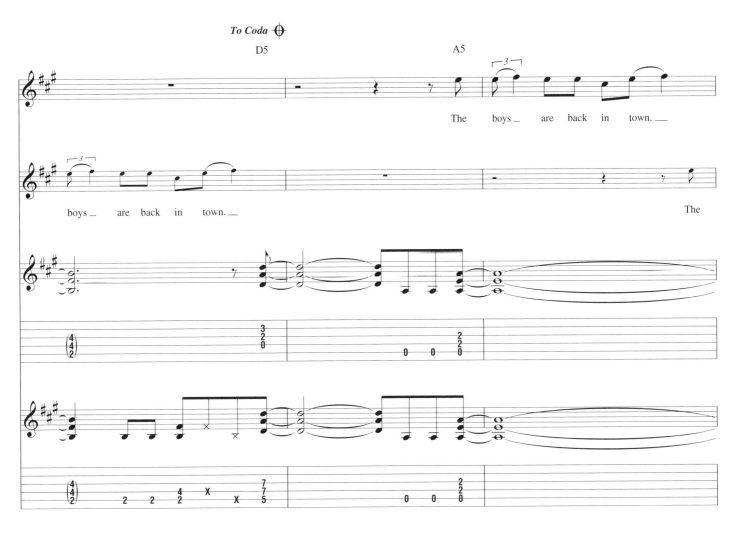

Spread the word ___ a-round.

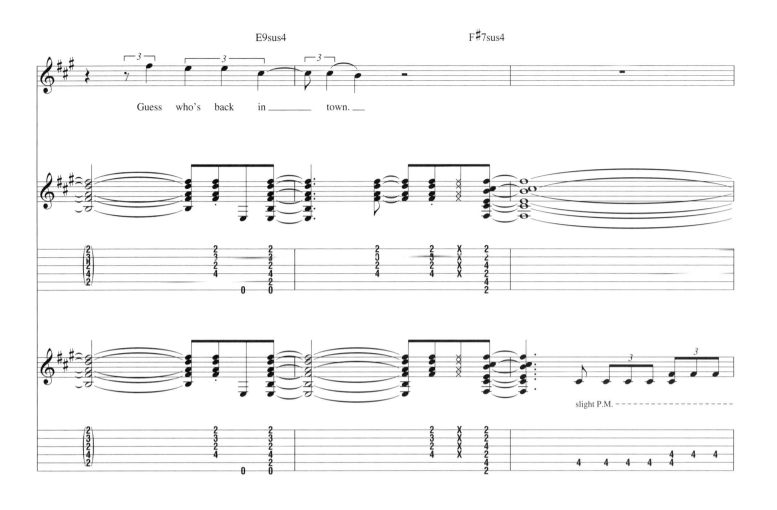

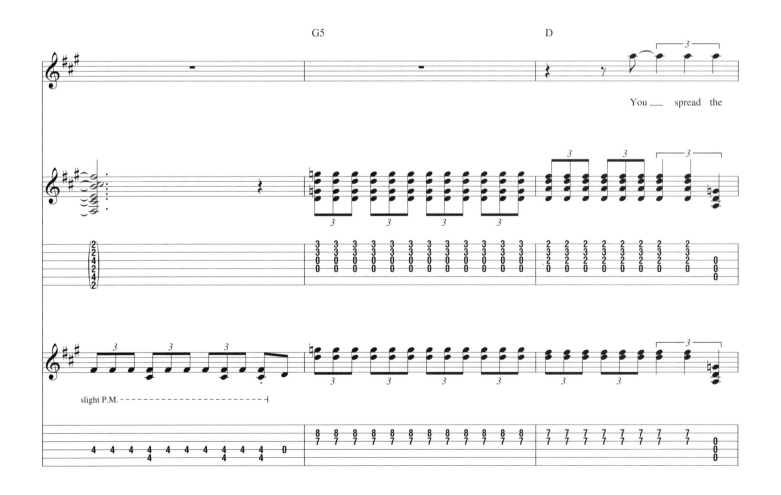

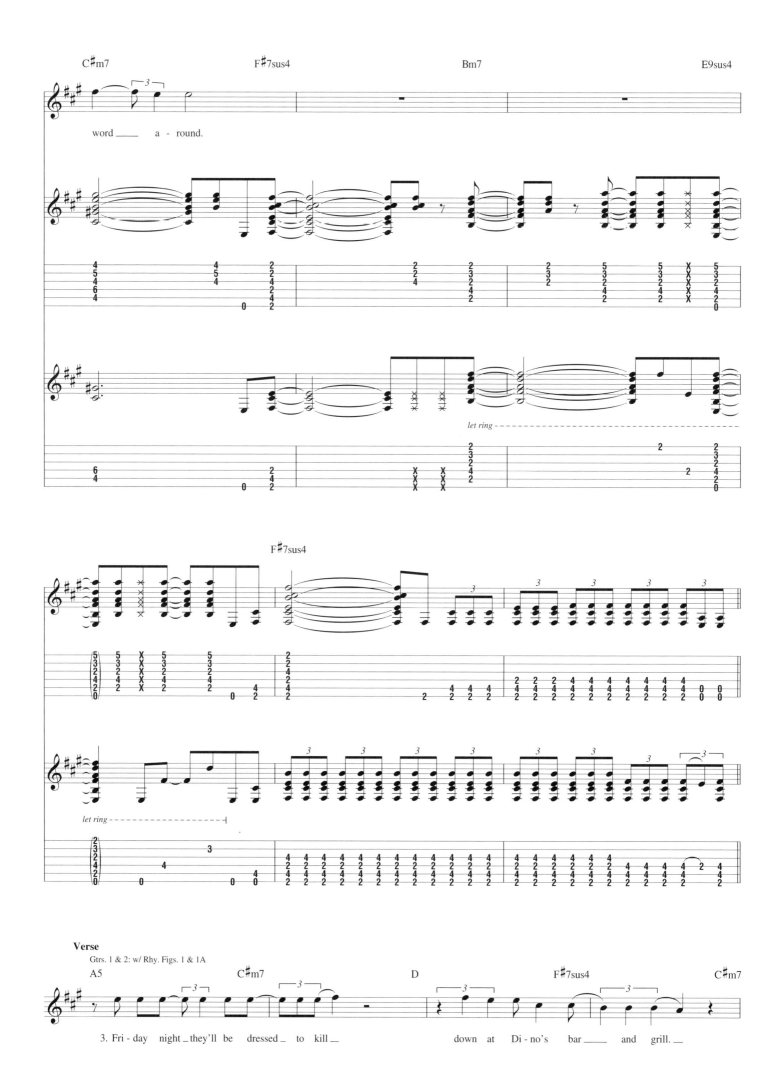

The drink will flow and blood will spill and if the boys want to fight you bet-ter let 'em.

That juke box in the cor-ner blast-ing out my fa-v'rite song, the nights are get-ting warm - er, it won't be long,

D.S. al Coda

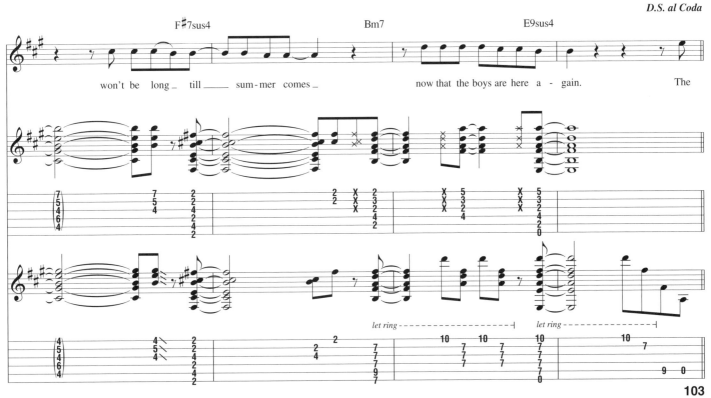

won't be long till sum-mer comes now that the boys are here a-gain. The

⊕ Coda

The boys are back in town.
The boys are back in town.

Spoken: Spread the word a - round.
The boys are back in town.
The

Whispered: The boys are back, the boys are back.

boys _ are back in town.) _

slight P.M. -

Interlude

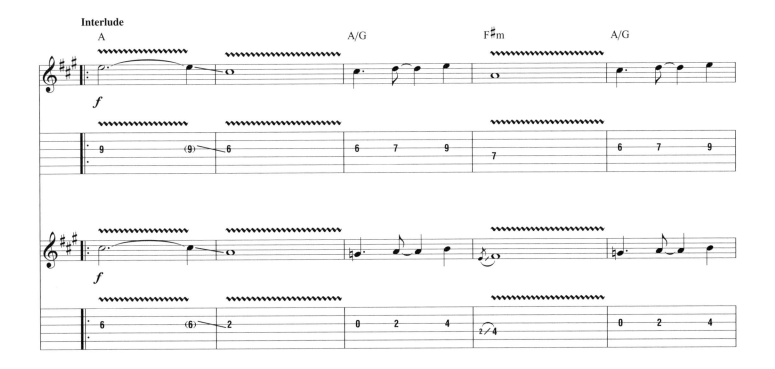

Outro

Gtr. 1: w/ Riff A (till fade)
Gtr. 2: w/ Riff A1 (1st 3 meas.)

Gtr. 2: w/ Fill 2

The boys _ are back _ in town _

Gtr. 2: w/ Riff A1 (till fade)

_ a - gain. _

Been _ hang - in' down _

Riff B
Gtr. 4 (dist.)

End Riff B

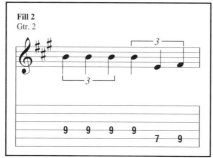

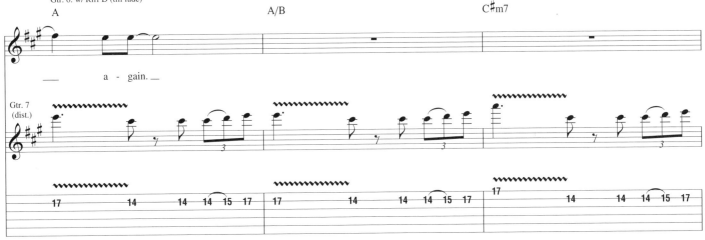

Carry On Wayward Son

Words and Music by Kerry Livgren

Carry on my way - ward son, _____ there'll be peace when you ___ are done. ___

Lay your wea - ry head ___ to rest. _____ Don't you cry no ___ more. _____

*Chord symbols reflect overall harmony.

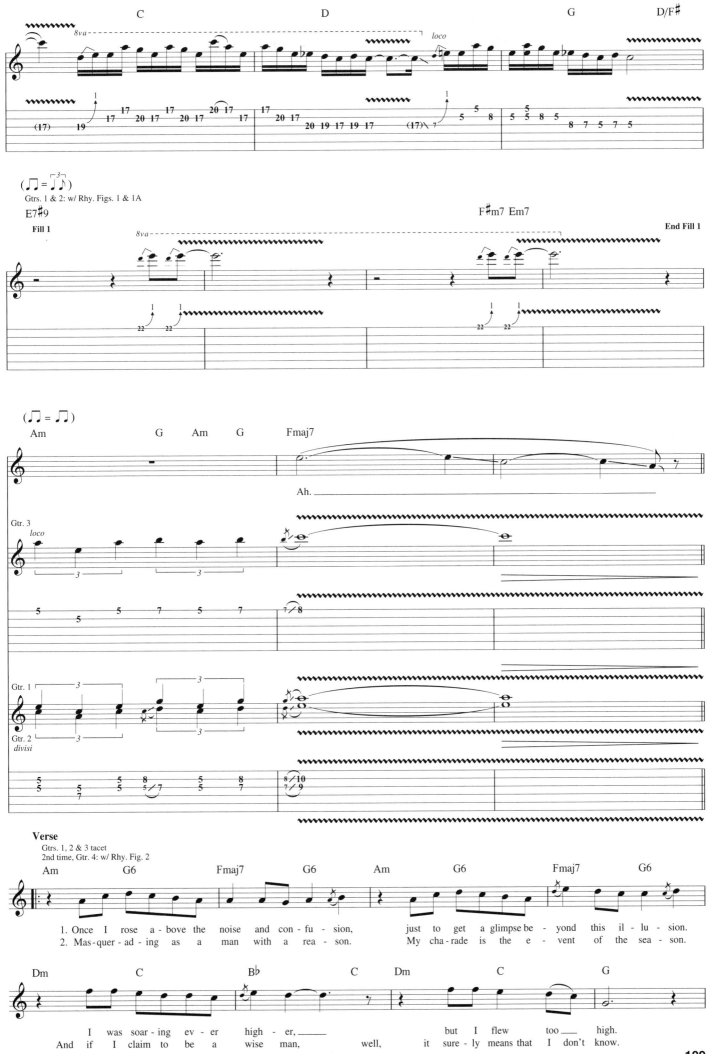

1. Once I rose a-bove the noise and con-fu-sion, just to get a glimpse be-yond this il-lu-sion.
2. Mas-quer-ad-ing as a man with a rea-son. My cha-rade is the e-vent of the sea-son.

I was soar-ing ev-er high-er, but I flew too high.
And if I claim to be a wise man, well, it sure-ly means that I don't know.

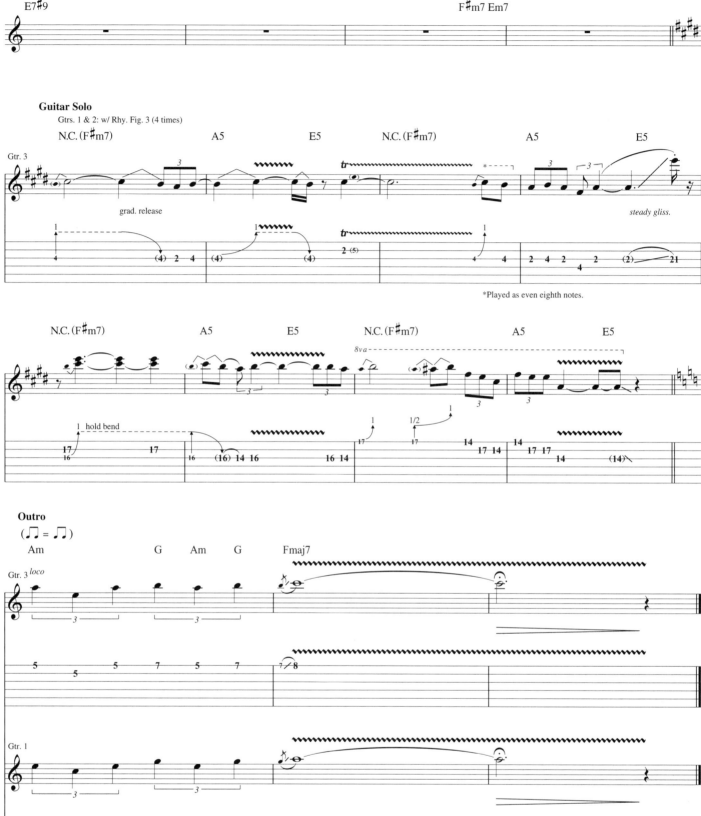

*Played as even eighth notes.

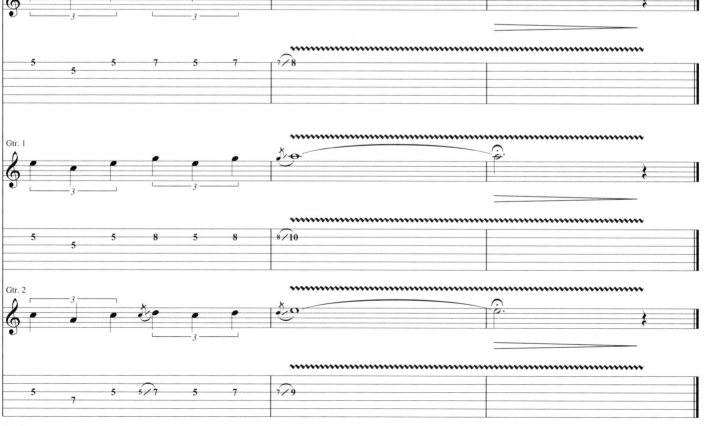

from Pink Floyd - *The Wall*

Comfortably Numb

Words and Music by Roger Waters and David Gilmour

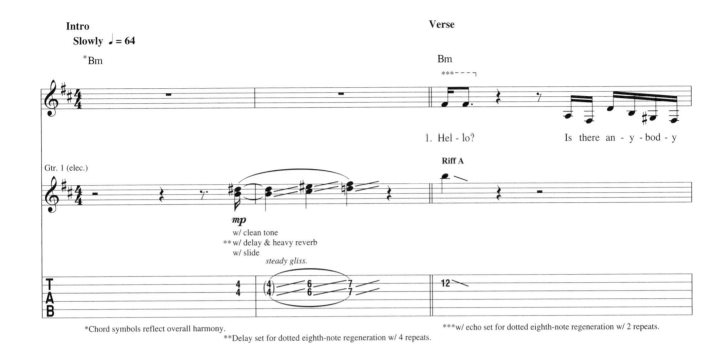

*Chord symbols reflect overall harmony.
**Delay set for dotted eighth-note regeneration w/ 4 repeats.
***w/ echo set for dotted eighth-note regeneration w/ 2 repeats.

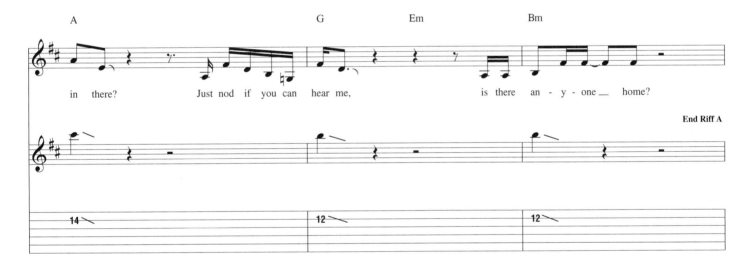

just the ba-sic facts, can you show me where it hurts?

Chorus

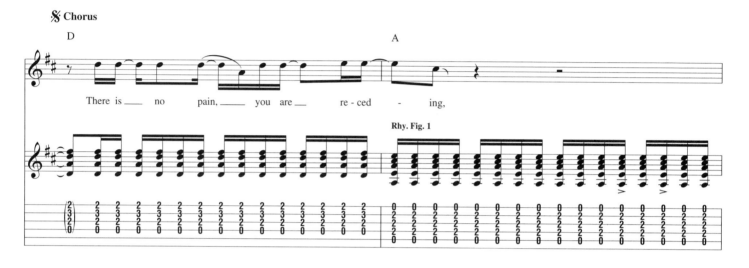

There is ___ no pain, ___ you are ___ re-ced-ing,

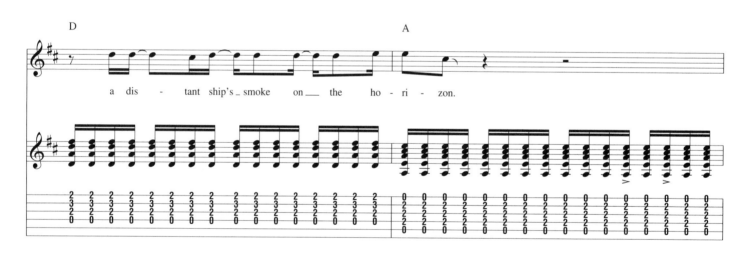

a dis-tant ship's _ smoke on ___ the ho-ri- zon.

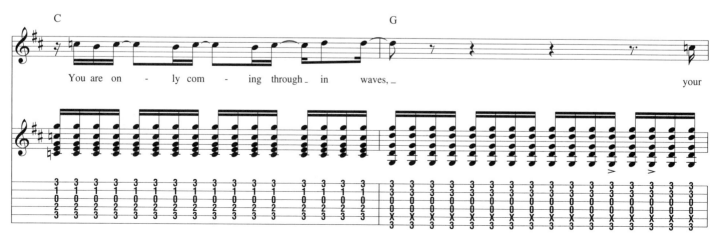

You are on-ly com-ing through _ in waves, _ your

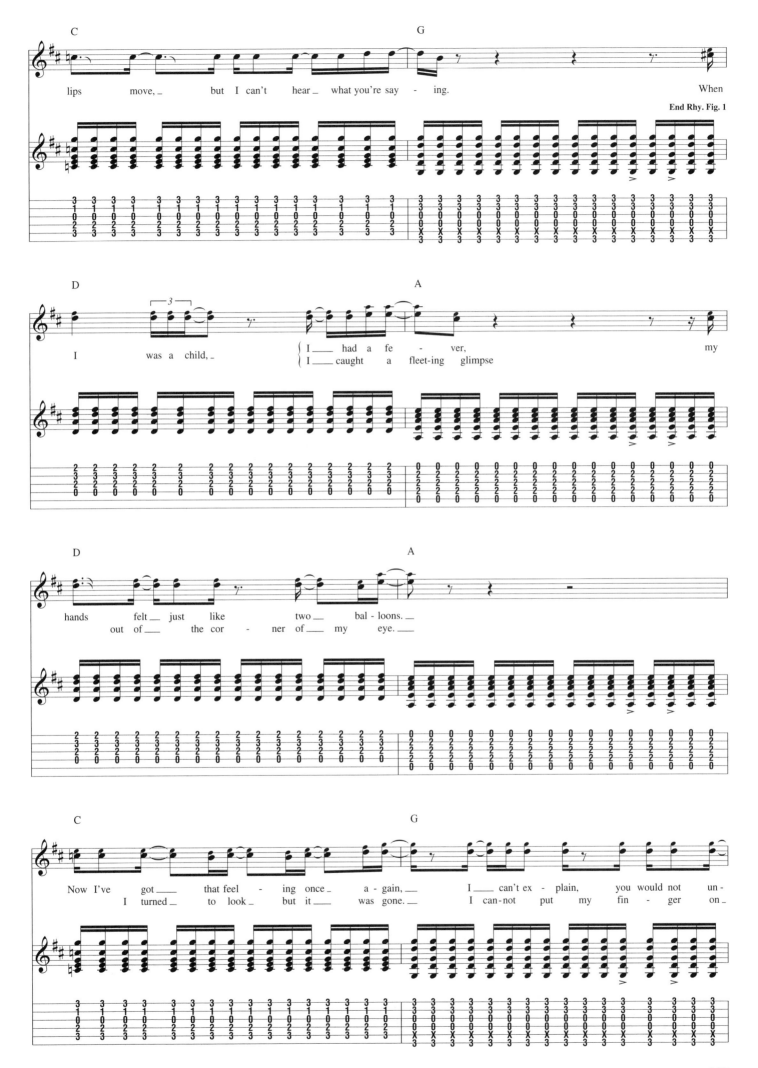

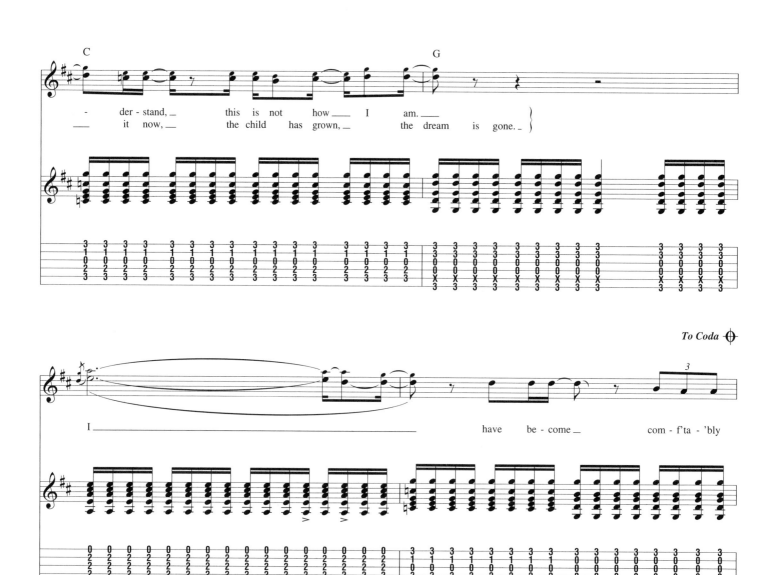

Guitar Solo

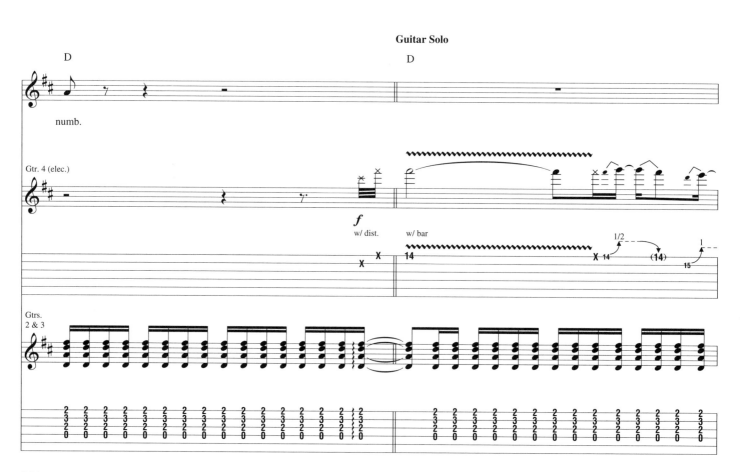

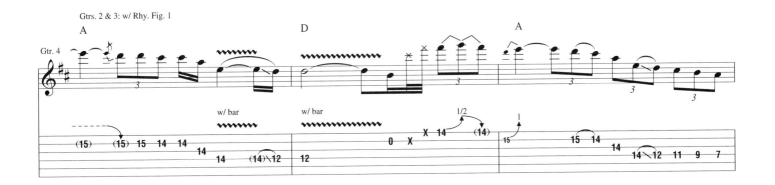

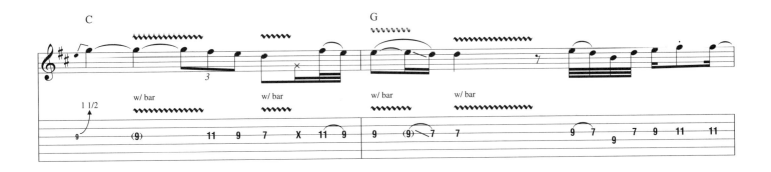

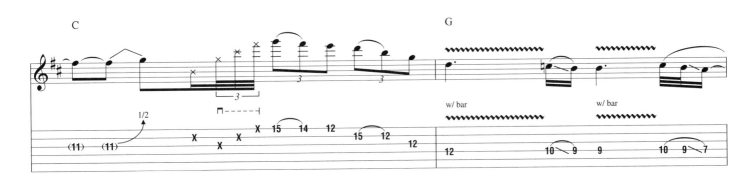

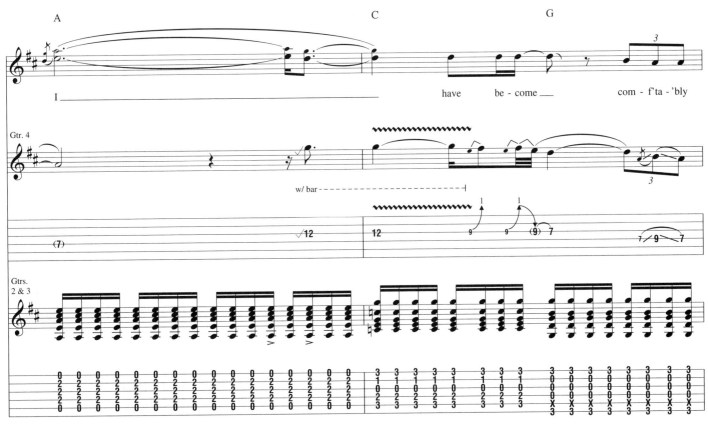

I _____ have be-come ____ com-f'ta-'bly

Verse

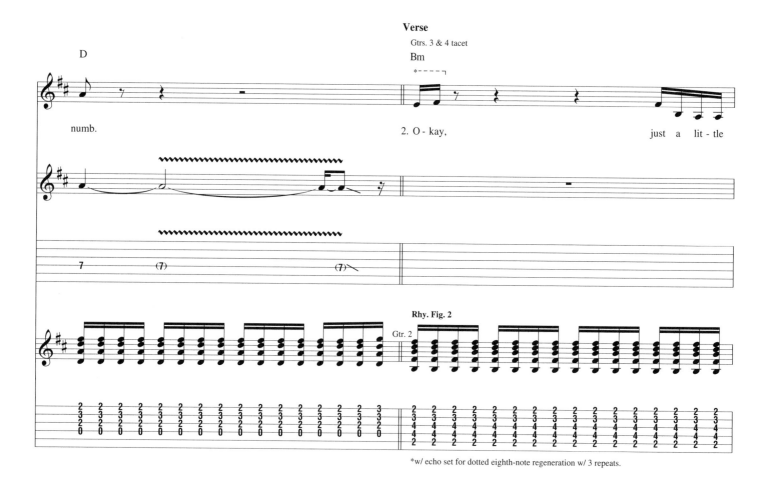

*w/ echo set for dotted eighth-note regeneration w/ 3 repeats.

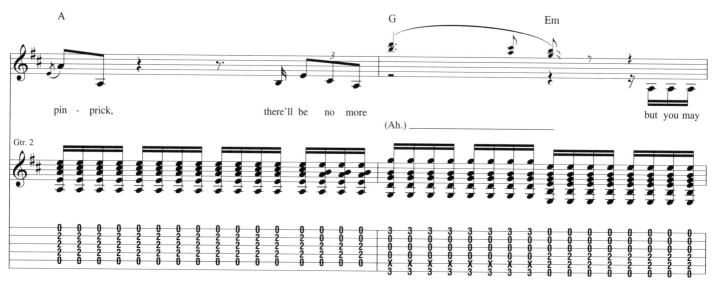

**As before

120

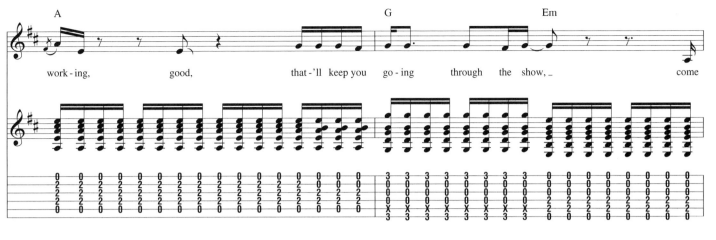

work-ing,   good,   that-'ll keep you go-ing   through the show, __   come

D.S. al Coda

Gtr. 3: w/ Rhy. Fill 1

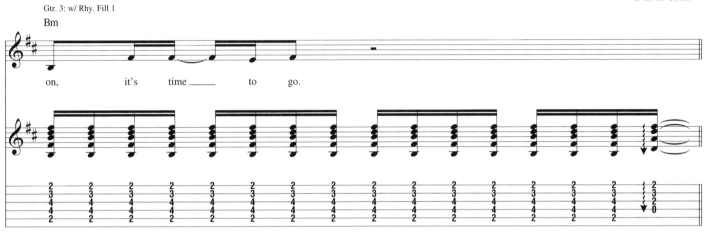

on,   it's   time ___   to   go.

$\oplus$ **Coda**

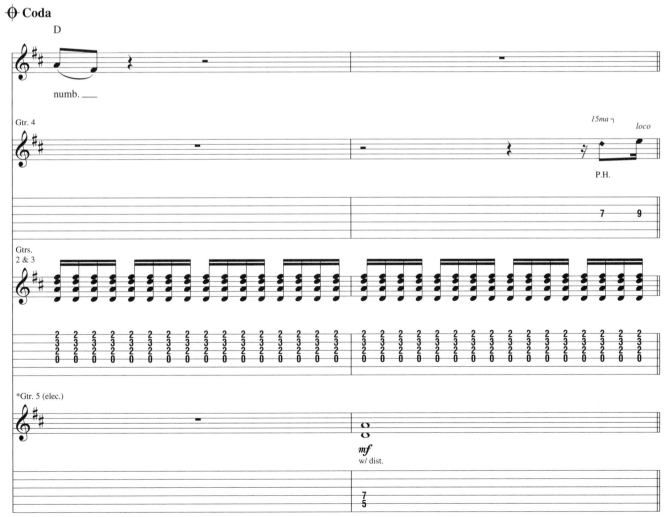

numb. ___

Gtr. 4

15ma

loco

P.H.

Gtrs.
2 & 3

*Gtr. 5 (elec.)

mf
w/ dist.

*Doubled throughout

121

Outro-Guitar Solo

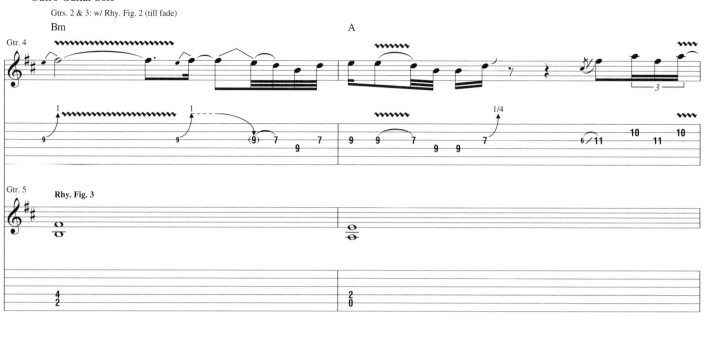

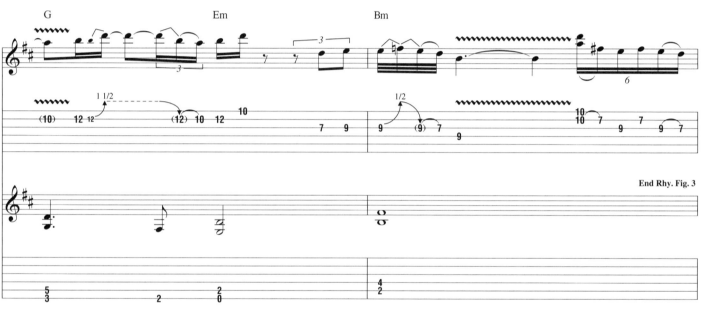

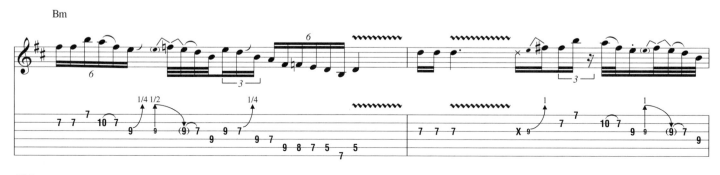

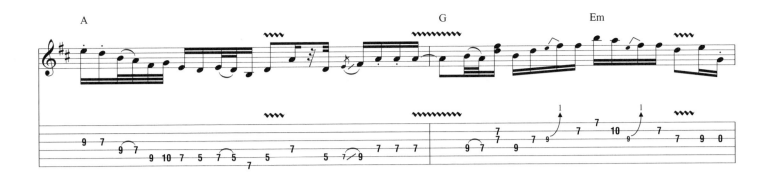

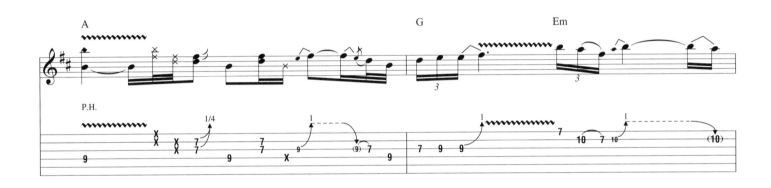

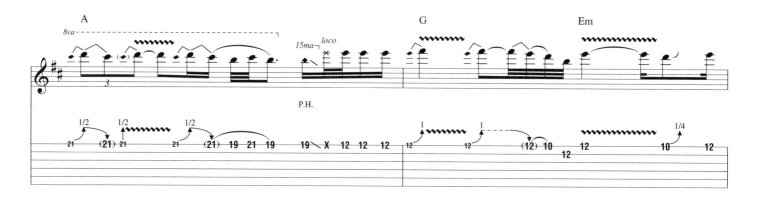

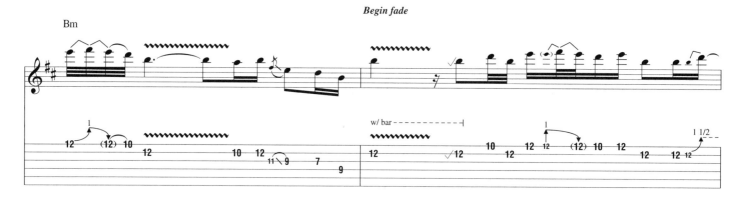

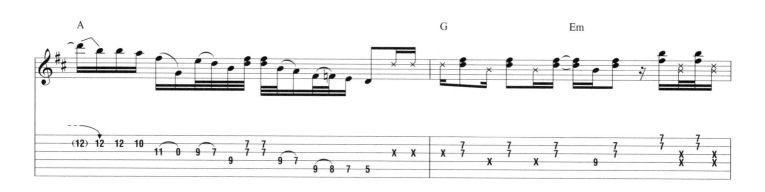

from Ozzy Osbourne - *Blizzard of Ozz*

Crazy Train

Words and Music by Ozzy Osbourne, Randy Rhoads and Bob Daisley

*w/ echo set for quarter-note regeneration w/ 7 repeats.
**Chords in parentheses implied by bass.

***Doubled throughout   †Microphonic fdbk., not caused by string vibration.

Lyrics:
1. Cra-zy, but that's how it goes. ___ I've
   lis-tened to preach-ers, I've lis-tened to fools. ___
3. Heirs of a cold war, that's what we've be-come. ___ In-

Mil-lions of peo-ple liv-ing as foes. ___
watched all the drop-outs who make their own rules. ___ One
her-it-ing trou-bles, I'm men-tal-ly numb.

126

Guitar Solo

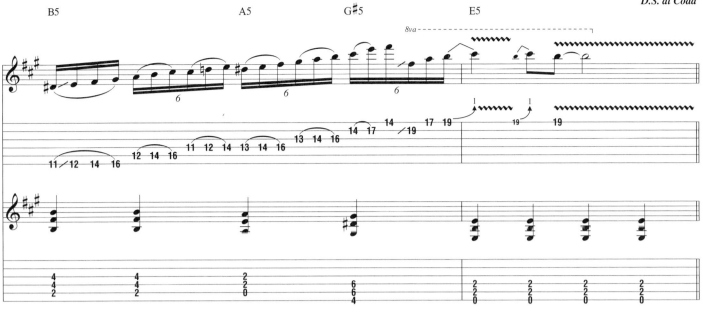

Coda

Outro

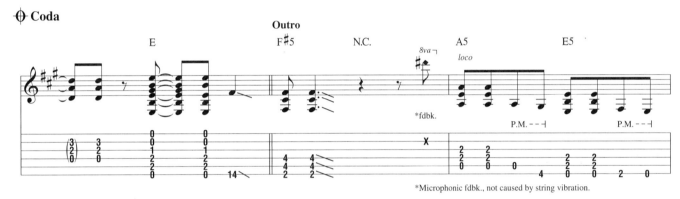

*Microphonic fdbk., not caused by string vibration.

Begin fade

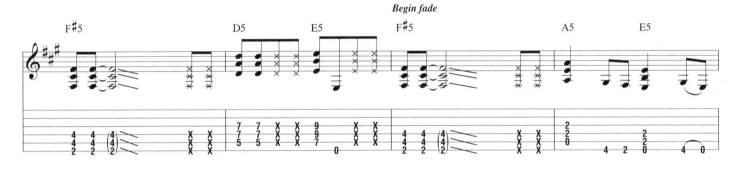

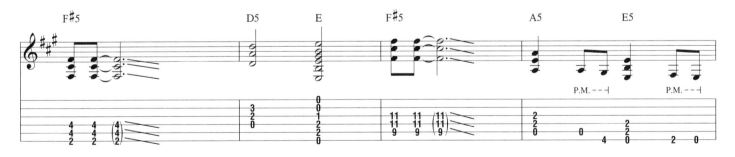

Fade out

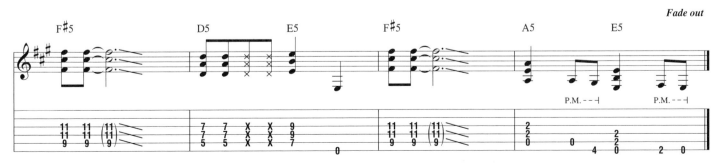

Cross Road Blues
(Crossroads)

Words and Music by Robert Johnson

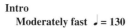

Intro
Moderately fast ♩ = 130

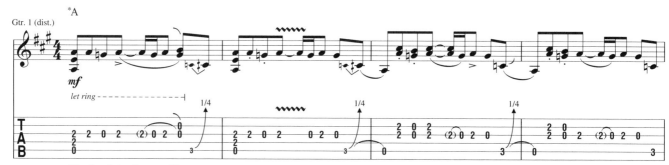

*Chord symbols reflect overall harmony.

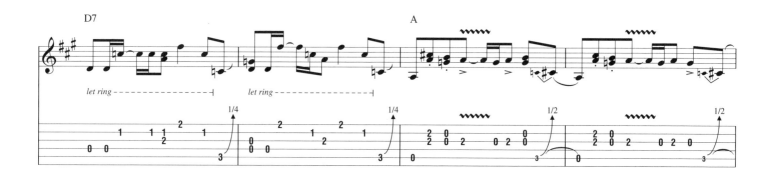

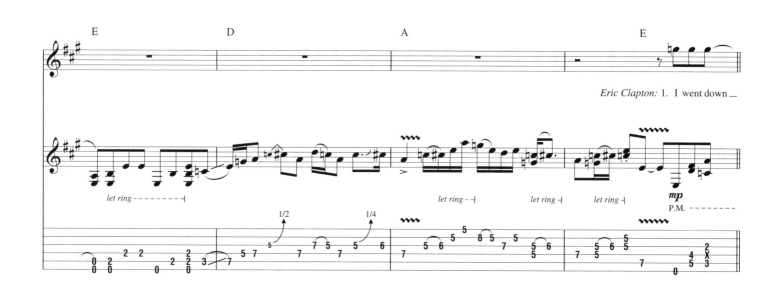

Eric Clapton: 1. I went down __

Day Tripper

Words and Music by John Lennon and Paul McCartney

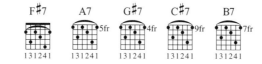

1. Got a good rea - son for tak - ing the eas - y way out. ___
2. She's a big teas - er, she took me half ___ the way there. ___
3. Tried to please ___ her, she on - ly played ___ one night stands. ___

***Paul - downstemmed notes (doubled),
John - upstemmed notes (next 8 meas.)

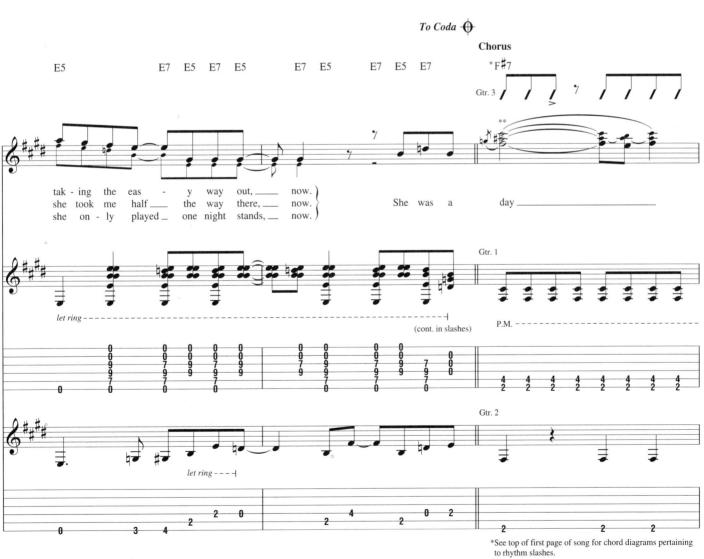

*See top of first page of song for chord diagrams pertaining to rhythm slashes.

**John - lead vocal,
George - harmony,
Paul - high harmony

2nd time, Gtr. 2: w/ Fill 1

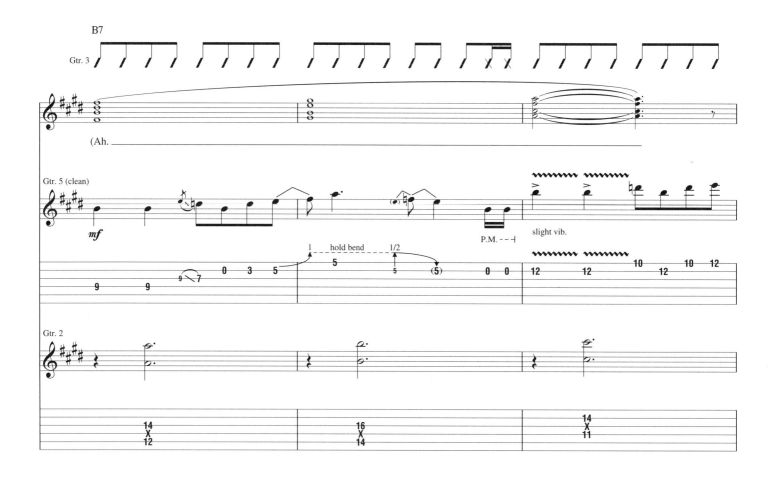

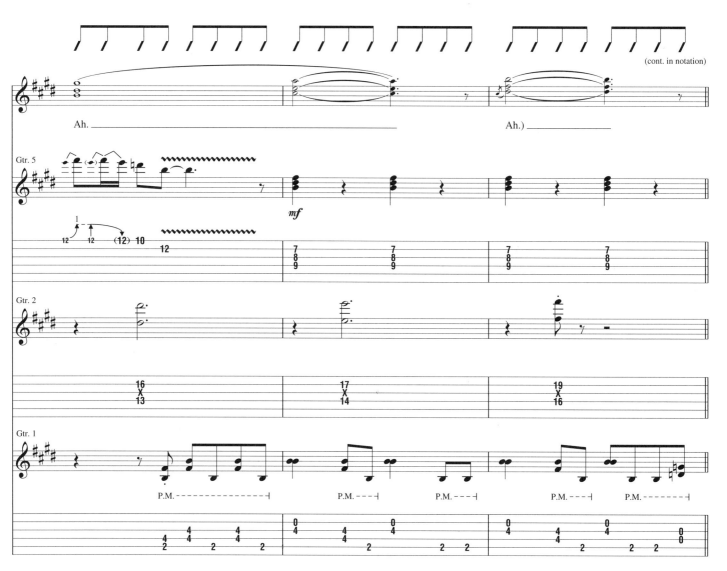

long   to find out, ___   and I found out.

Breakdown

(Bass enters)

Outro-Chorus   *Repeat & fade*

Day   trip-per,   day   trip-per,   yeah. ___

from Kiss - *Destroyer*

Detroit Rock City

Words and Music by Paul Stanley and Bob Ezrin

Tune down 1/2 step:
(low to high) Eb-Ab-Db-Gb-Bb-Eb

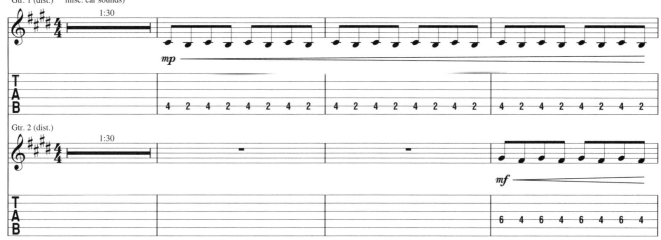

*Chord symbols reflect implied harmony.

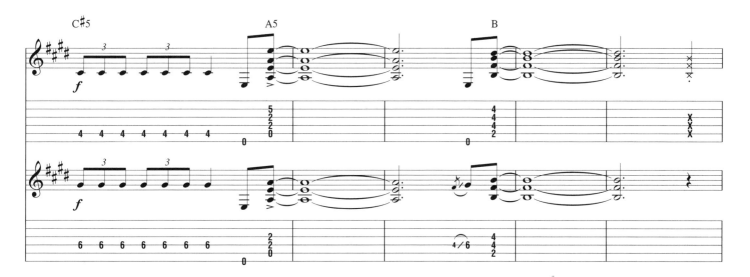

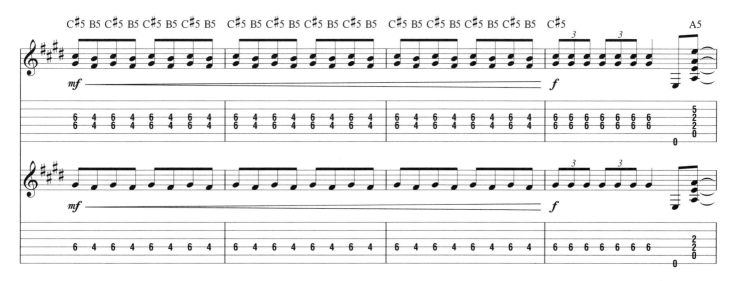

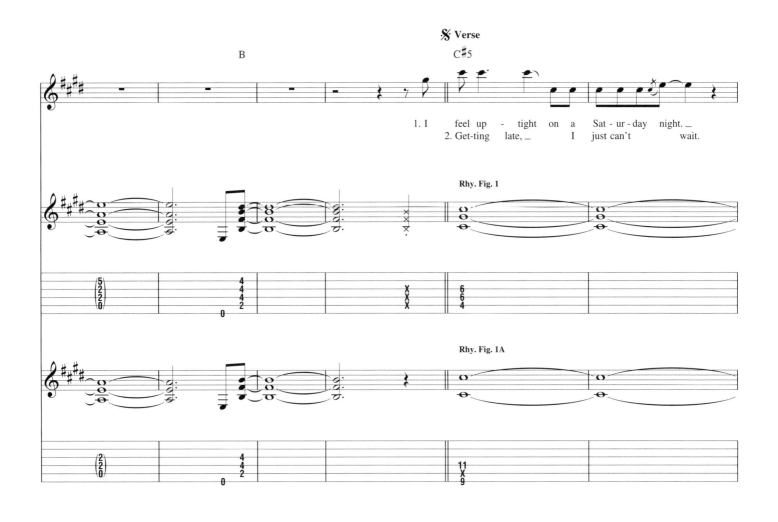

§ Verse

1. I feel up - tight on a Sat - ur - day night. _
2. Get-ting late, _ I just can't wait.

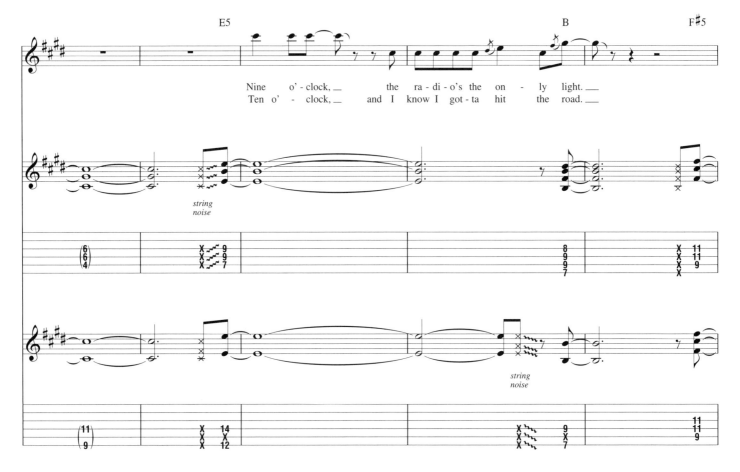

Nine o' - clock, _ the ra - di - o's the on - ly light. _
Ten o' - clock, _ and I know I got - ta hit the road. _

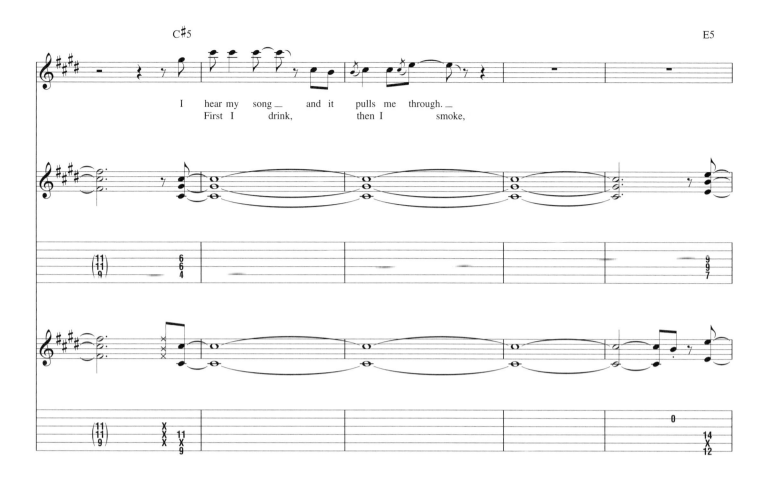

I hear my song____ and it pulls me through.____
First I drink, then I smoke,

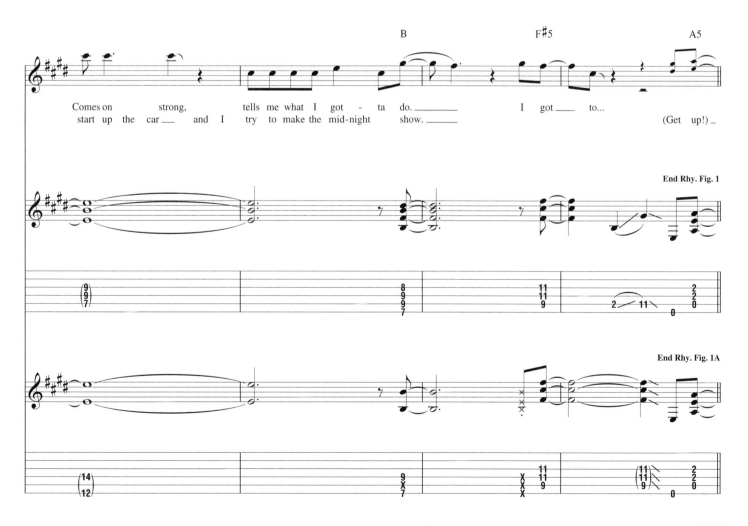

Comes on strong, tells me what I got - ta do._____ I got____ to...
start up the car___ and I try to make the mid-night show.____ (Get up!)__

End Rhy. Fig. 1

End Rhy. Fig. 1A

Chorus

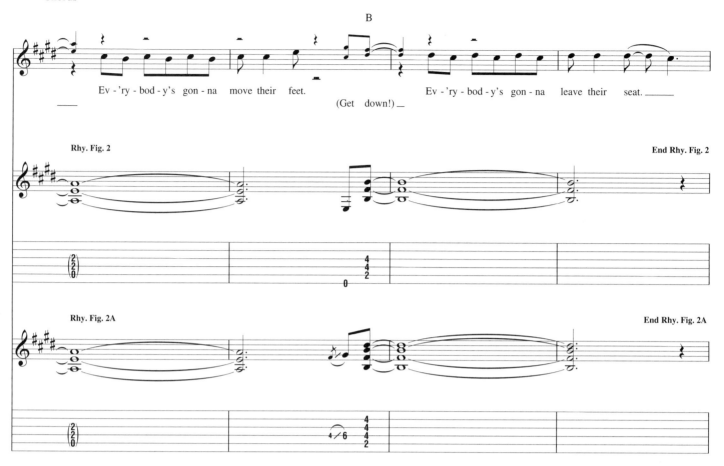

Ev-'ry-bod-y's gon-na move their feet. Ev-'ry-bod-y's gon-na leave their seat. _____

Get down!) _____

*Microphonic fdbk., not caused by string vibration.

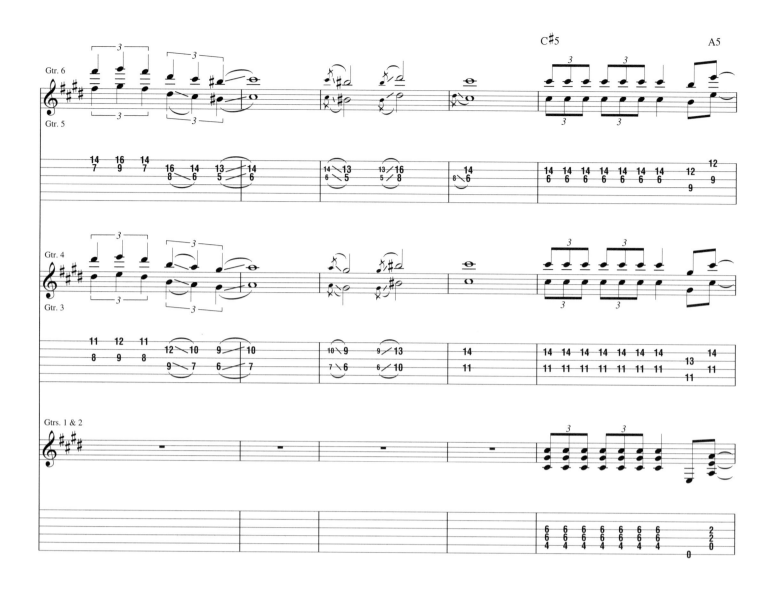

Gtrs. 1 & 2: w/ Rhy. Figs. 2 & 2A

Gtrs. 1 & 2: w/ Riff A

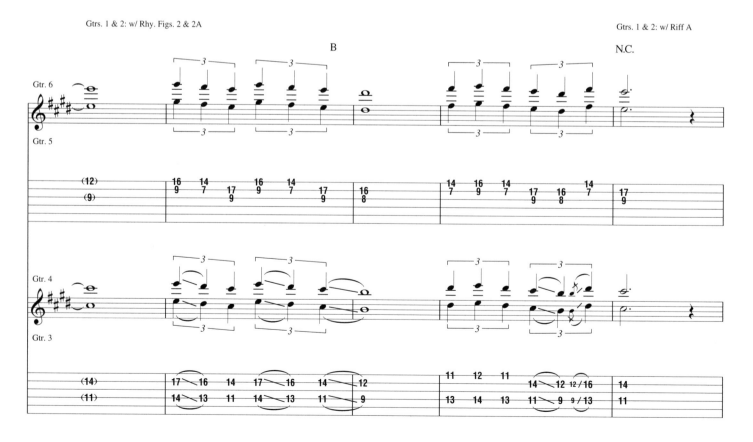

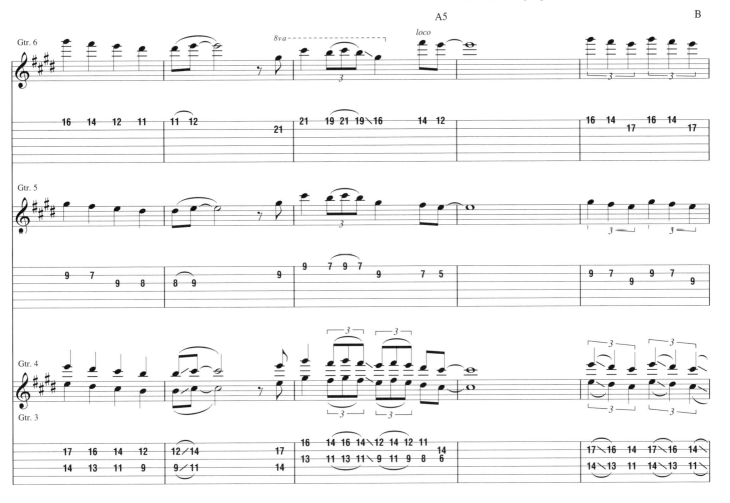

Verse

Gtr. 1: w/ Rhy. Fig. 1
Gtr. 2: w/ Riff B
Gtrs. 5 & 6 tacet

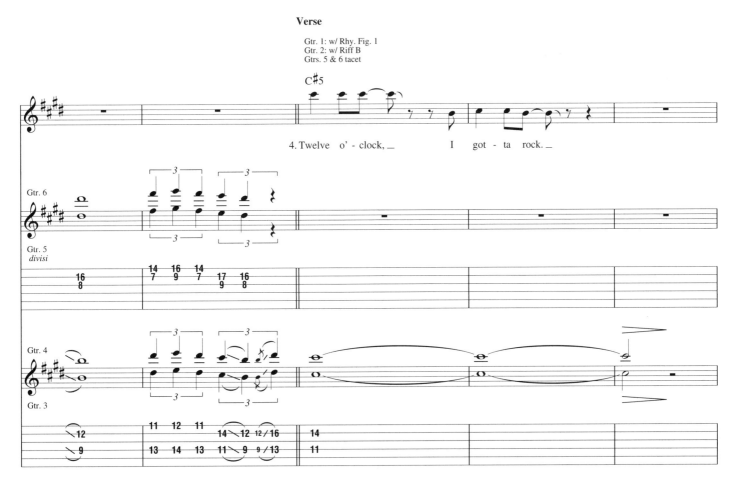

4. Twelve o'-clock, __ I got-ta rock. __

Gtrs. 3 & 4 tacet

E5 ⋯ B ⋯ F#5

There's a truck a - head, ___ lights star - in' at my eyes. _____

C#5 ⋯ E5

Oh, my God, __ no time to turn. __ I

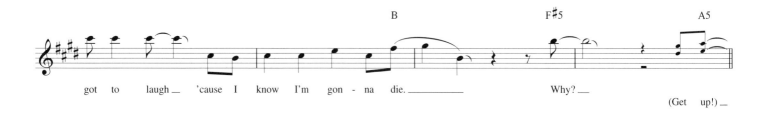

B ⋯ F#5 ⋯ A5

got to laugh __ 'cause I know I'm gon - na die. _____ Why? __

(Get up!) __

Outro-Chorus

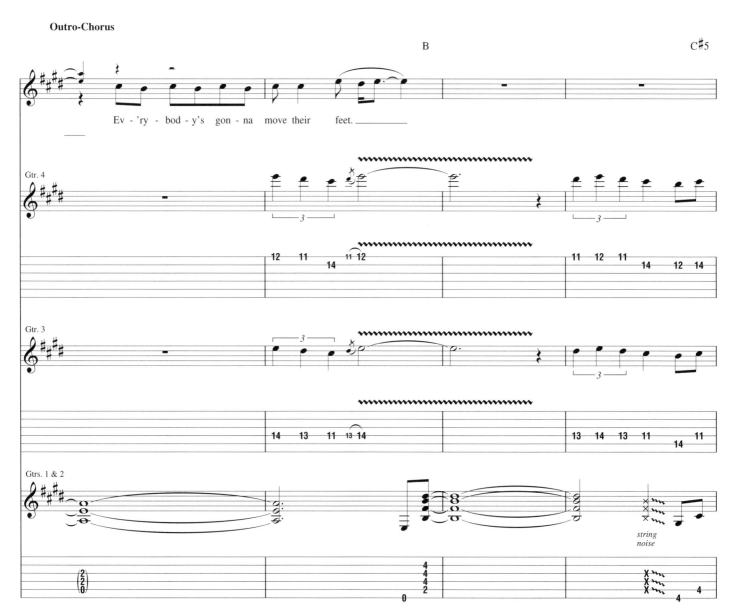

B ⋯ C#5

Ev - 'ry - bod - y's gon - na move their feet. _____

154

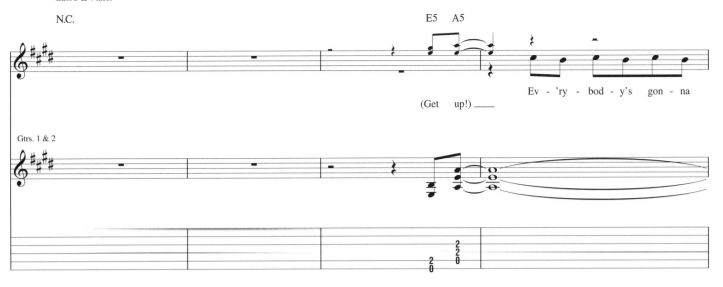

155

from Mötley Crüe - *Dr. Feel Good*

Dr. Feel Good

Words by Nikki Sixx
Music by Mick Mars and Nikki Sixx

Tune down 1 step:
(low to high) D-G-C-F-A-D

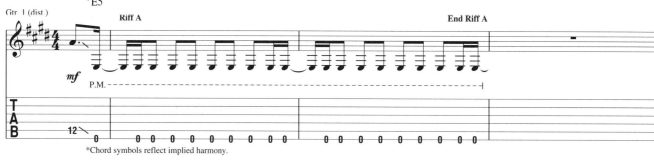

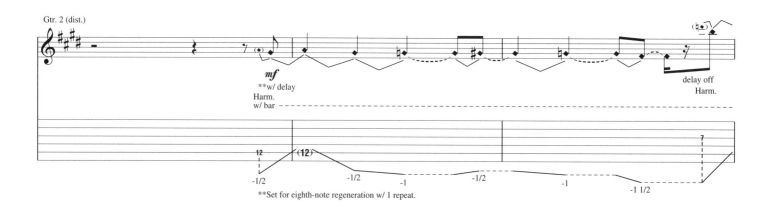

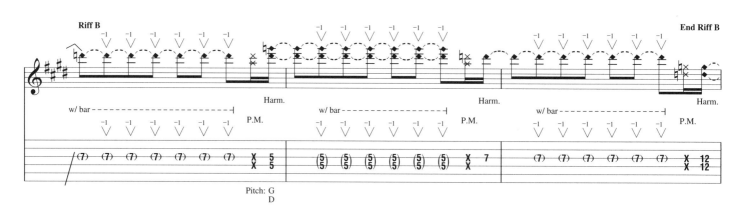

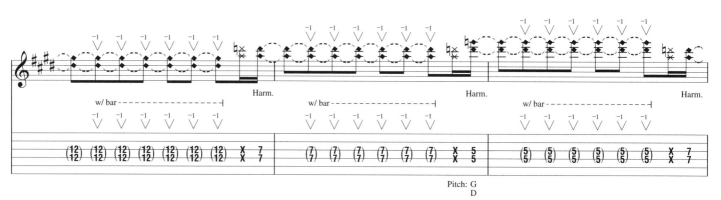

*Harmonic located six-tenths the distance between 2nd & 3rd frets.
**Set for dotted quarter-note regeneration w/ 1 repeat.

1. Rat - tailed Jim-my is a sec-ond-hand hood, deals __ out in Hol - ly - wood. Got a
__ on the cor - ner al - ways ig - nore, some - bod-y's get-ting paid. __ Jim -

Interlude

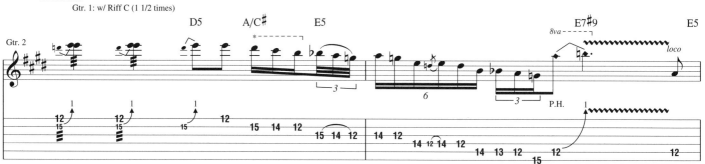

*Played as even sixteenth-notes.

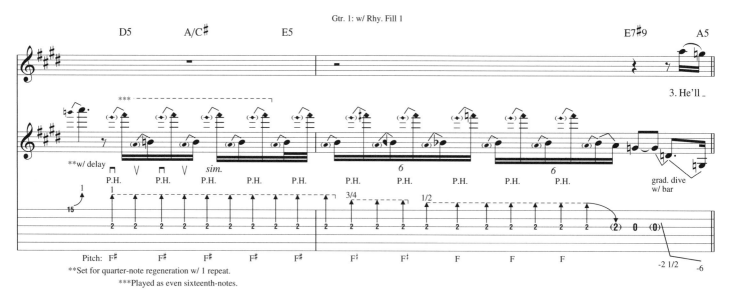

**Set for quarter-note regeneration w/ 1 repeat.
***Played as even sixteenth-notes.

Verse

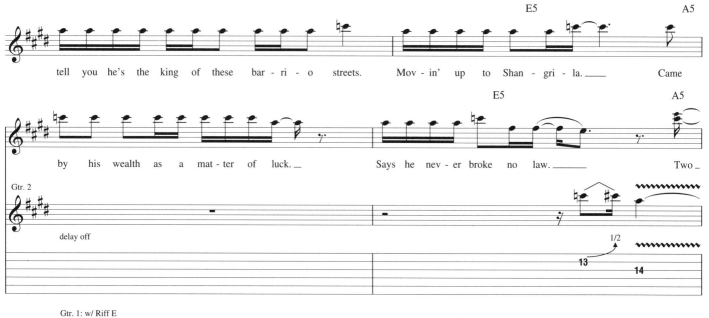

tell you he's the king of these bar-ri-o streets. Mov-in' up to Shan-gri-la.___ Came

by his wealth as a mat-ter of luck.___ Says he nev-er broke no law._____ Two

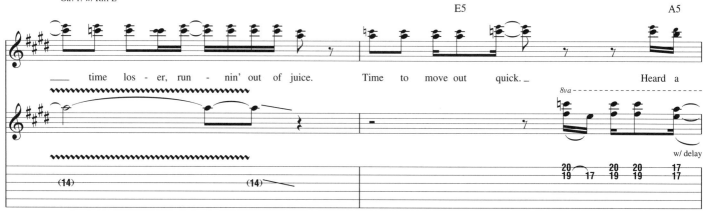

___ time los-er, run-nin' out of juice. Time to move out quick.___ Heard a

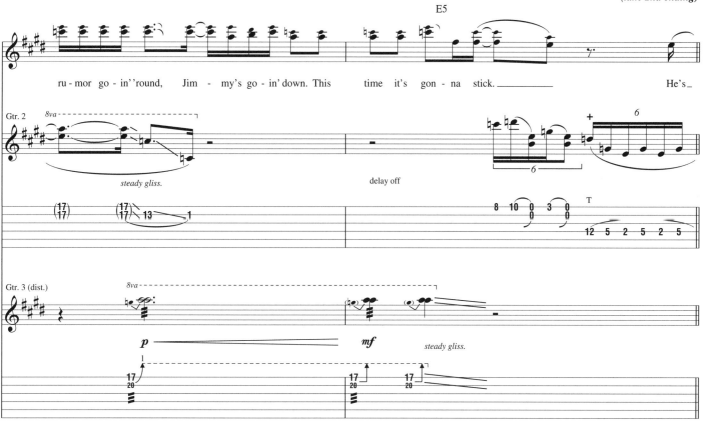

ru - mor go - in' 'round, Jim - my's go - in' down. This   time it's gon - na stick._____   He's_

$\oplus$ **Coda 1**

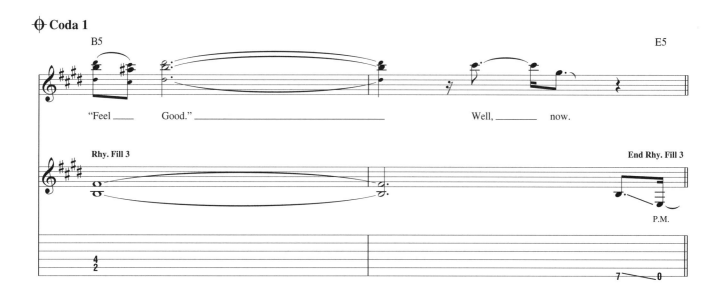

"Feel ___ Good." _____ Well, _____ now.

Interlude

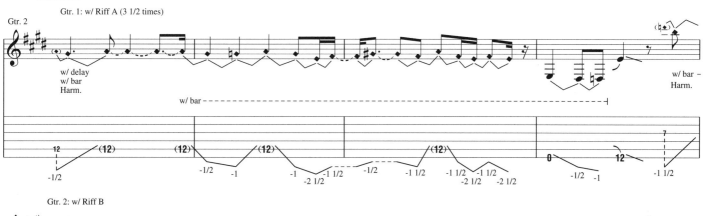

from Metallica - *Metallica*

Enter Sandman

Words and Music by James Hetfield, Lars Ulrich and Kirk Hammett

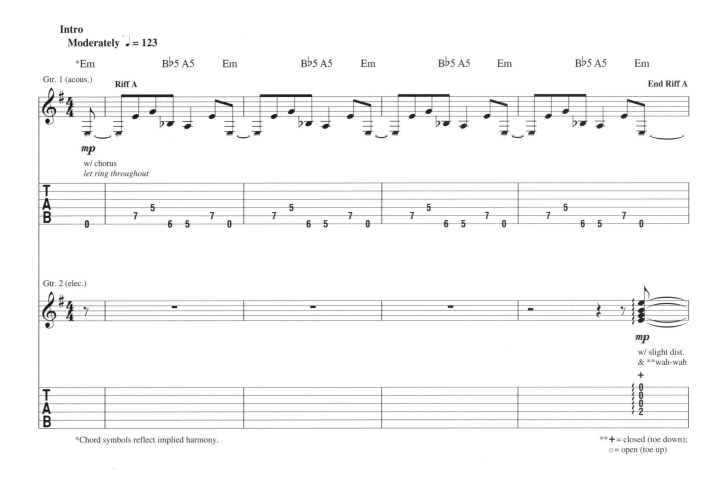

*Chord symbols reflect implied harmony.

**+ = closed (toe down);
∘ = open (toe up)

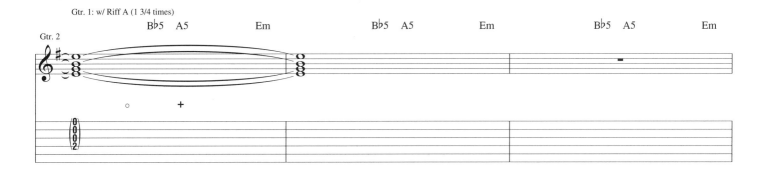

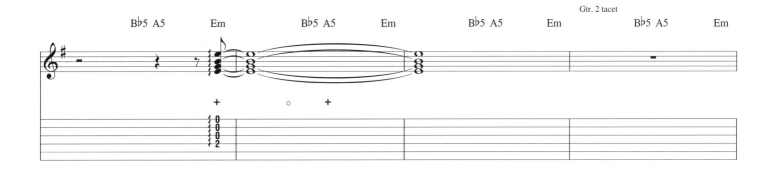

165

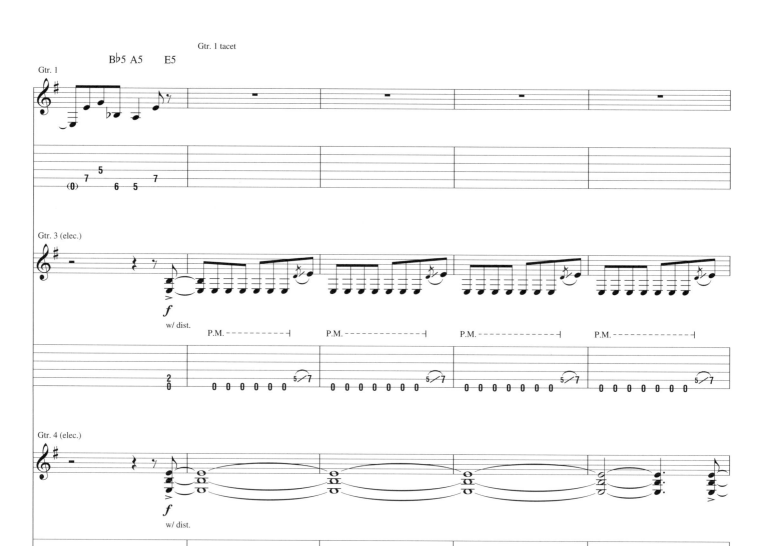

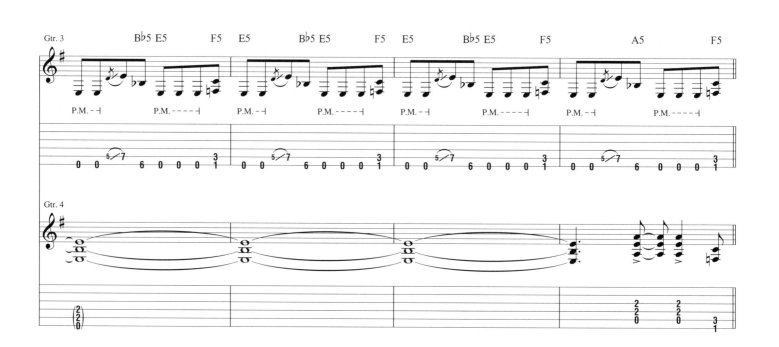

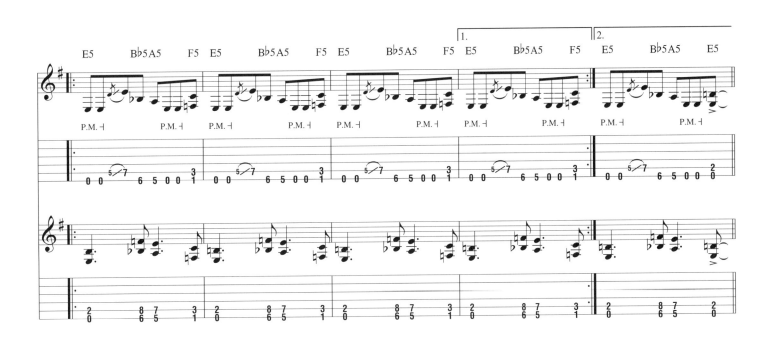

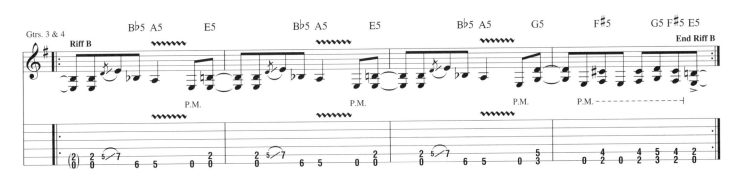

𝄋 Verse

2nd time, Gtr. 2: w/ Fill 1

2nd time, Gtr. 2: w/ Fill 2

1. Say your prayers, lit - tle one. Don't for - get, my son, ___ to in - clude ev - 'ry - one. ___
2. Some - thing's wrong. Shot the light. Heav - y thoughts to - night, ___ and they aren't of Snow White. ___

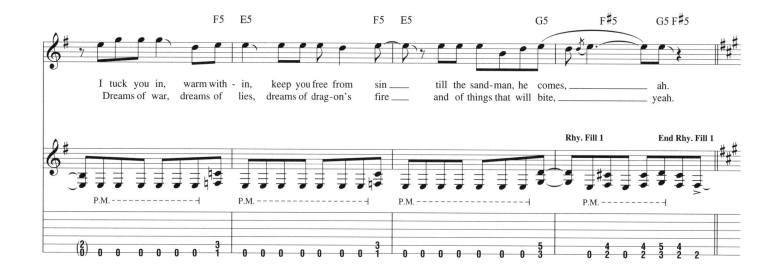

I tuck you in, warm with - in, keep you free from sin ___ till the sand-man, he comes, ___ ah.
Dreams of war, dreams of lies, dreams of drag-on's fire ___ and of things that will bite, ___ yeah.

Sleep with one ___ eye o - pen, grip-ping your pil - low tight. ___

Ex - it: light. ___ En - ter: night. ___

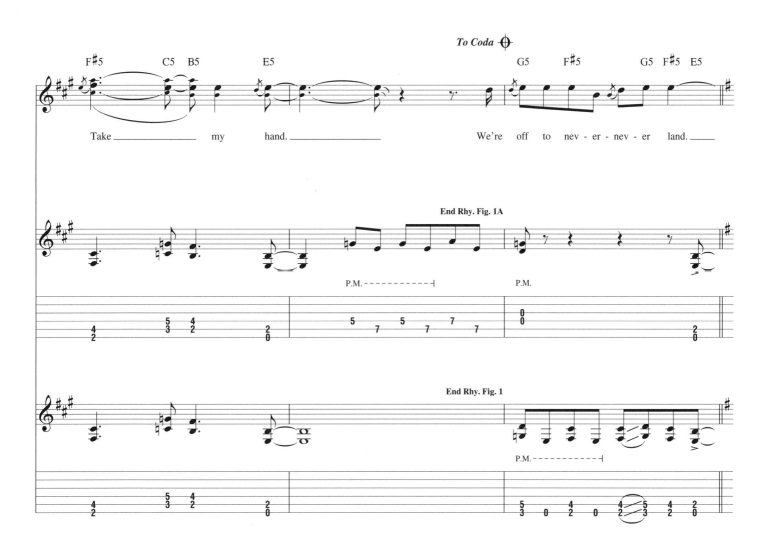

Take ____ my hand. _____ We're off to nev - er - nev - er land. ____

Interlude

Gtrs. 3 & 4: w/ Riff B (2 times)

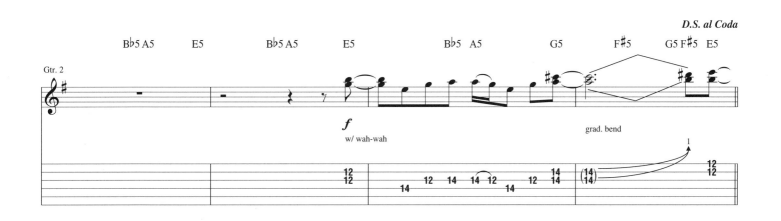

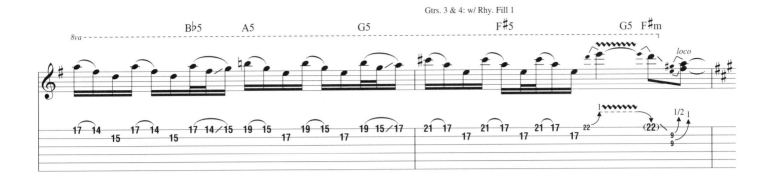

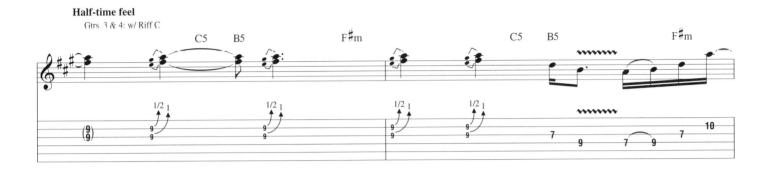

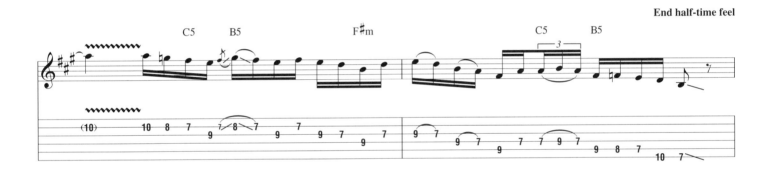

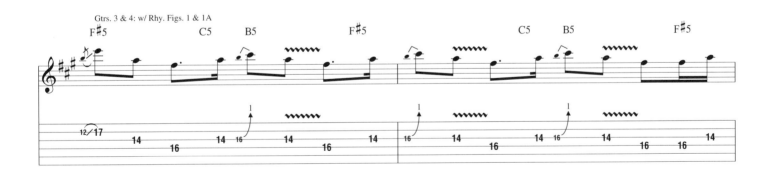

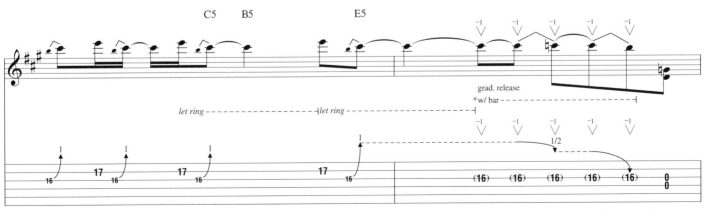

*Gradually release bend while articulating w/ trem. bar.

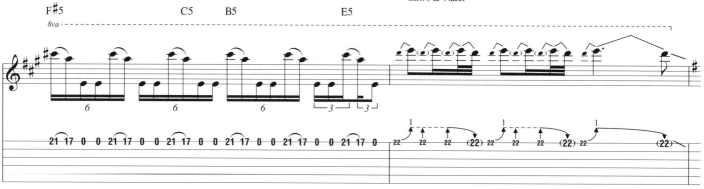

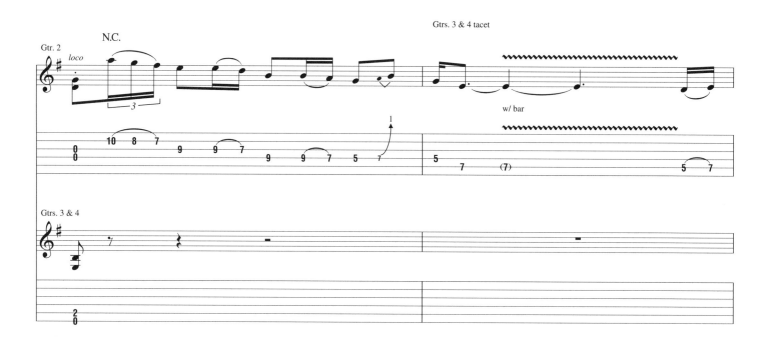

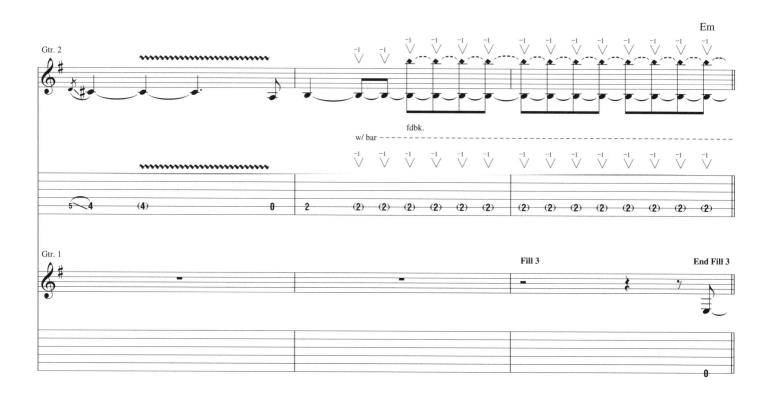

Interlude

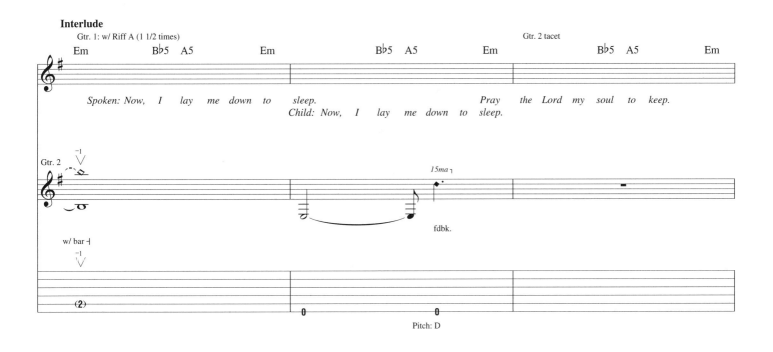

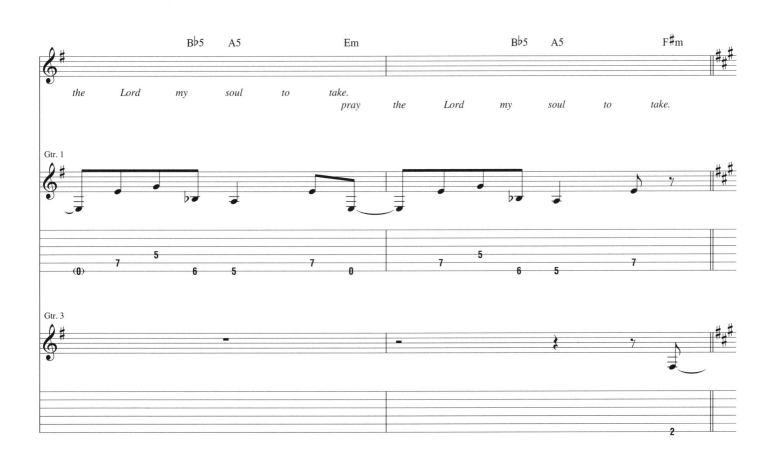

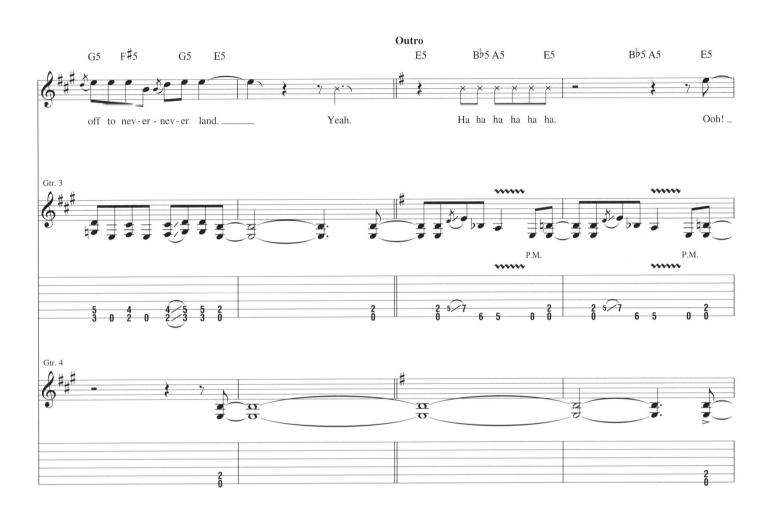

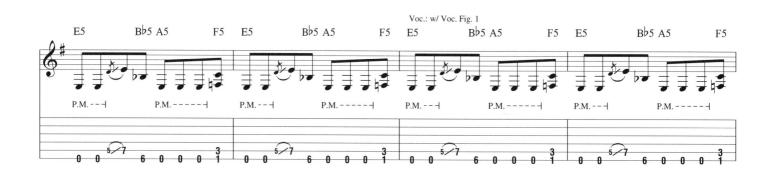

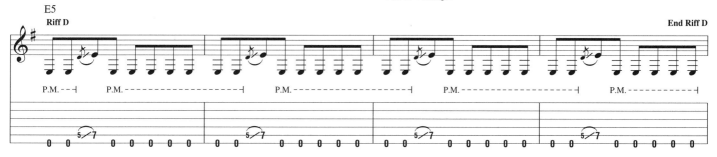

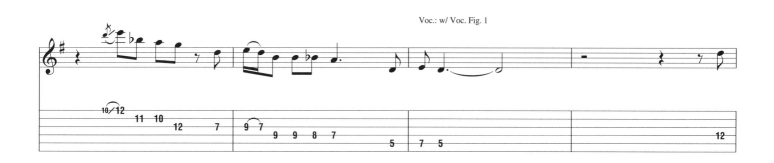

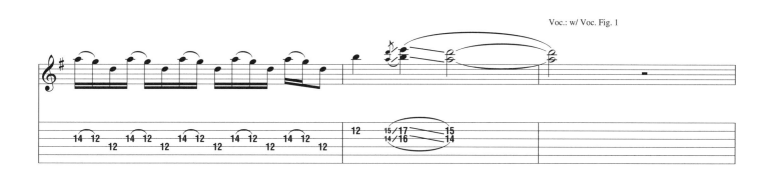

Free Bird

Words and Music by Allen Collins and Ronnie Van Zant

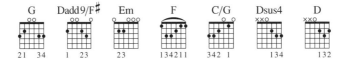

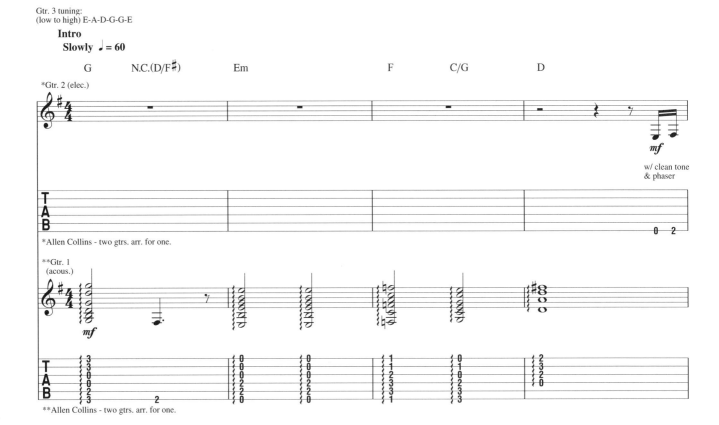

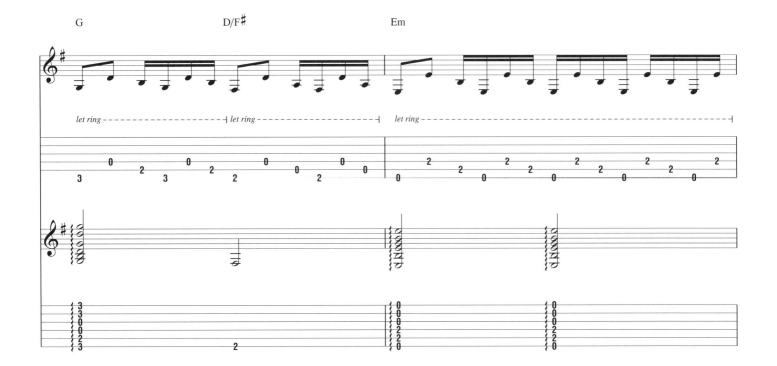

F　　　　　　　　C/G　　　　　　　　　　　D　　　　　Dsus4 D　　　Dsus4 D　　　Dsus4 D

*Gtr. 3 (elec.)

w/ dist.
w/ slide
w/ fingers

*Gary Rossington - two gtrs. arr. for one.

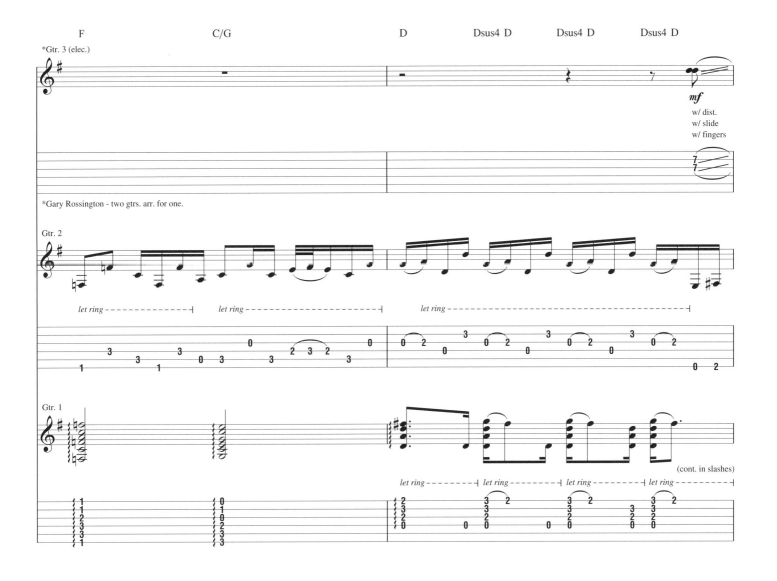

(cont. in slashes)

**G　　　　　　　　Dadd9/F#　　　　　　　Em

Rhy. Fig. 1

Riff A

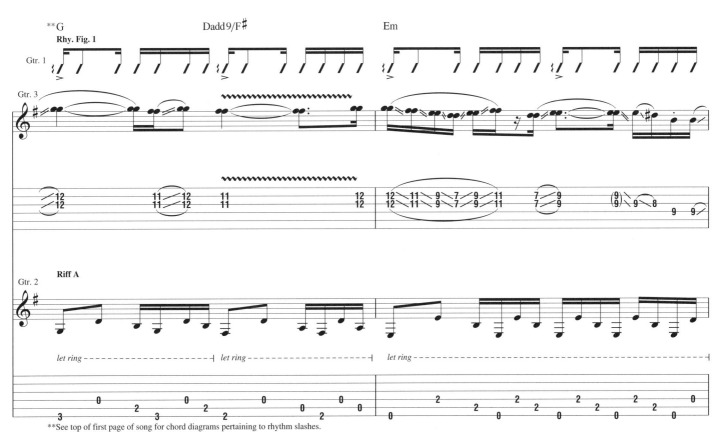

**See top of first page of song for chord diagrams pertaining to rhythm slashes.

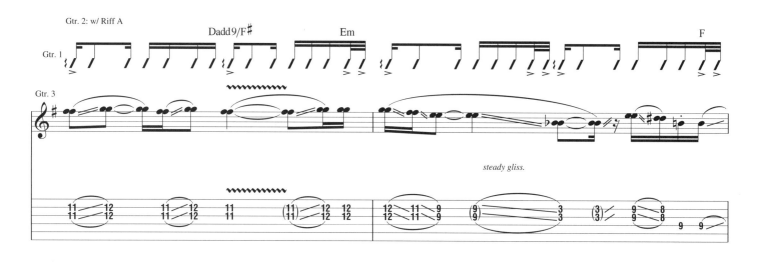

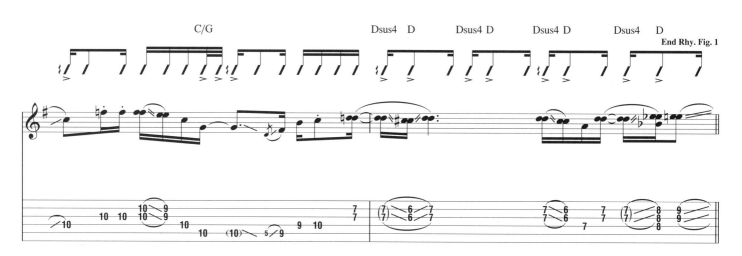

Verse

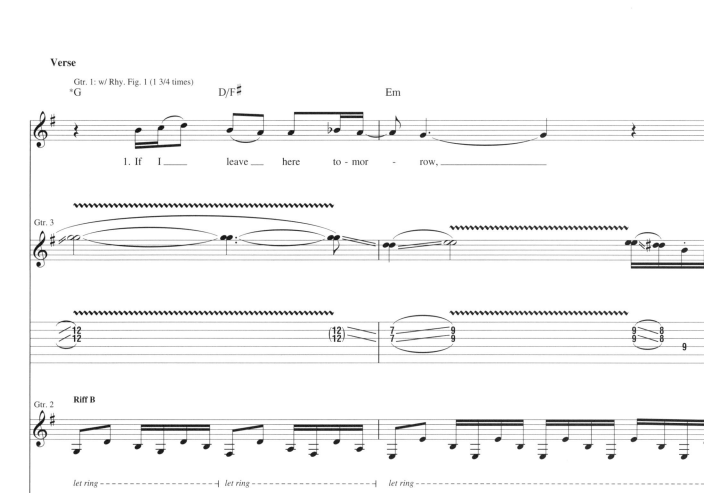

*Chord symbols reflect basic harmony.

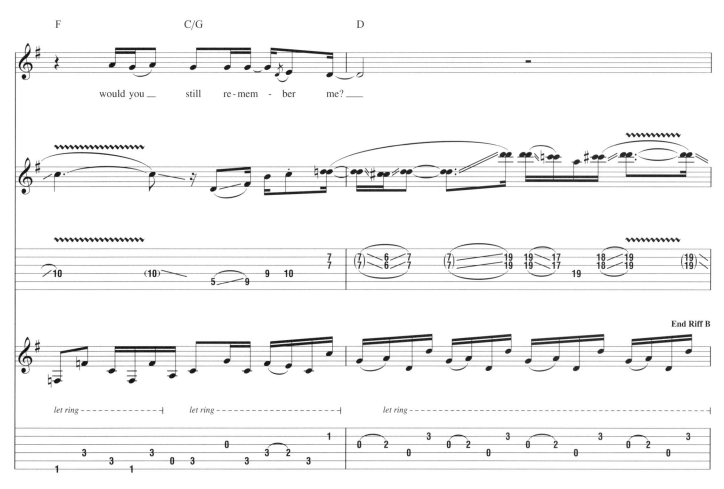

182

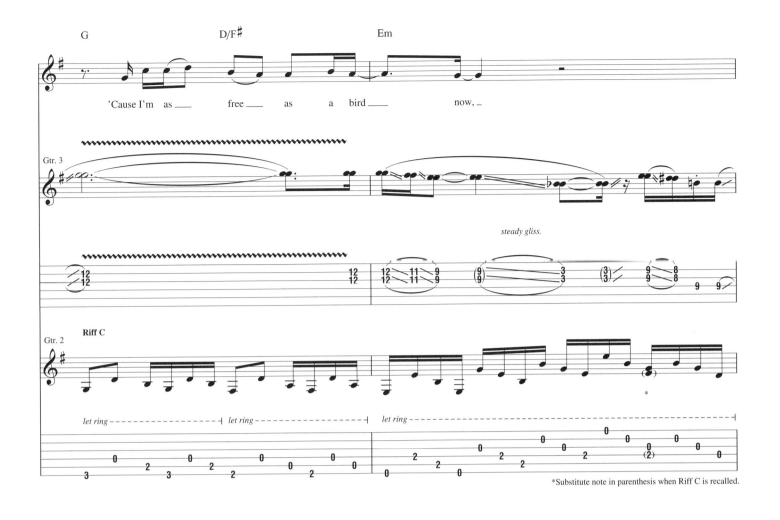

*Substitute note in parenthesis when Riff C is recalled.

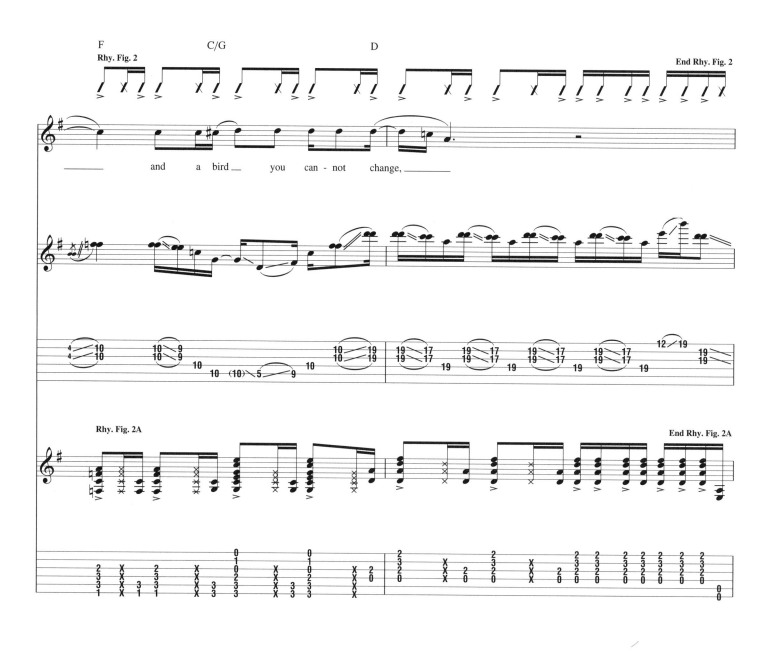

and a bird___ you can not change,___

and this bird___ you can not change.___

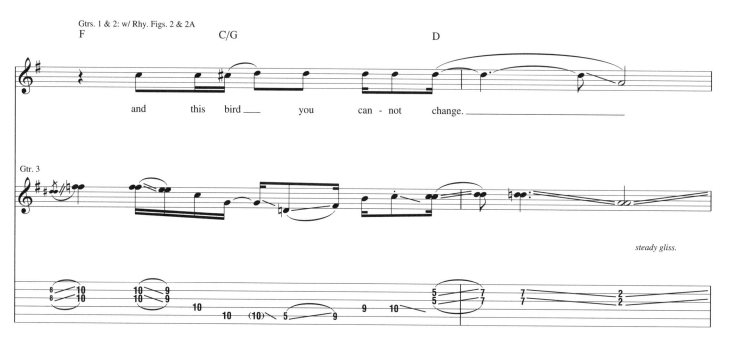

184

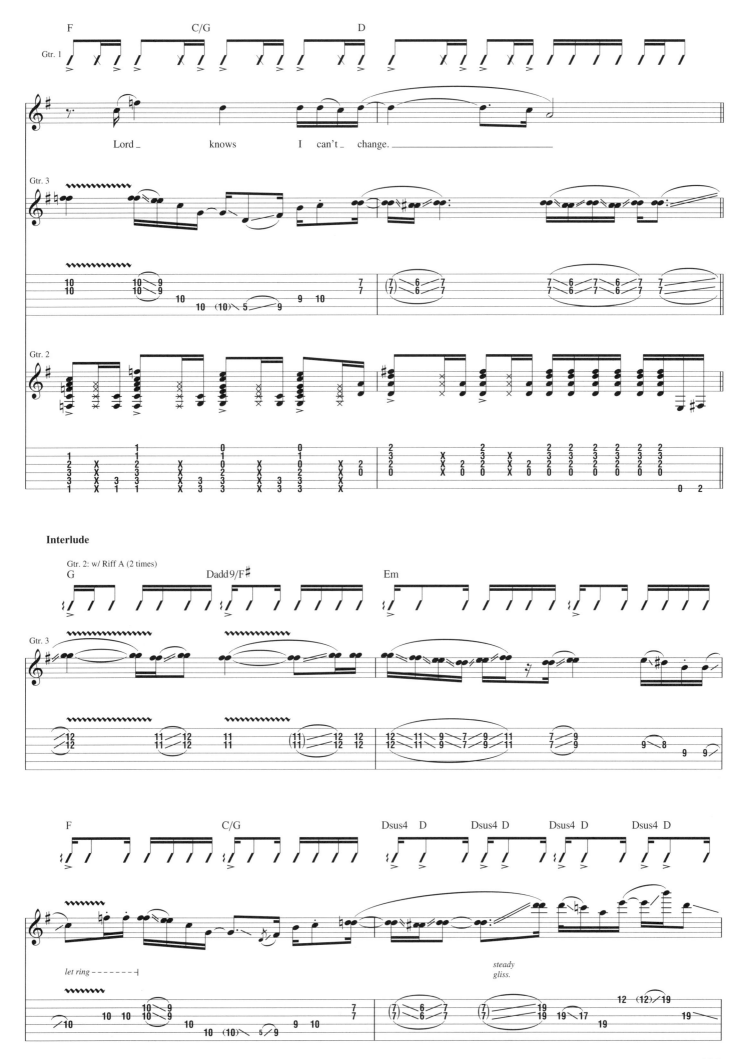

Lord __ knows I can't __ change. _____

Interlude

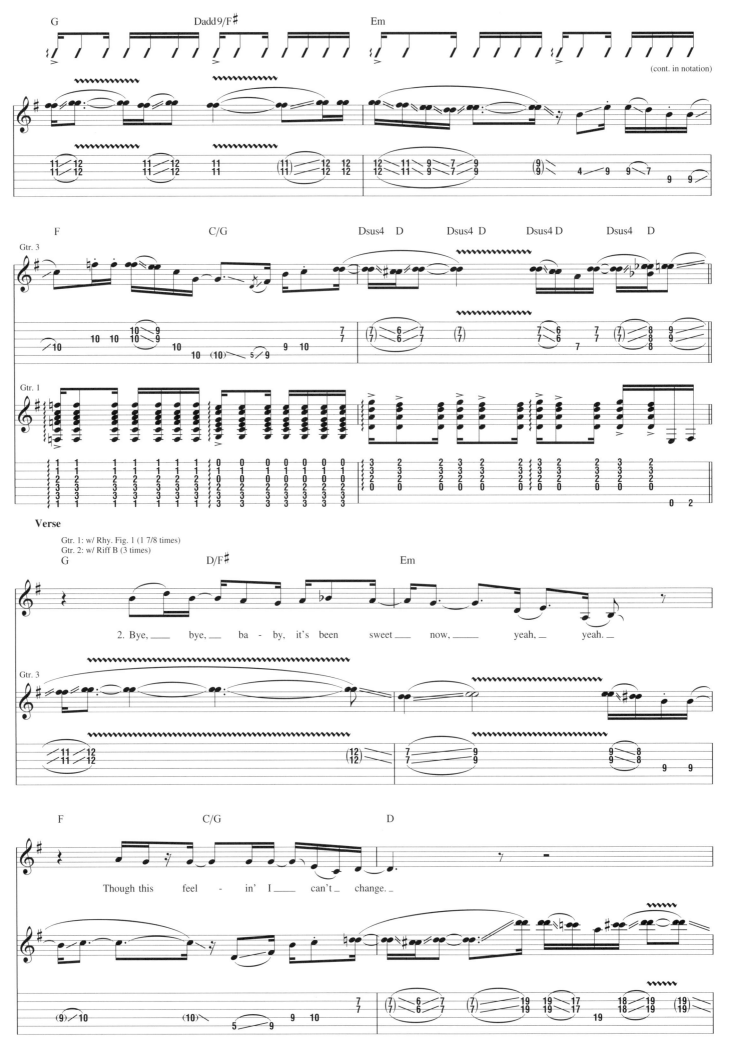

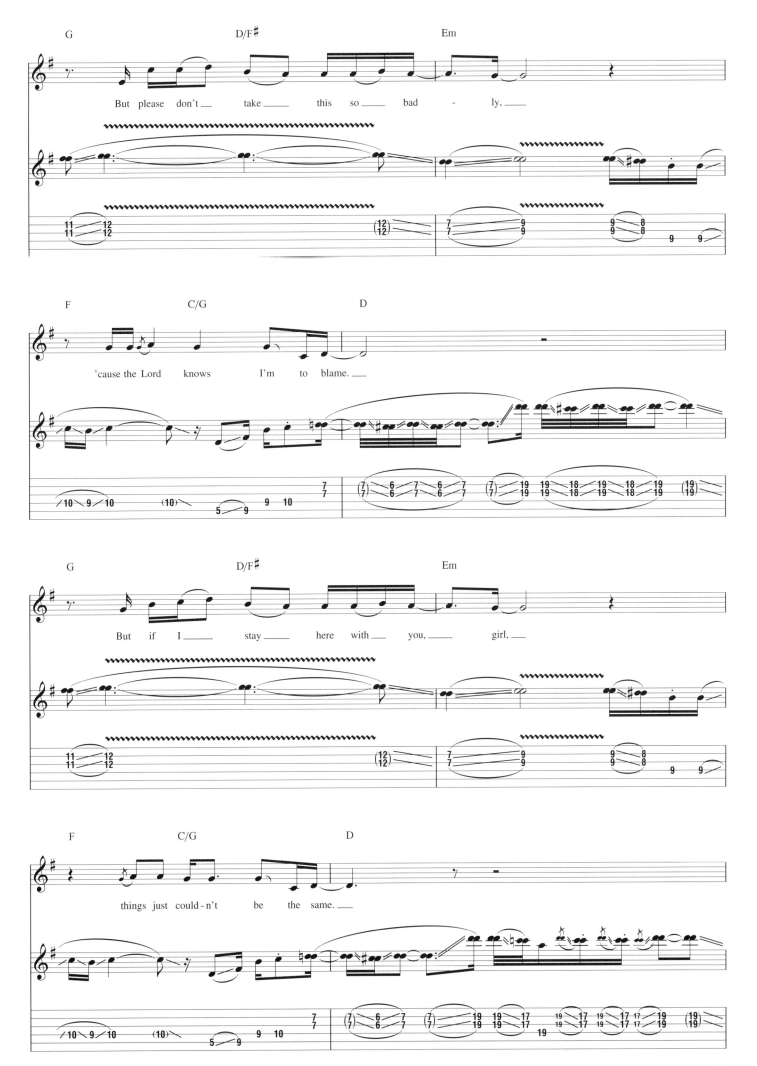

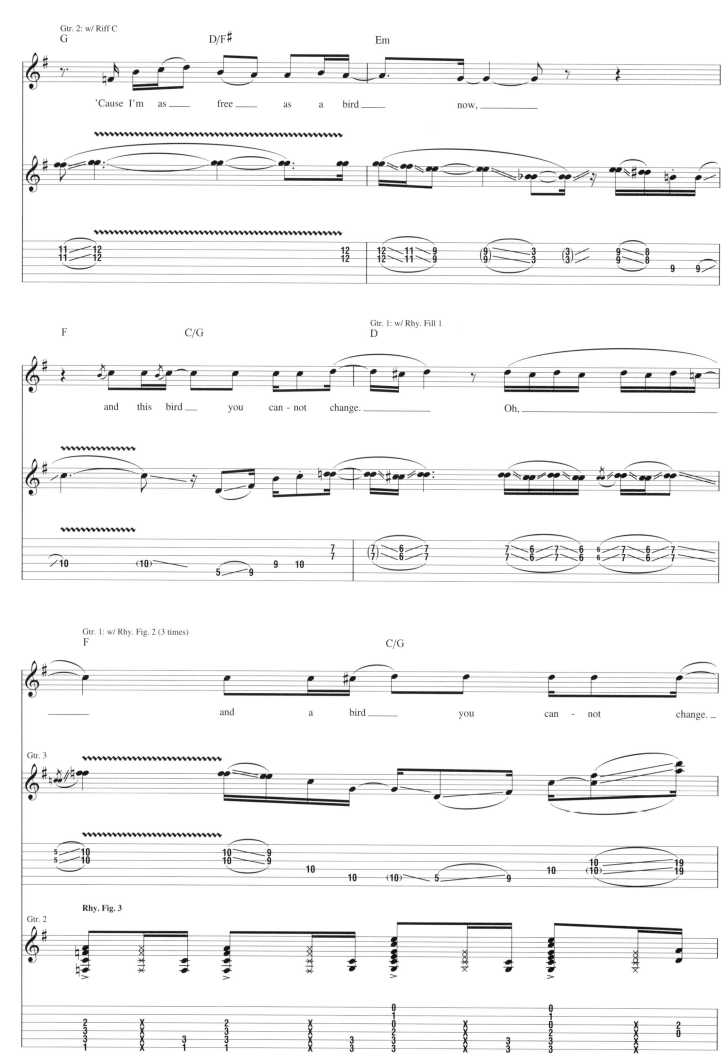

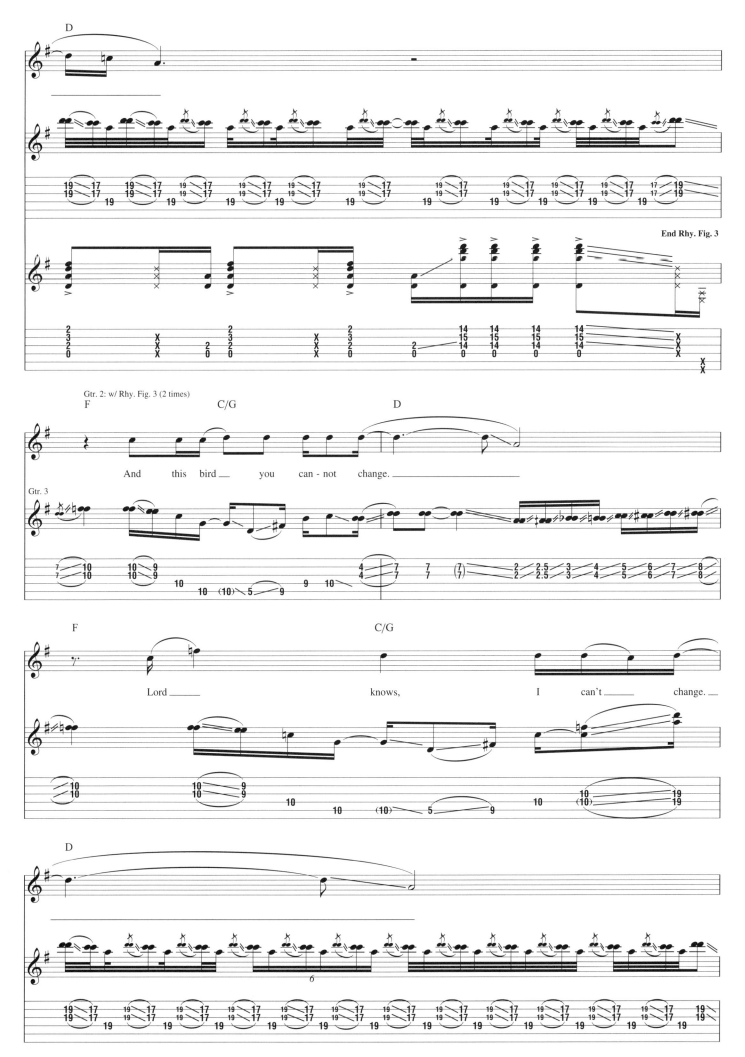

Lord, help me, I can't ___ change. ___

Lord, ___ I can't ___ change. ___ Won't you

Bridge
Faster ♩ = 150

*Composite arrangement

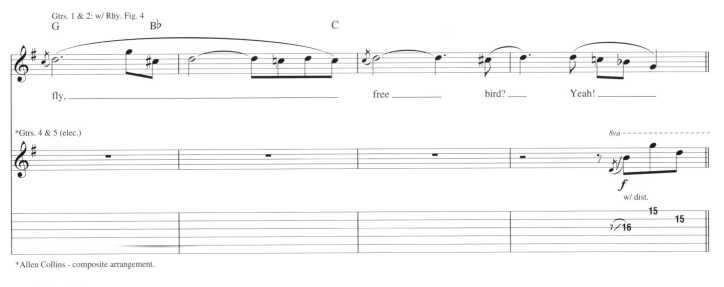

fly, _____ free _____ bird? ____ Yeah! _____

*Gtrs. 4 & 5 (elec.)

*Allen Collins - composite arrangement.

Guitar Solo

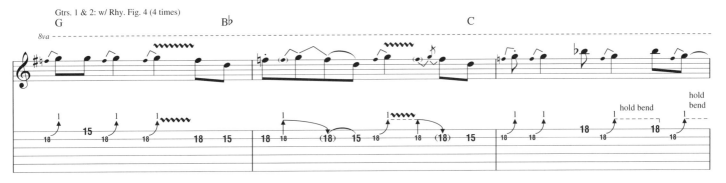

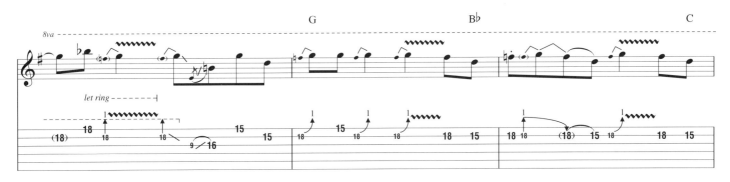

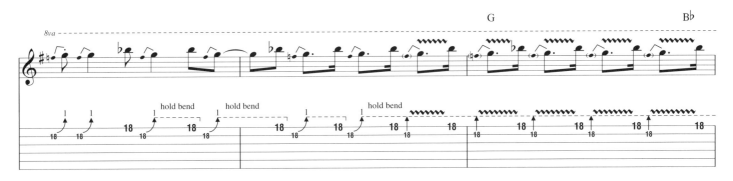

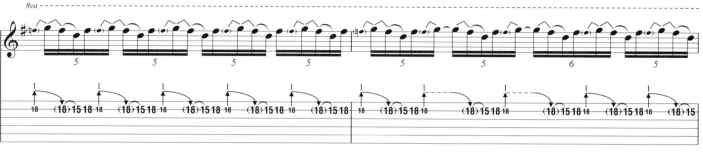

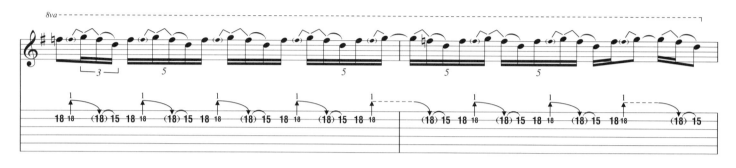

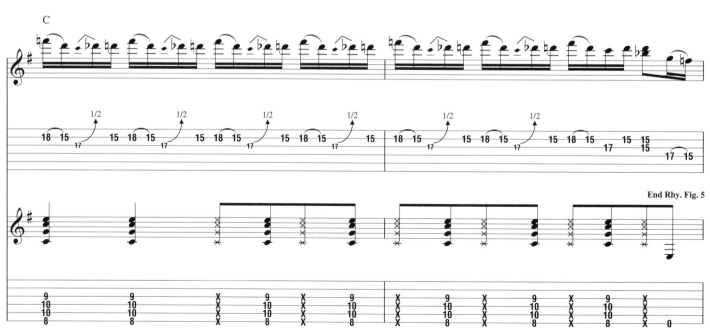

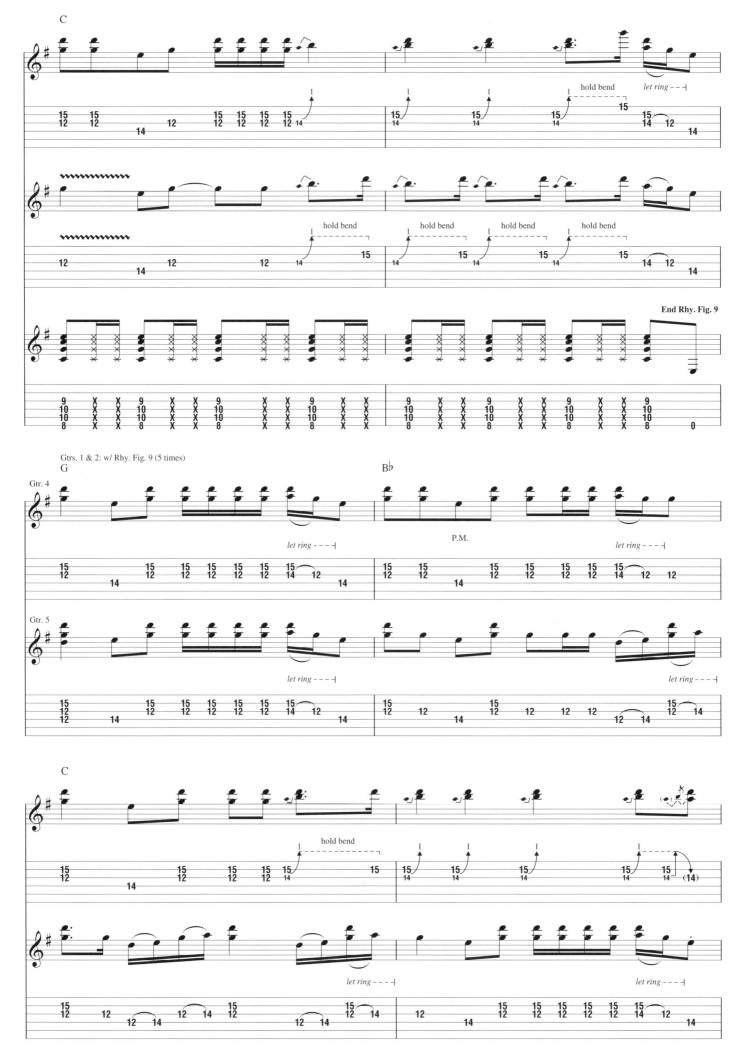

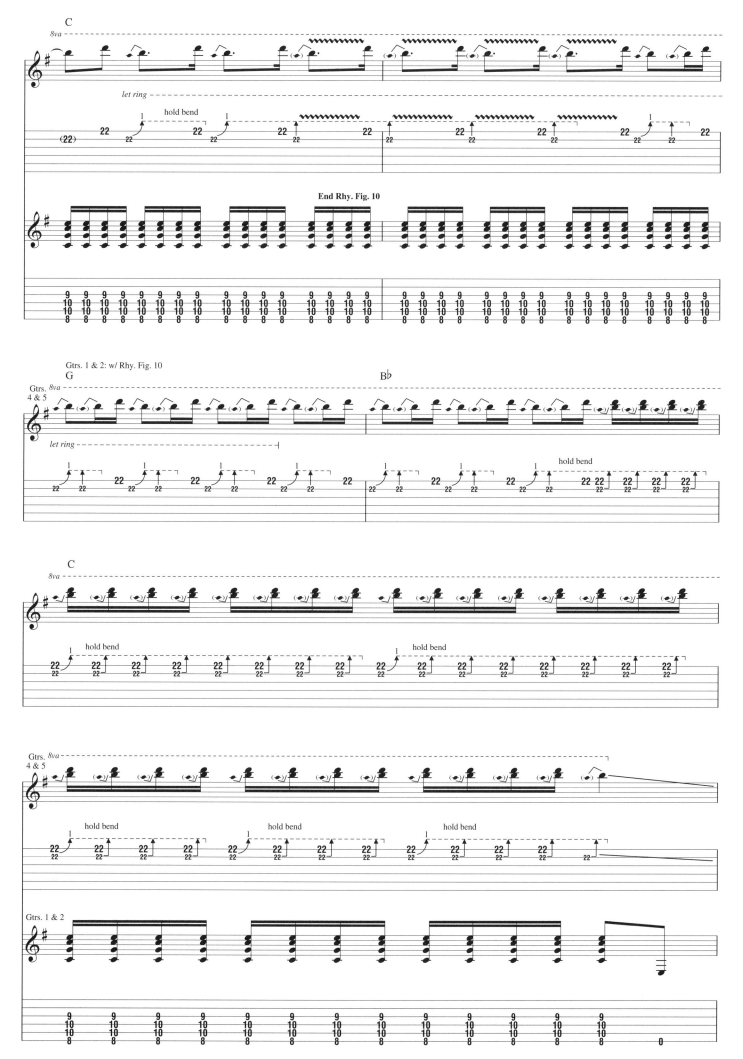

207

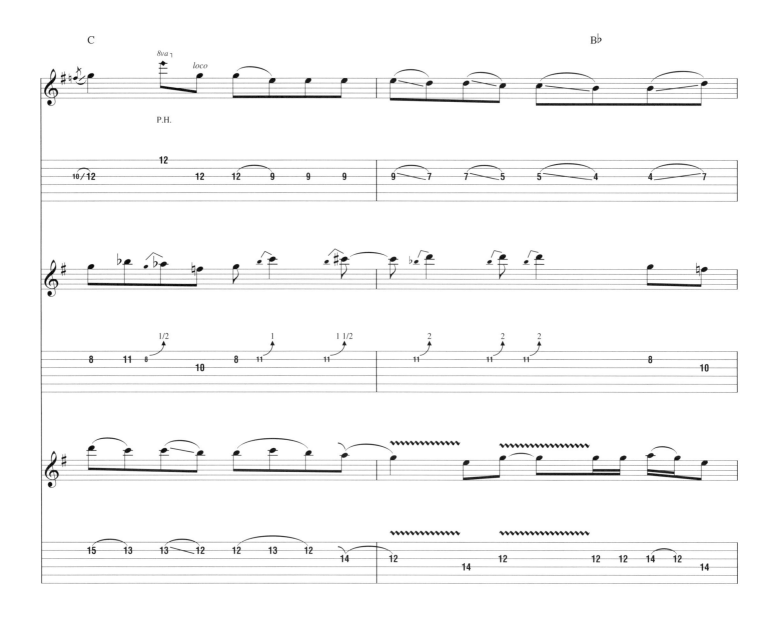

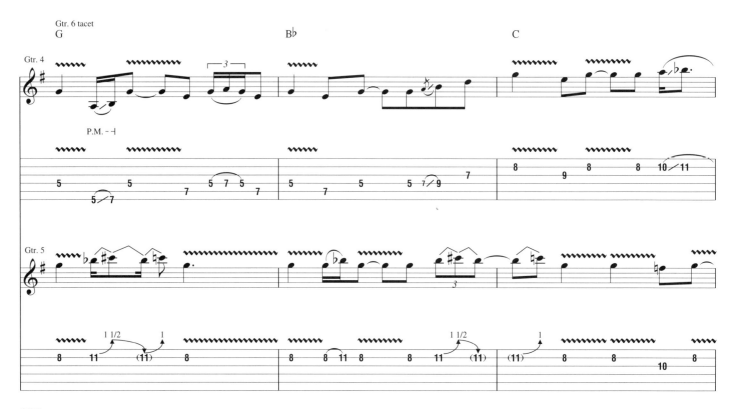

from James Gang - *Rides Again*

Funk #49

Words and Music by Joe Walsh, Dale Peters and James Fox

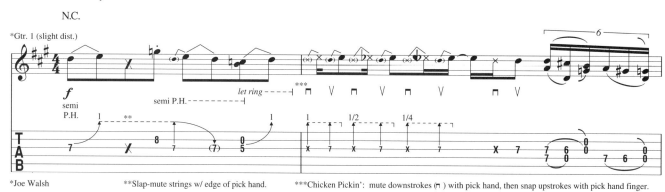

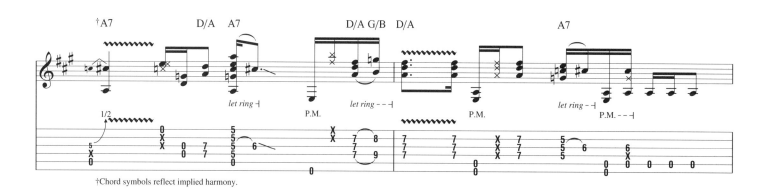

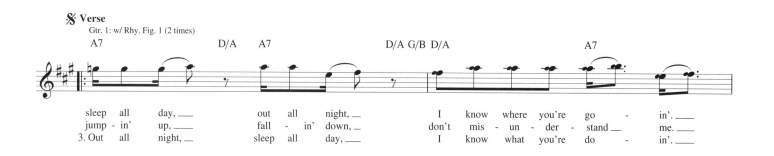

sleep all day, ___ out all night, ___ I know where you're go - in'. ___
jump - in' up, ___ fall - in' down, ___ don't mis - un - der - stand ___ me. ___
3. Out all night, ___ sleep all day, ___ I know what you're do - in'. ___

I don't think ___ that's a, act - in' right, ___   you don't think it's show - in'. ___
You don't think ___ that I know your plan;   what you try'n' to hand ___ me?
If you're gon - na a, act that way, ___   I think there's trou - ble brew - in'. ___

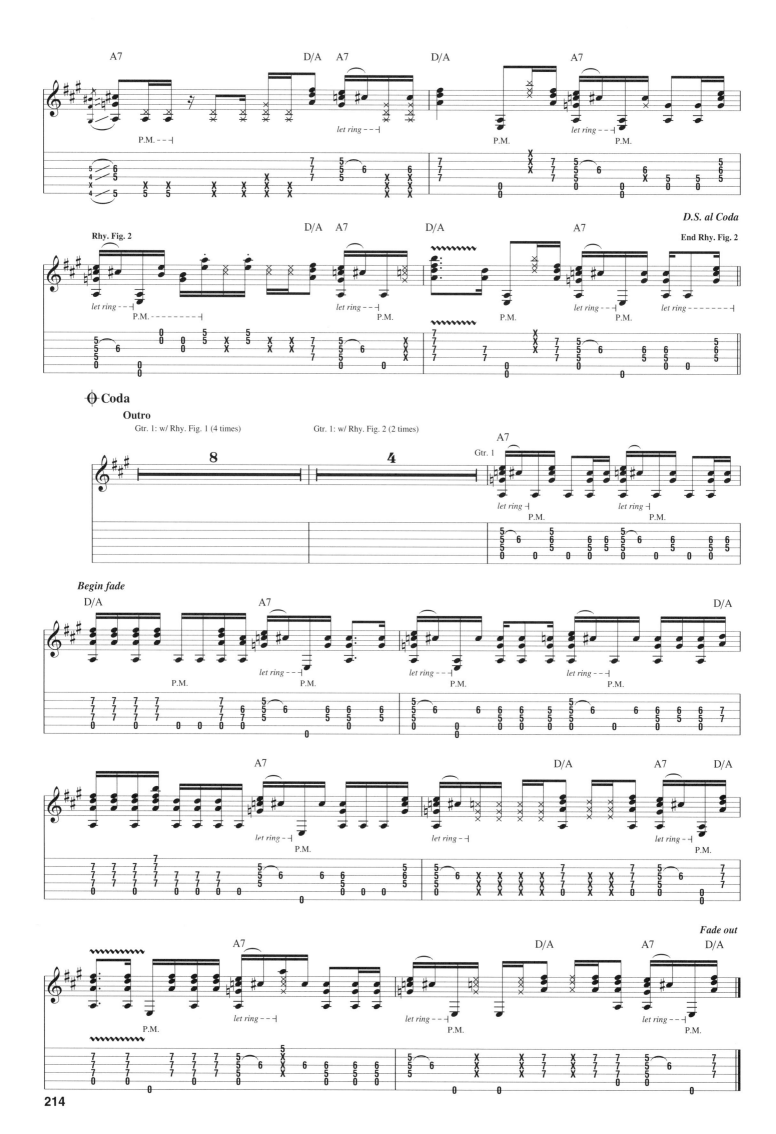

214

Highway to Hell

Words and Music by Angus Young, Malcolm Young and Bon Scott

Guitar Solo

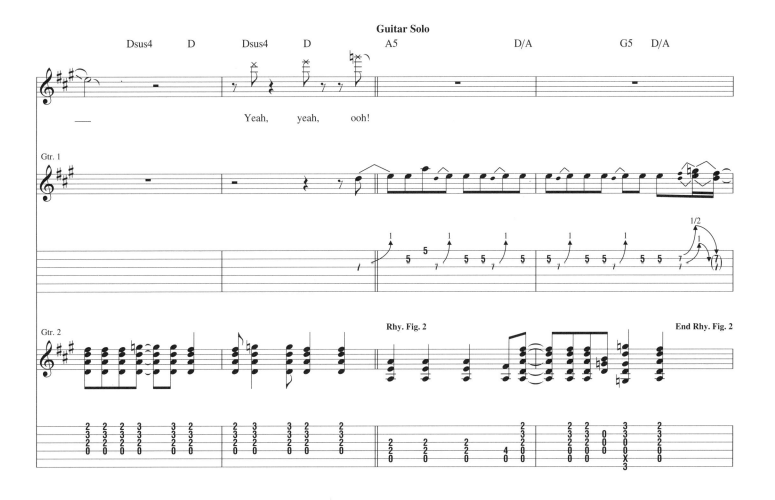

Yeah, yeah, ooh!

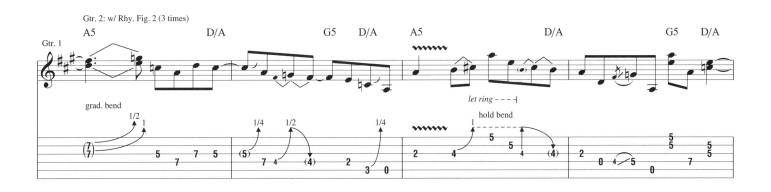

Outro-Chorus

Bkgd. Voc.: w/ Voc. Fig. 1
Gtr. 2: w/ Rhy. Fig. 2 (2 1/2 times)

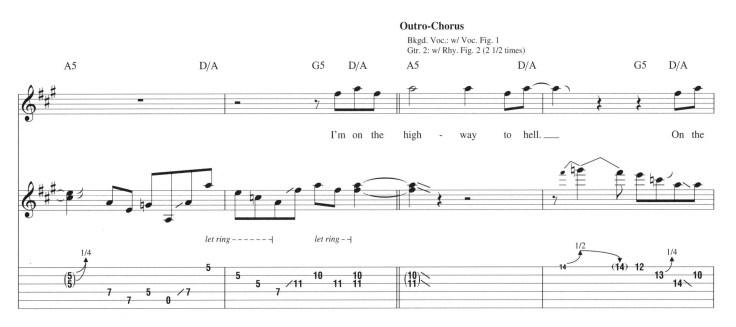

I'm on the high-way to hell. __ On the

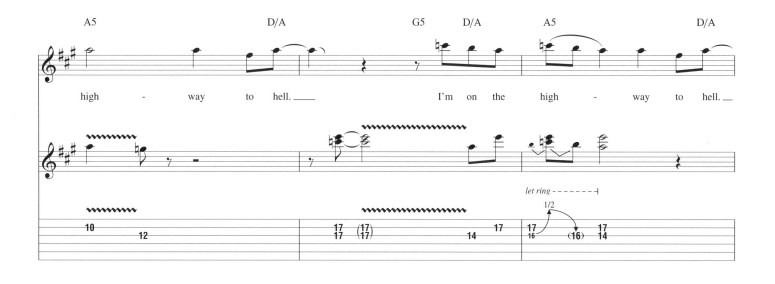

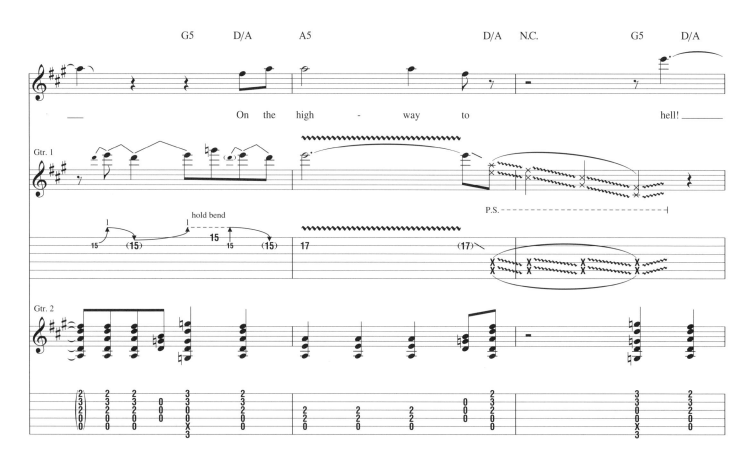

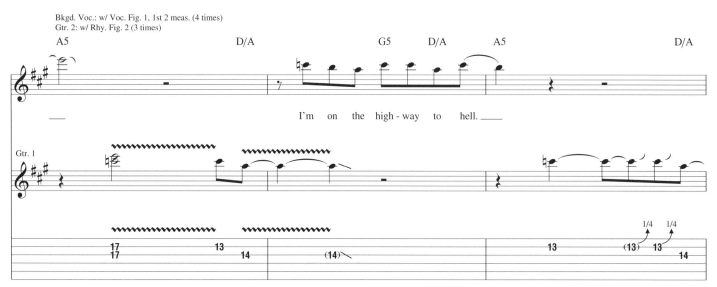

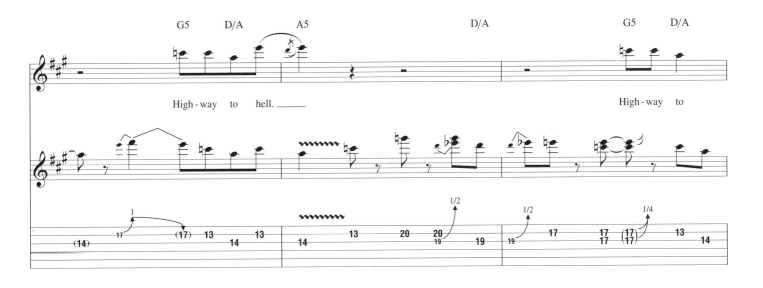

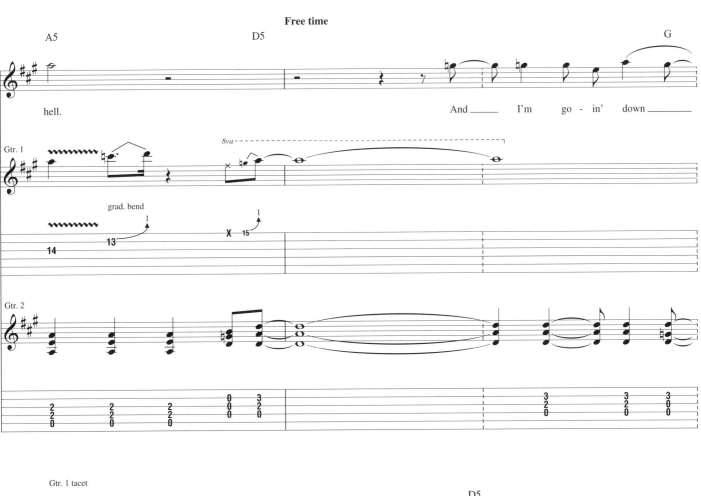

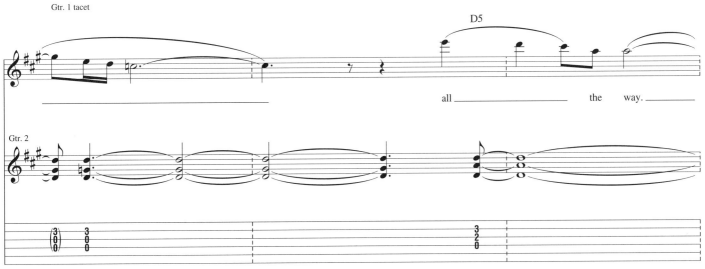

A5

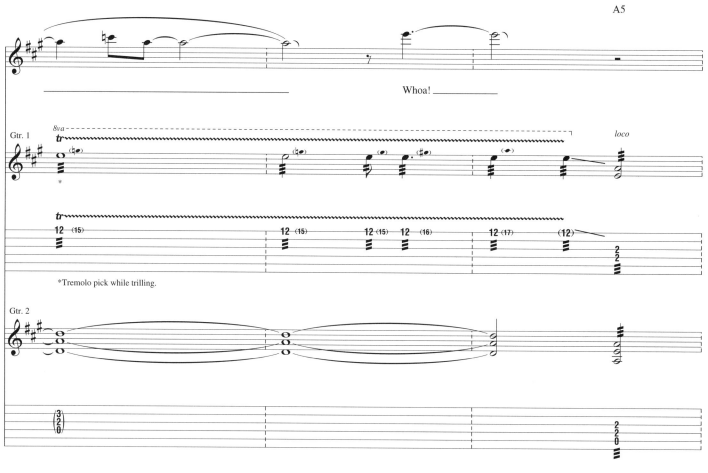

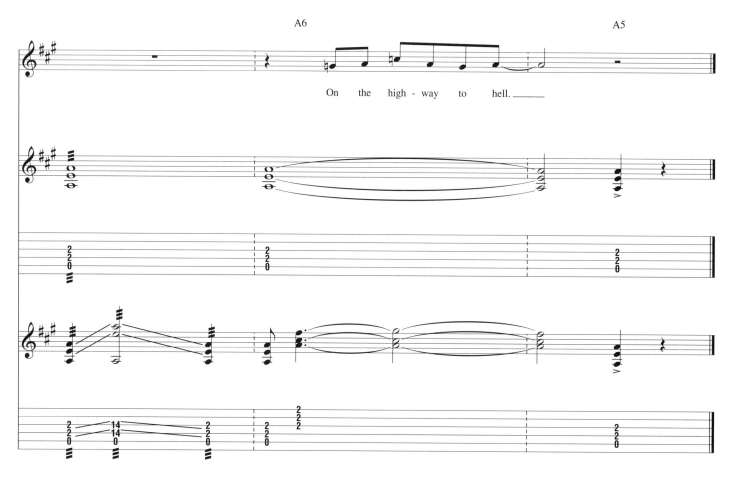

220

from Eagles - *Hotel California*

Hotel California

Words and Music by Don Henley, Glenn Frey and Don Felder

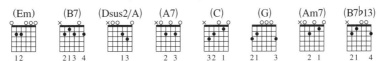

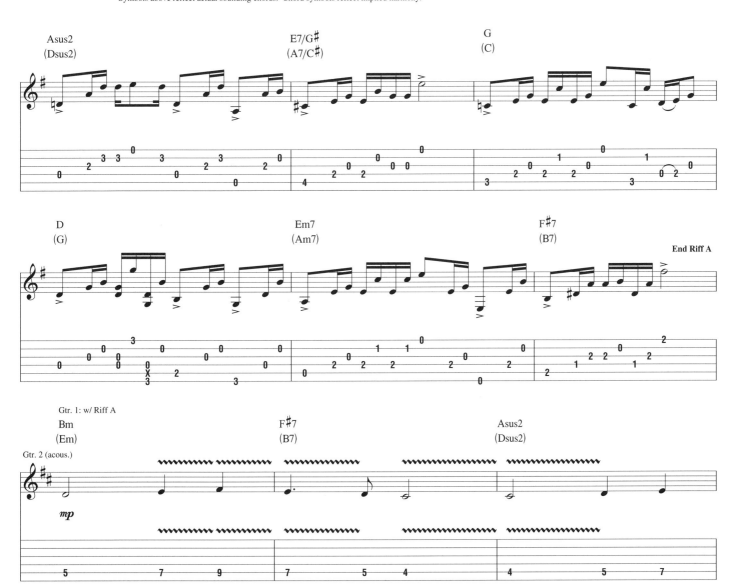

*Symbols in parentheses represent chord names respective to capoed gtr.
Symbols above reflect actual sounding chords. Chord symbols reflect implied harmony.

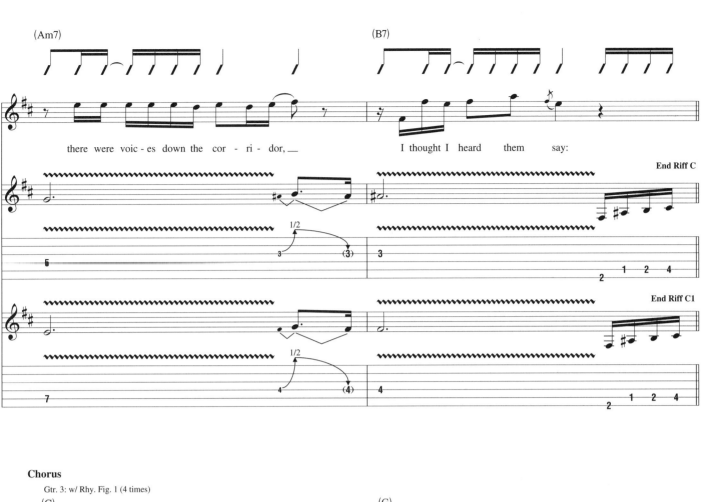

there were voic - es down the cor - ri - dor, ___ I thought I heard them say:

End Riff C

End Riff C1

Chorus
Gtr. 3: w/ Rhy. Fig. 1 (4 times)

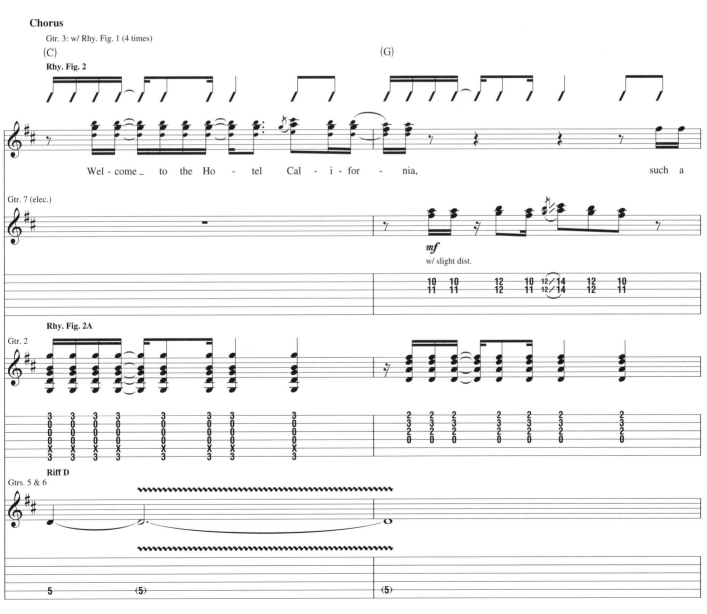

Wel - come _ to the Ho - tel Cal - i - for - nia,   such a

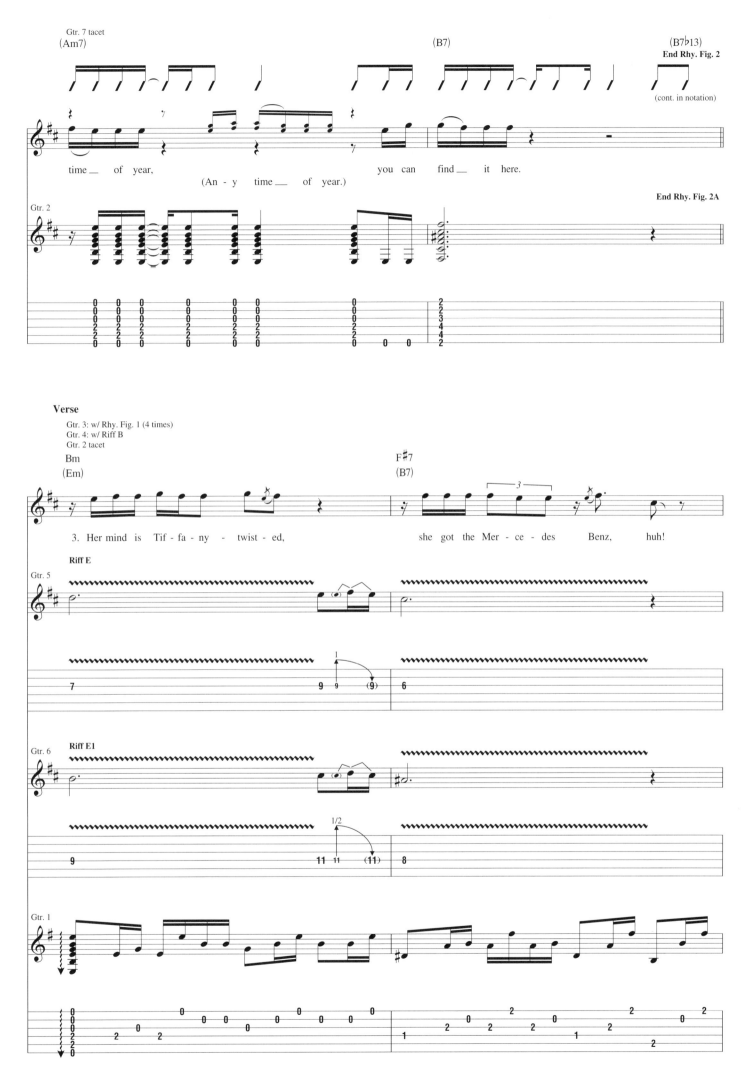

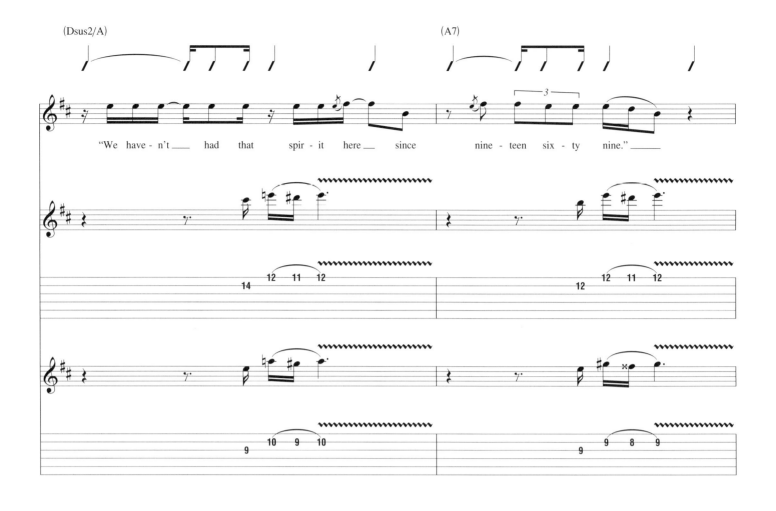

"We have -n't ____ had that spir - it here ____ since nine - teen six - ty nine." ____

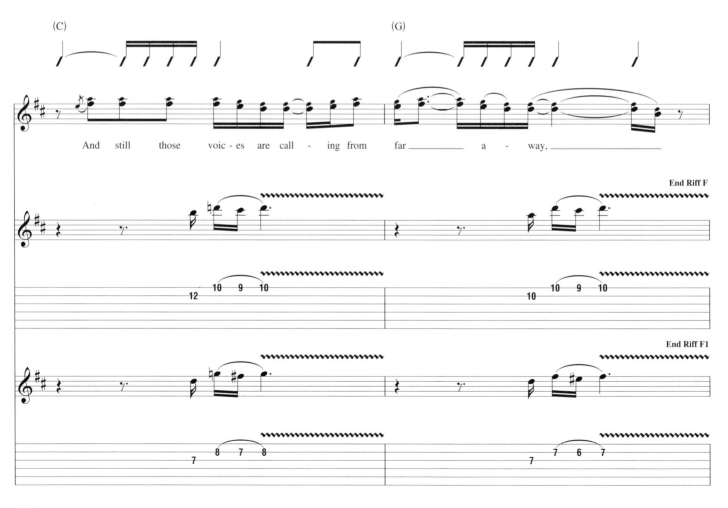

And still those voic - es are call - ing from far ____ a - way, ____

End Riff F

End Riff F1

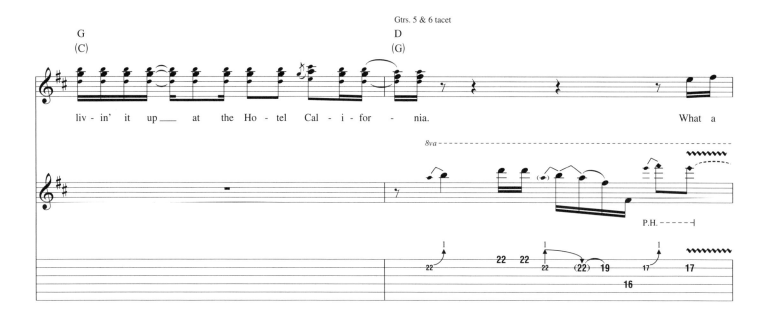

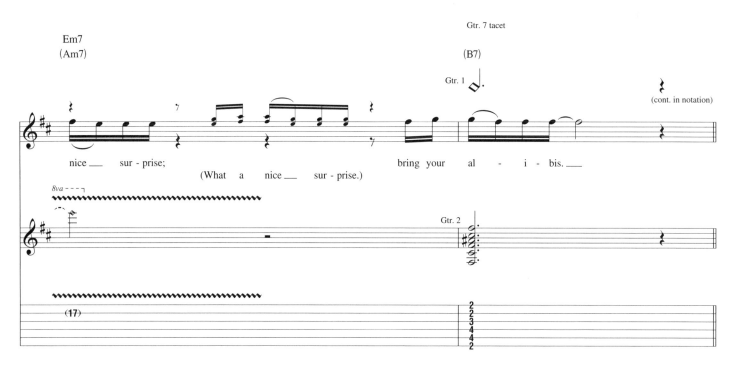

Guitar Solo

Gtr. 1: w/ Rhy. Fig. 3 (till fade)
Gtr. 3: w/ Rhy. Fig. 1 (till fade)
Gtr. 4: w/ Riff B (till fade)
Gtrs. 5 & 6: w/ Riffs C & C1 (1st 6 meas.)

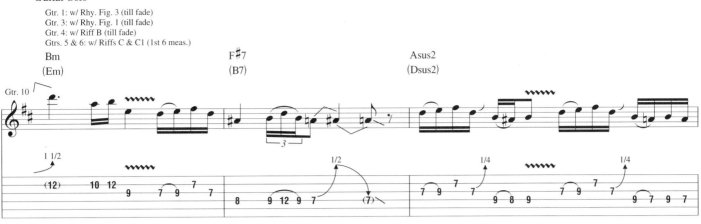

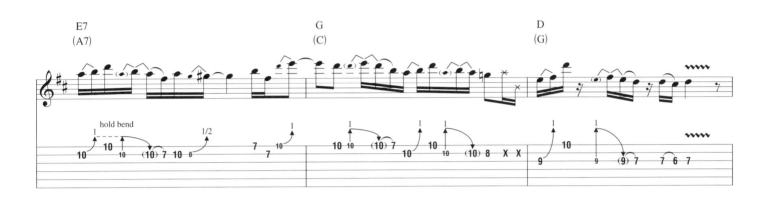

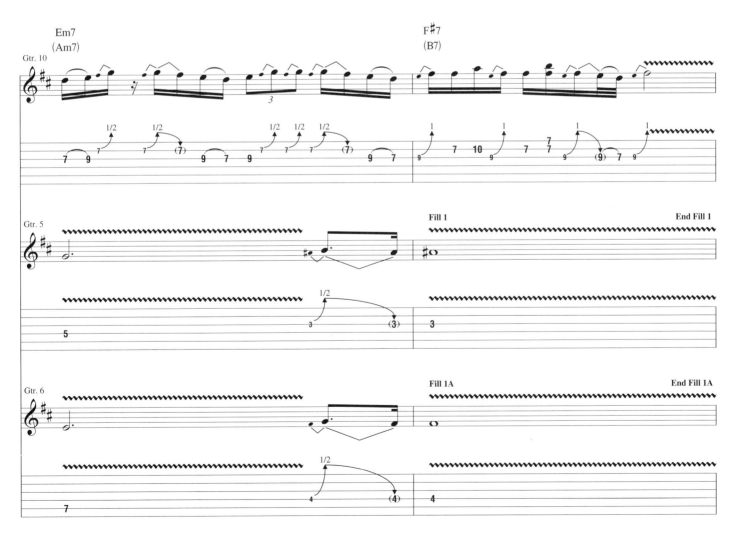

from Black Sabbath - *Paranoid*

Iron Man

Words and Music by Frank Iommi, John Osbourne, William Ward and Terence Butler

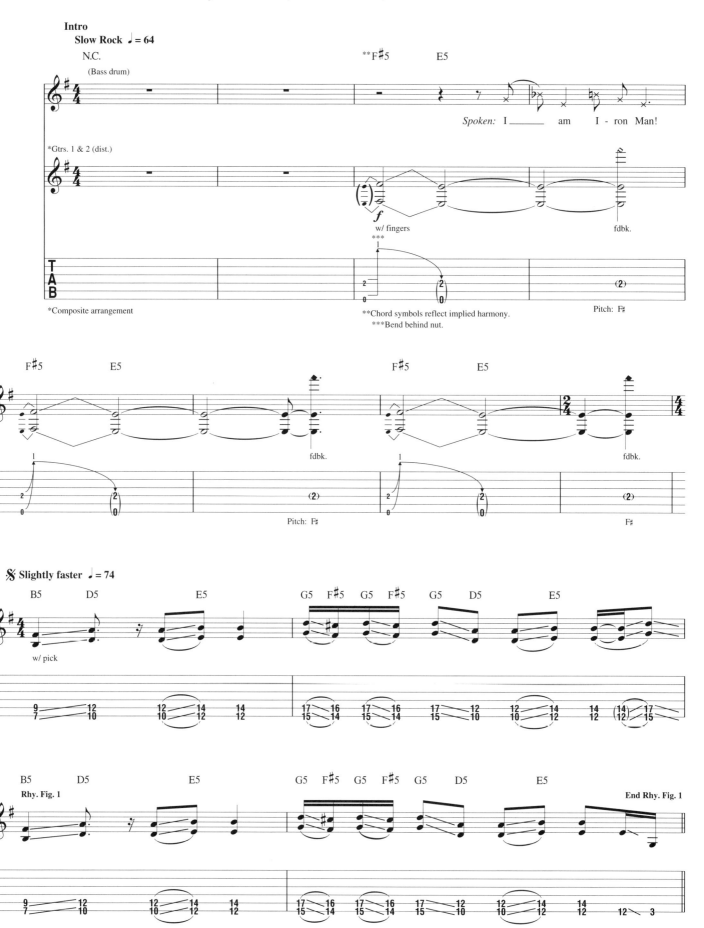

Verse

Gtrs. 1 & 2: w/ Riff A (2 times)

3. He was turned to steel in ___ the ___ great ___ mag - net - ic field,
4. Now the time is here for ___ I - ron Man ___ to spread fear.

when he trav - elled time for ___ the ___ fu - ture of man - kind.
Ven - geance from the grave, kills ___ the ___ peo - ple he once saved.

Bridge

No - bod - y wants ___ him, ___ he just stares ___ at the world. ___
No - bod - y wants ___ him, ___ they just turn ___ their ___ heads. ___

Rhy. Fig. 2   **End Rhy. Fig. 2**   **Riff B**   **End Riff B**

Gtrs. 1 & 2

Gtrs. 1 & 2: w/ Rhy. Fig. 2   Gtrs. 1 & 2: w/ Riff B

Plan - ning his ven - geance ___ that he will ___ soon un - furl. ___
No - bod - y helps ___ him, ___ now he has ___ his re - venge. ___

Interlude
Double-time (♪ = ♩)

N.C.

Riff C   **End Riff C**

Gtrs. 1 & 2

Guitar Solo
Gtr. 2 tacet

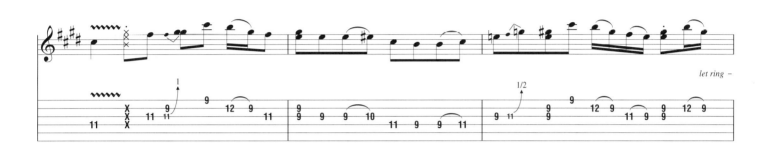

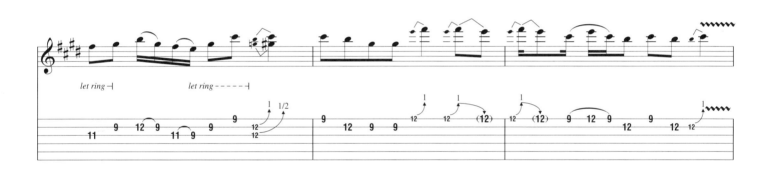

Interlude
Gtrs. 1 & 2: w/ Riff C

A tempo
Gtrs. 1 & 2: w/ Riff B (2 times)

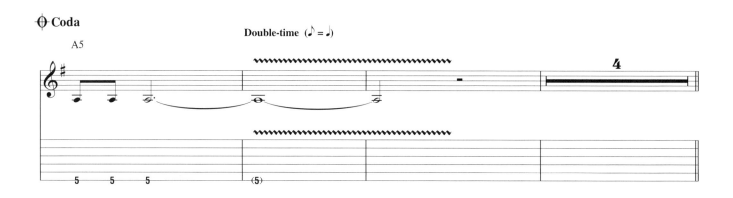

⊕ Coda

Double-time (♪ = ♩)

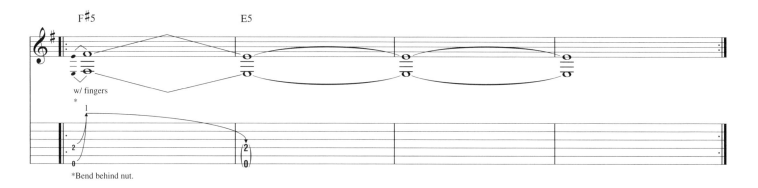

w/ fingers
*
*Bend behind nut.

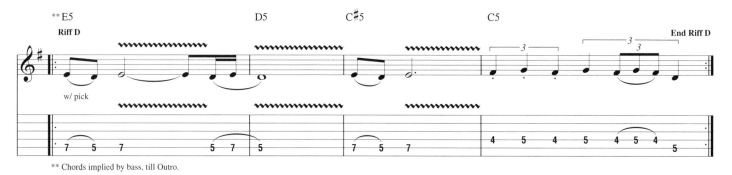

** Chords implied by bass, till Outro.

Guitar Solo

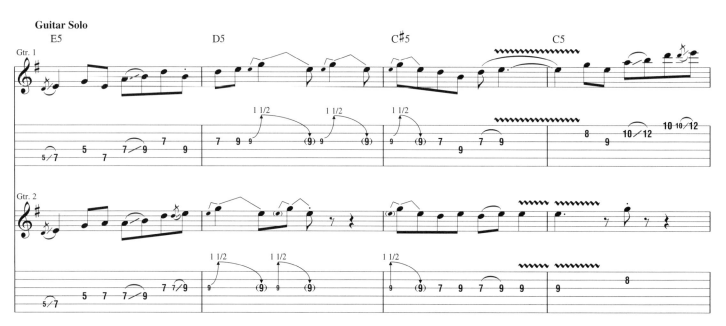

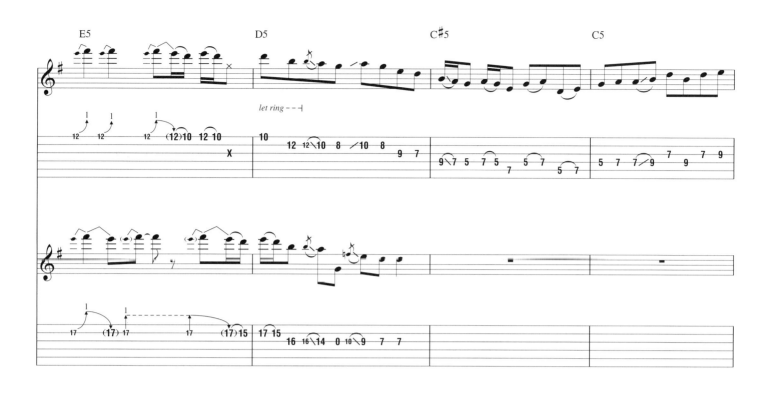

Outro

Gtrs. 1 & 2: w/ Riff D (3 times)

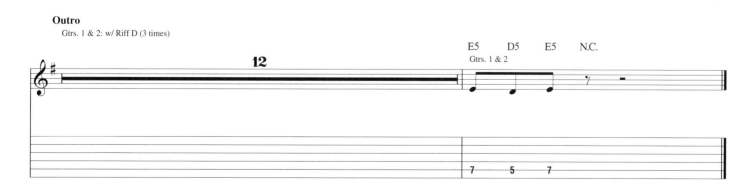

from Elvis Presley - *Elvis: 30 #1 Hits*

Jailhouse Rock

Words and Music by Jerry Leiber and Mike Stoller

Tune down 1/2 step:
(low to high) E♭-A♭-D♭-G♭-B♭-E♭

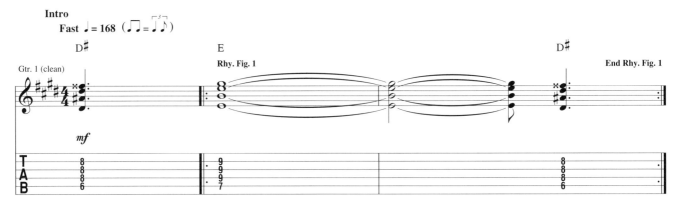

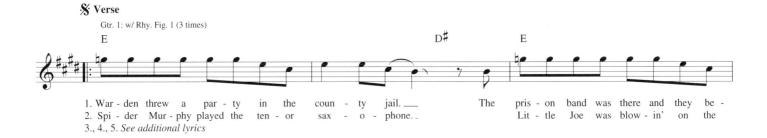

1. War - den threw a par - ty in the coun - ty jail.___ The pris - on band was there and they be -
2. Spi - der Mur - phy played the ten - or sax - o - phone.__ Lit - tle Joe was blow - in' on the
3., 4., 5. *See additional lyrics*

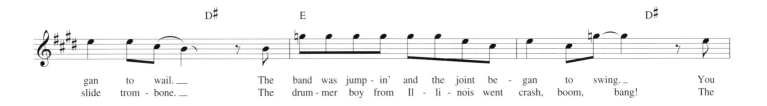

gan to wail.___ The band was jump - in' and the joint be - gan to swing.__ You
slide trom - bone.___ The drum - mer boy from Il - li - nois went crash, boom, bang! The

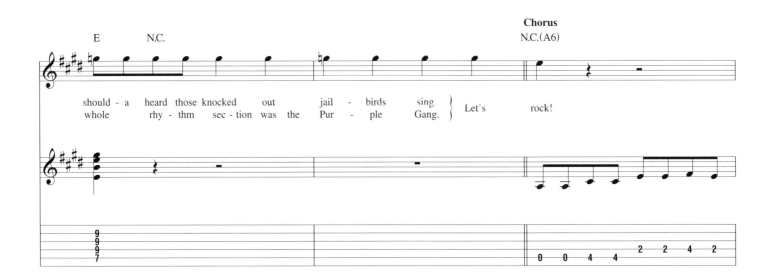

should - a heard those knocked out jail - birds sing. } Let's rock!
whole rhythm sec - tion was the Pur - ple Gang.

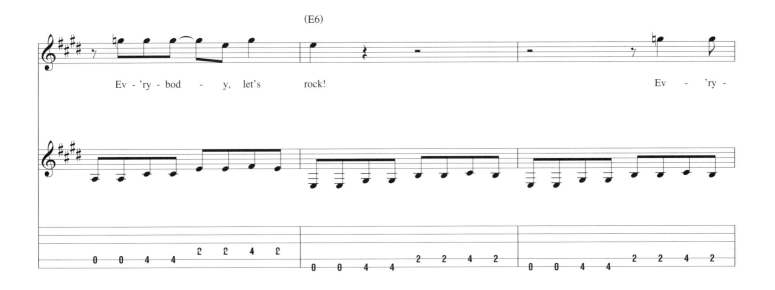

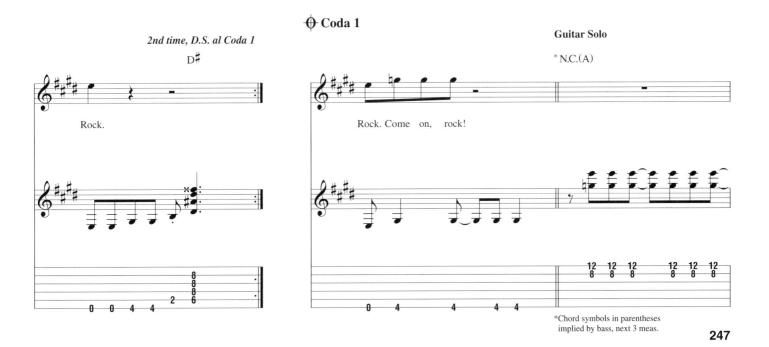

*Chord symbols in parentheses
implied by bass, next 3 meas.

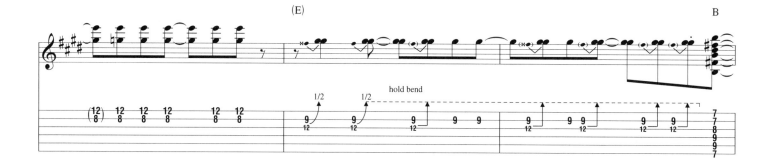

D.S. al Coda 2
(take repeat)

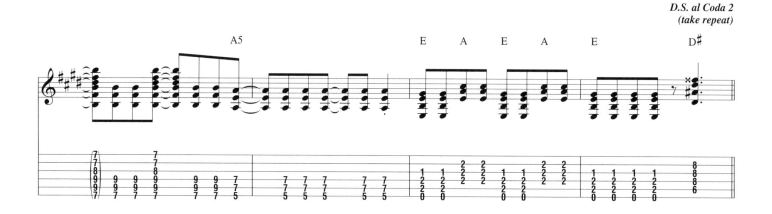

⊕ Coda 2

Outro

Play 8 times and fade

Rock.   Danc - in' to the Jail - house   Rock.   Danc -

Additional Lyrics

3. Number forty-seven said to number three,
   "You the cutest jailbird I ever did see.
   I sure would be delighted with your company.
   Come on and do the Jailhouse Rock with me."

4. Sad Sack was sittin' on a block of stone,
   Way over in the corner weepin' all alone.
   The warden said, "Hey, buddy, don't you be no square.
   If you can't find a partner use a wooden chair."

5. Shifty Henry said to Bugs, "For heaven's sake,
   No one's lookin', now's our chance to make a break."
   Bugs, he turned to Shifty and he said, "Nix, nix,
   I wanna stick around awhile to get my kicks."

Layla

Words and Music by Eric Clapton and Jim Gordon

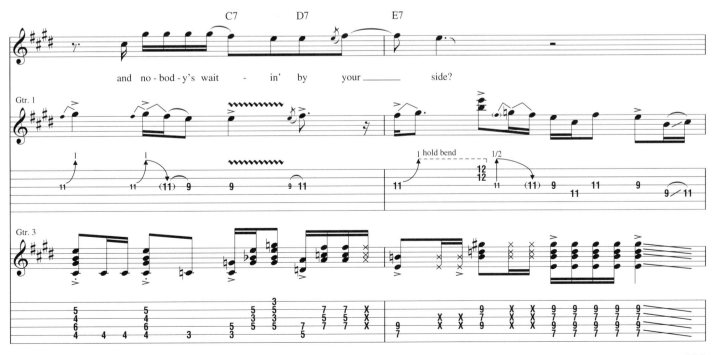

I beg you, dar - lin', please, Lay - la, _____
la.) _____

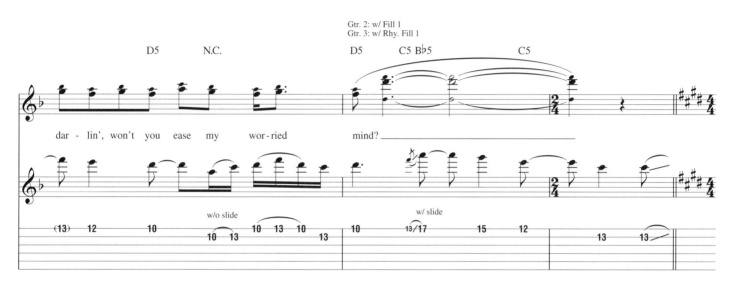

Gtr. 2: w/ Fill 1
Gtr. 3: w/ Rhy. Fill 1

dar - lin', won't you ease my wor - ried mind? _____

Verse

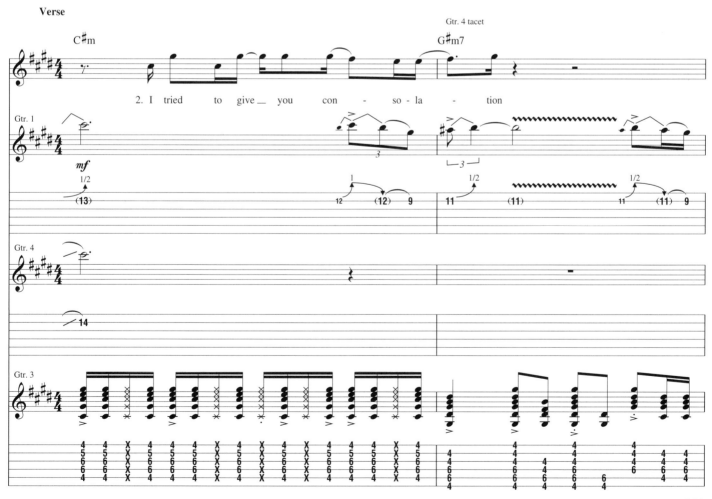

Gtr. 4 tacet

2. I tried to give _ you con - so - la - tion

Gtr. 1

Gtr. 4

Gtr. 3

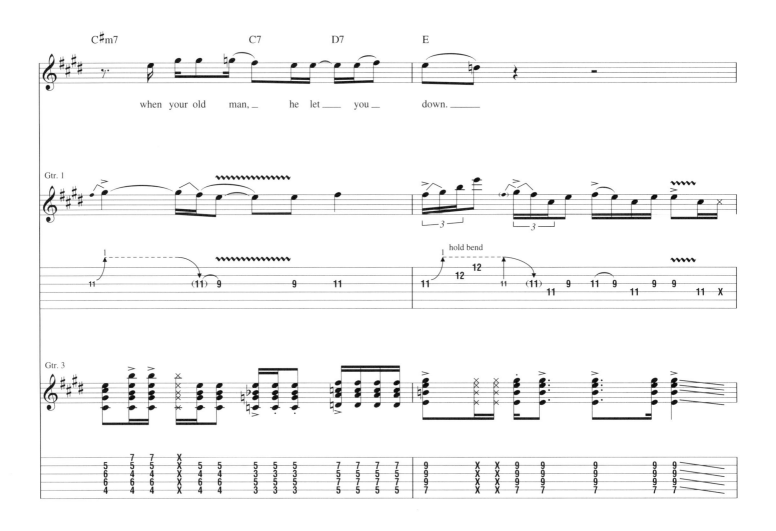

when your old man, ___ he let ___ you ___ down. ___

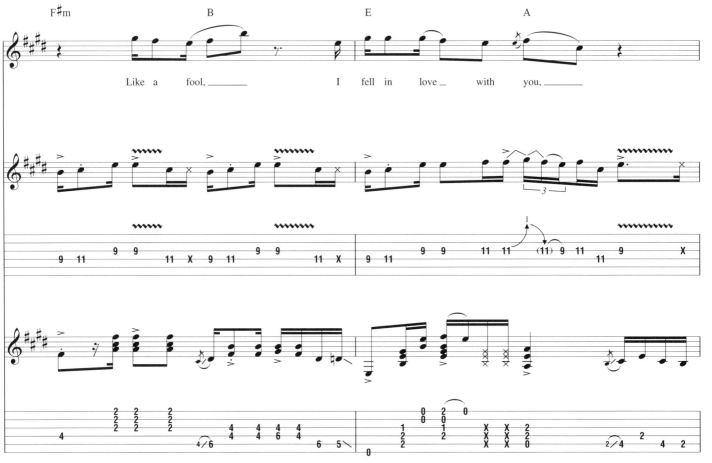

Like a fool, ___ I fell in love ___ with you, ___

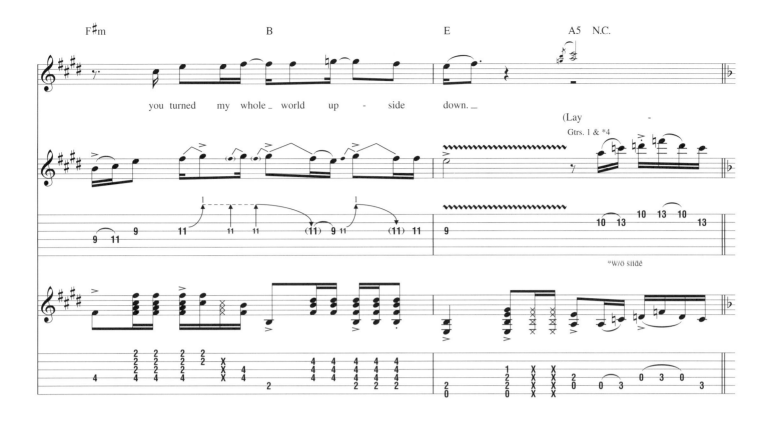

you turned my whole world up - side down. (Lay -

Chorus

Gtr. 1: w/ Riff B
Gtr. 2: w/ Riff A (3 times)
Gtr. 3: w/ Rhy. Fig. 1 (3 times)
Gtrs. 5 & 6: w/ Riffs C & C1

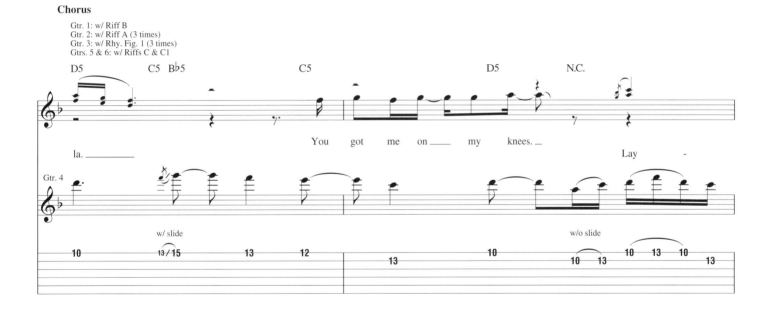

You got me on my knees. Lay -

la. Gtr. 4

w/ slide   w/o slide

I beg you, dar - lin', please, Lay - la,

la.)

w/ slide   w/o slide   w/ slide

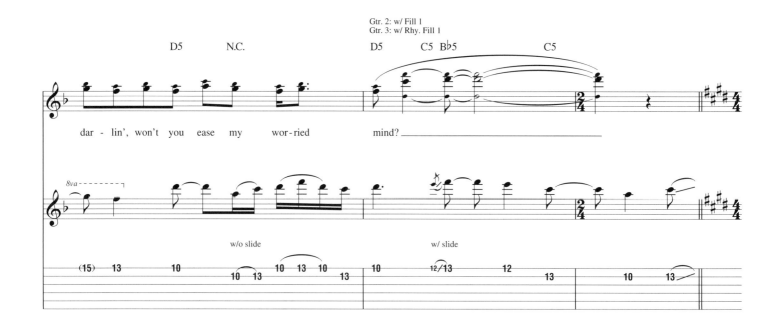

darlin', won't you ease my wor-ried mind? _____

Verse

3. So make the best __ of the sit - u - a - tion,

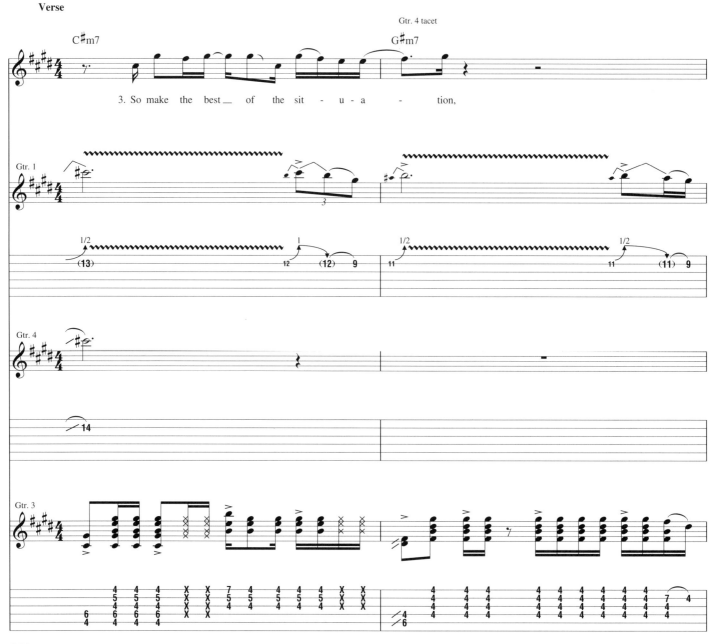

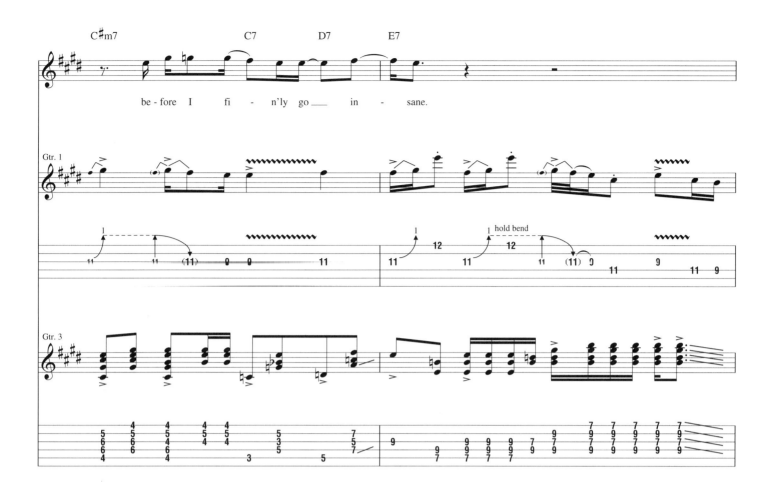

be - fore I fi - n'ly go —— in - sane.

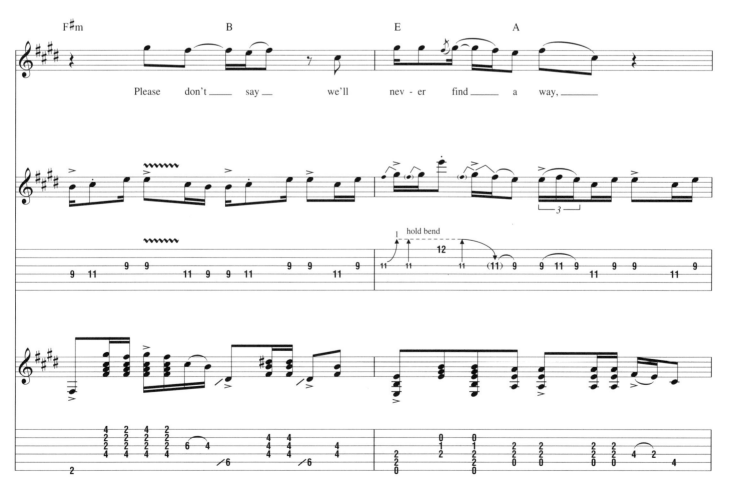

Please don't —— say —— we'll nev - er find —— a way, ——

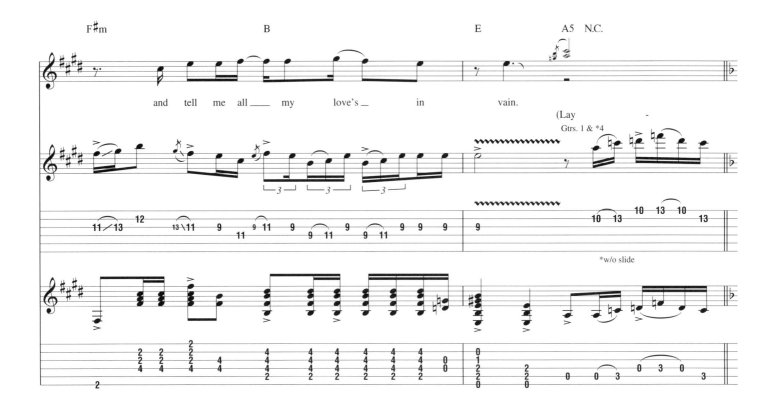

Chorus

Gtr. 1: w/ Riff B (1st 6 meas.)
Gtr. 2: w/ Riff A (3 times)
Gtr. 3: w/ Rhy. Fig. 1 (8 times)
Gtrs. 5 & 6: w/ Riffs C & C1 (1st 6 meas.)

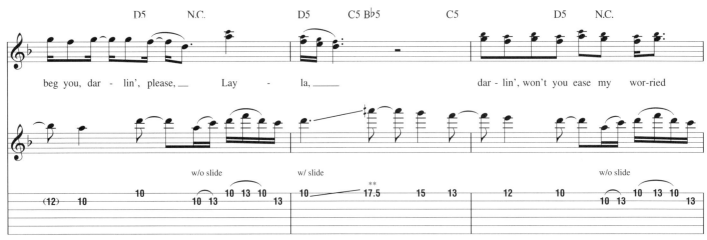

**Slide positioned halfway between 17th & 18th frets.

Guitar Solo

Gtr. 1: w/ Riff B (1st 7 meas.)
Gtr. 2: w/ Riff A (3 1/2 times)
Gtr. 3: w/ Rhy. Fig. 1 (11 1/2 times)
Gtrs. 5 & 6: w/ Riffs C & C1 (1st 7 meas.)

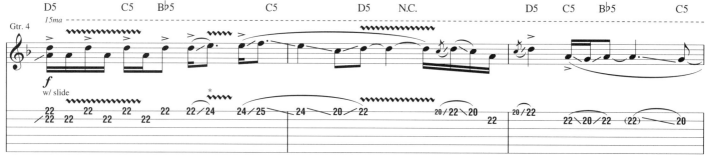

*Hypothetical fret locations throughout.

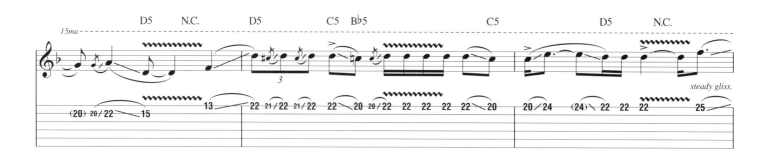

Gtrs. 1, 2, 5 & 6: w/ Riffs D, D1, D2 & D3

Gtr. 1: w/ Riff B (1st 7 meas.)
Gtr. 2: w/ Riff A (3 1/2 times)
Gtrs. 5 & 6: w/ Riffs C & C1 (1st 7 meas.)

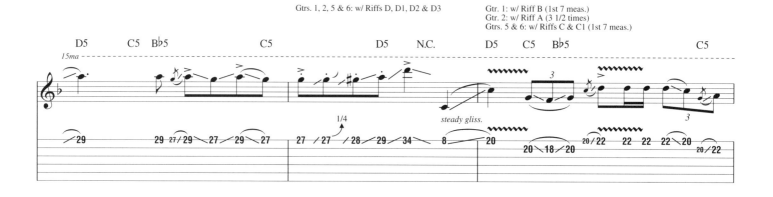

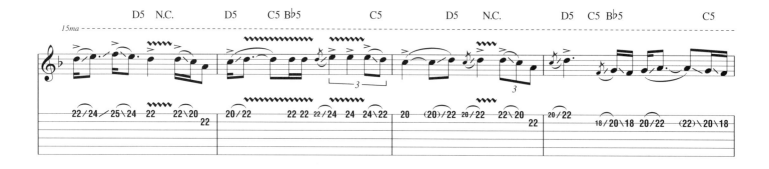

Gtrs. 1, 2, 5 & 6: w/ Riffs D, D1, D2 & D3

Gtr. 1: w/ Riff B (1st 7 meas.)
Gtr. 2: w/ Riff A (3 1/2 times)
Gtrs. 5 & 6: w/ Riffs C & C1 (1st 7 meas.)

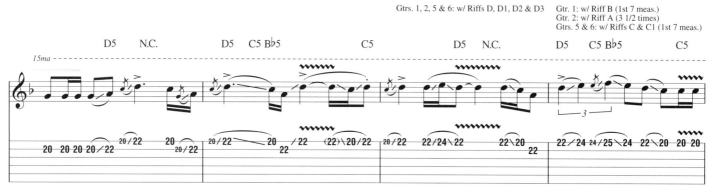

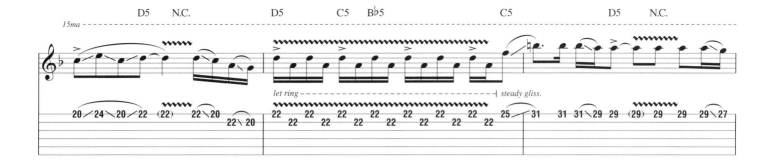

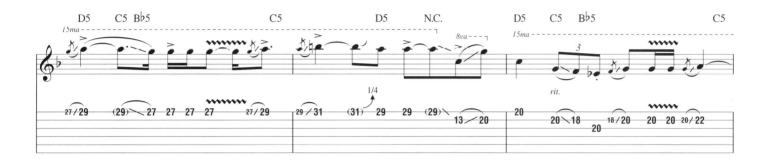

Interlude

Slower ♩ = 112

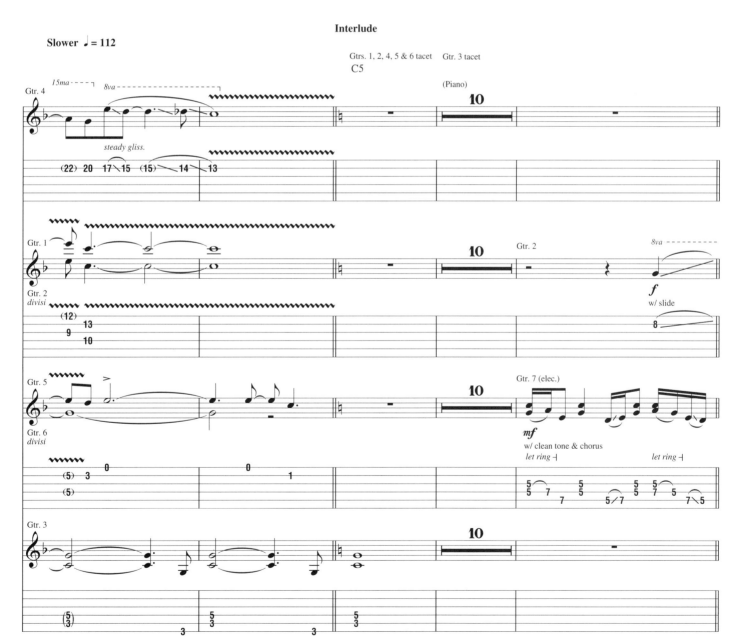

Outro

*Chord symbols reflect overall harmony.

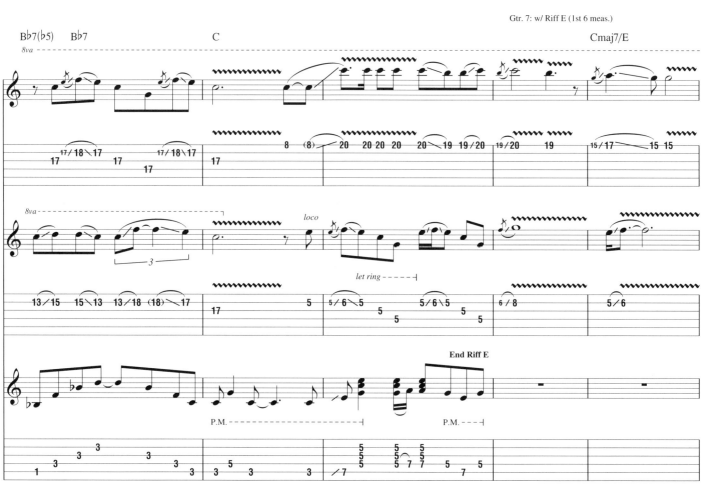

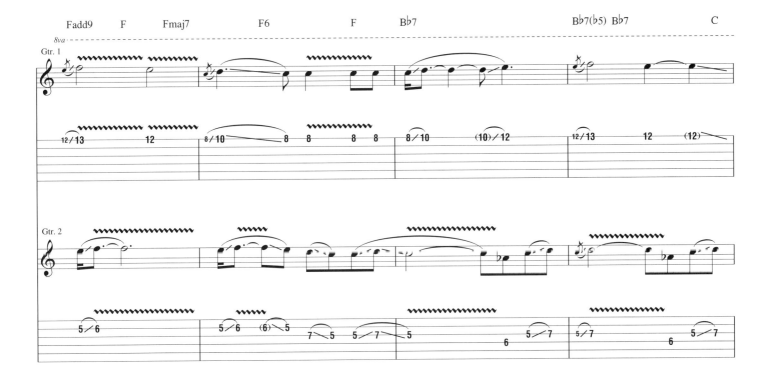

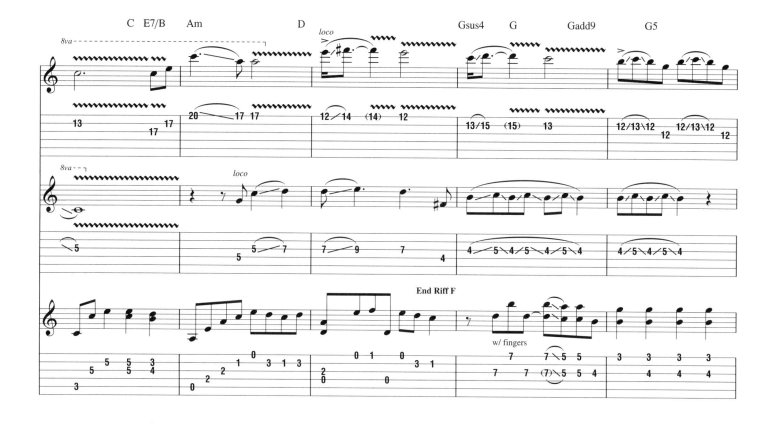

Gtr. 7: w/ Riff E (1st 4 meas., 2 times)

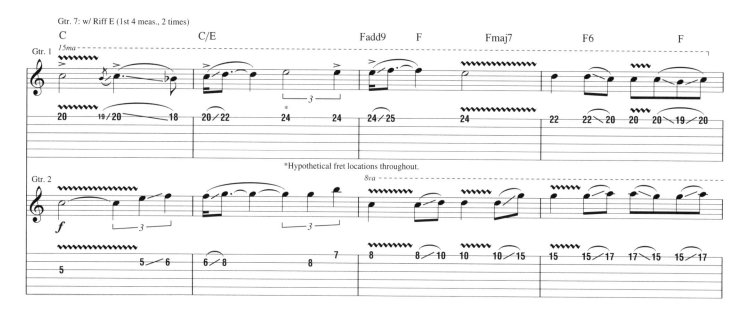

*Hypothetical fret locations throughout.

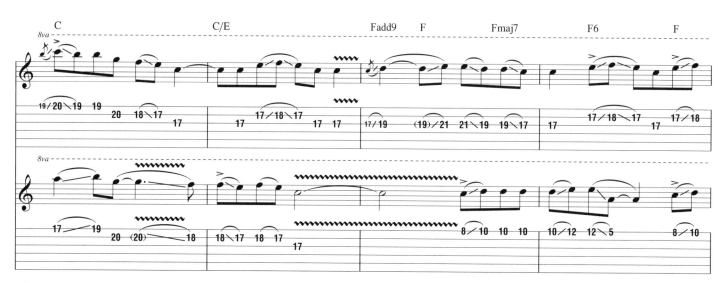

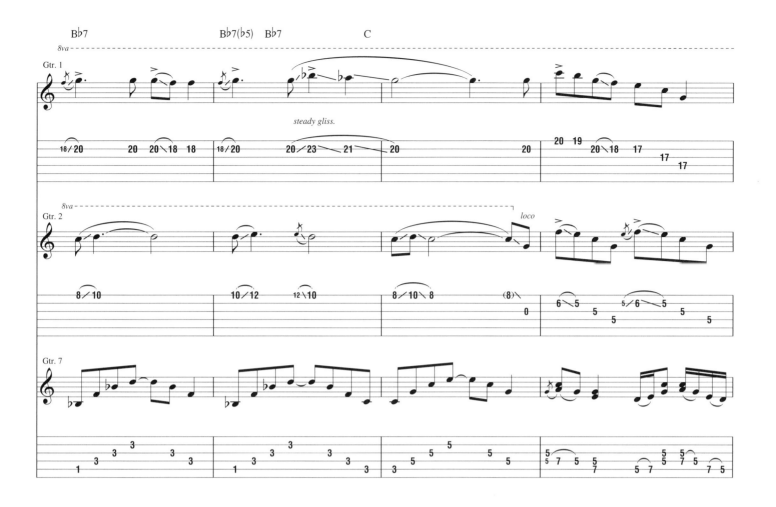

End Riff G

Gtr. 7: w/ Riff E (1st 6 meas.)
Gtr. 8: w/ Riff G

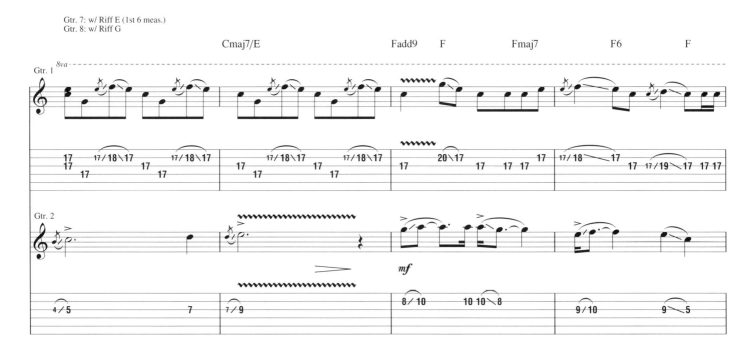

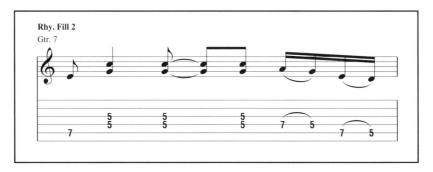

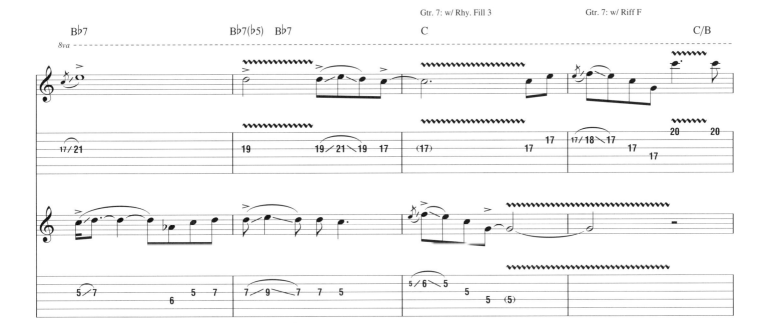

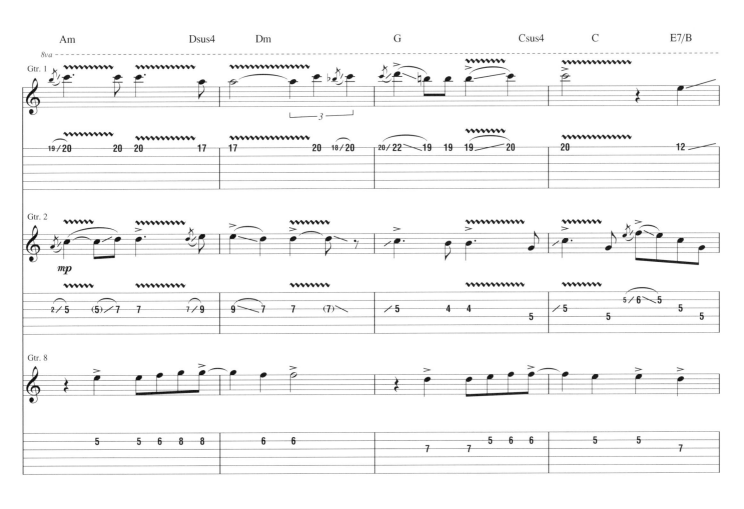

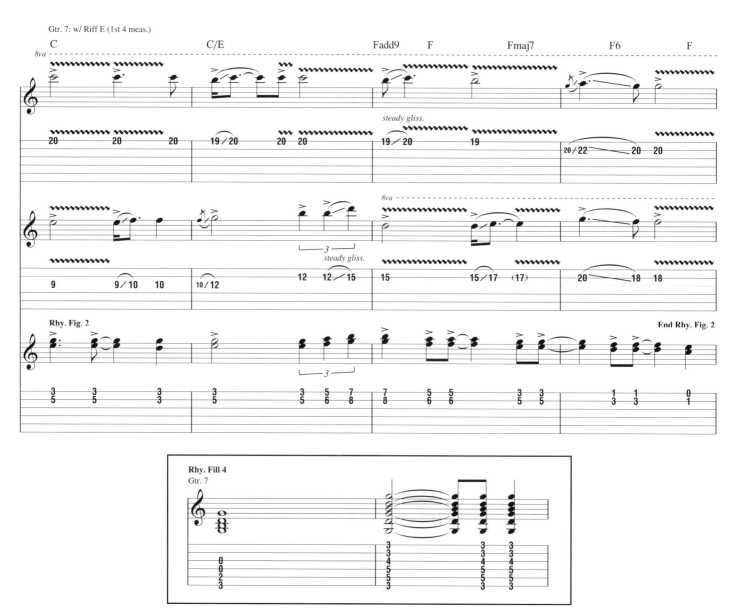

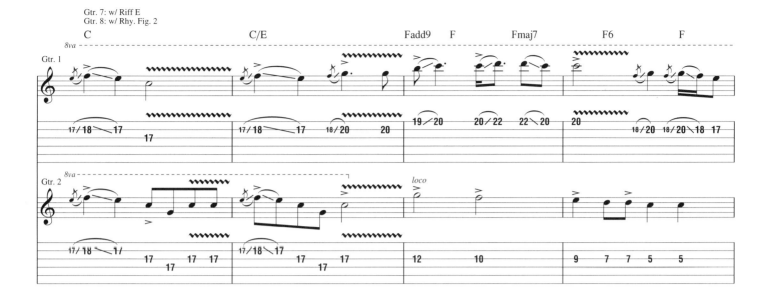

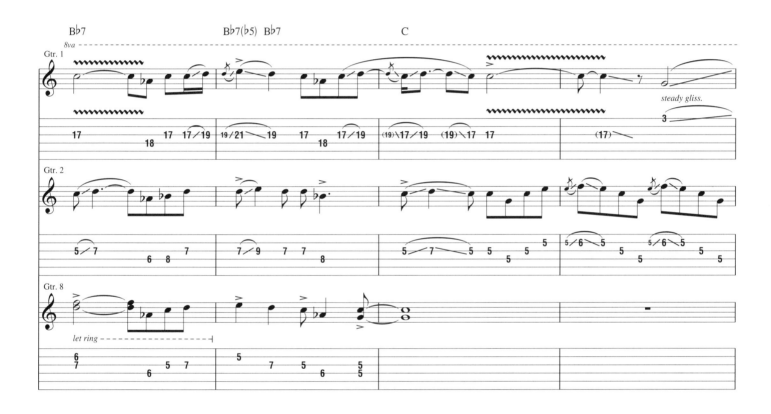

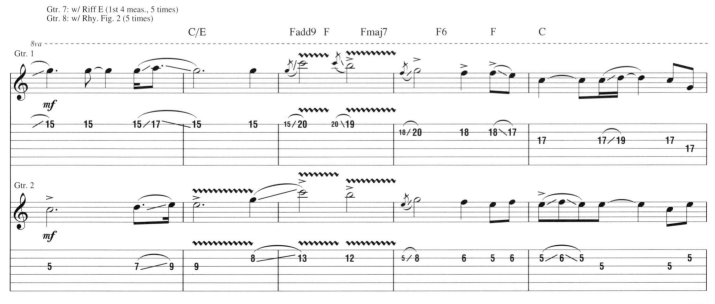

269

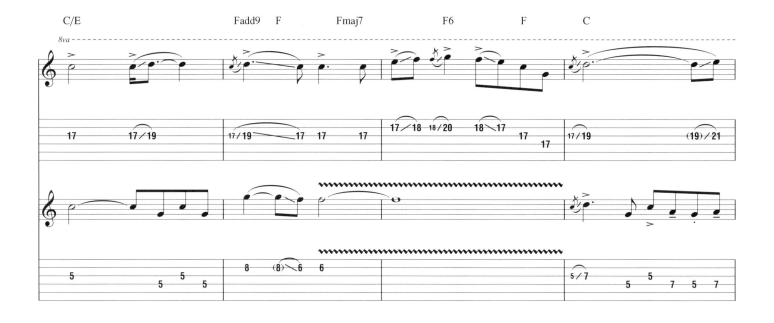

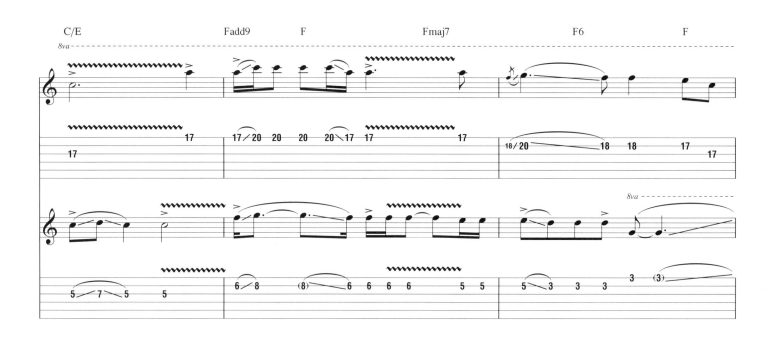

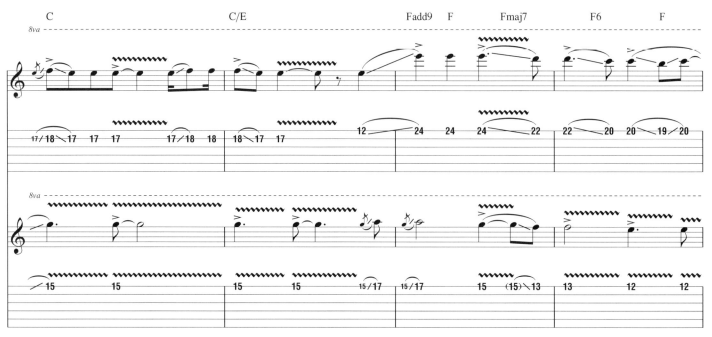

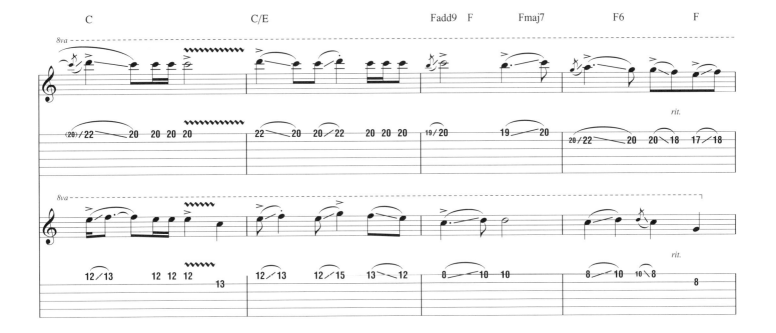

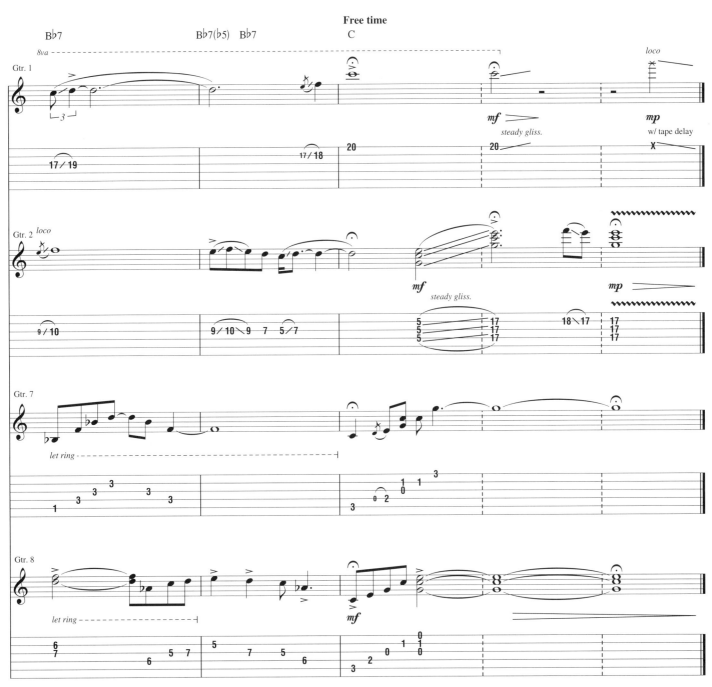

from Rush - *Moving Pictures*

Limelight

Words by Neil Peart
Music by Geddy Lee and Alex Lifeson

long a - wait - ed friend. _____

All the world's _ in - deed _ a stage, we are mere - ly _____ play - ers, _____ per -

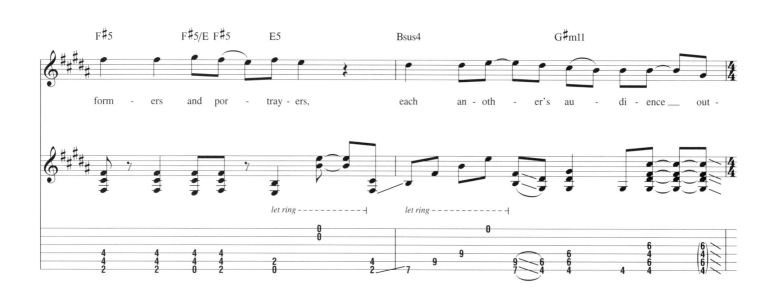

form - ers and por - tray - ers, each an - oth - er's au - di - ence _____ out -

D.S. al Coda 1

side the gild - ed _____ cage. _____

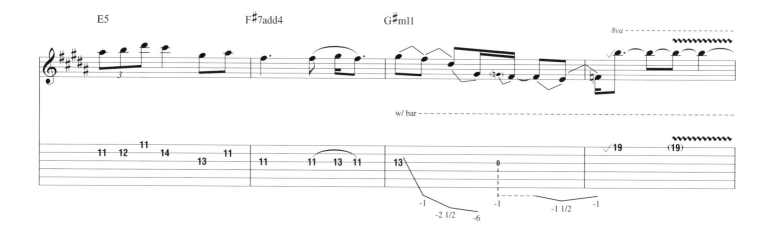

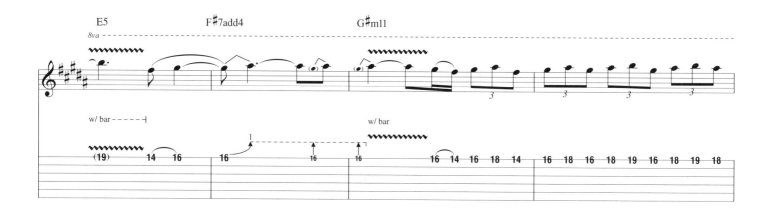

Gtr. 2: w/ Riff A

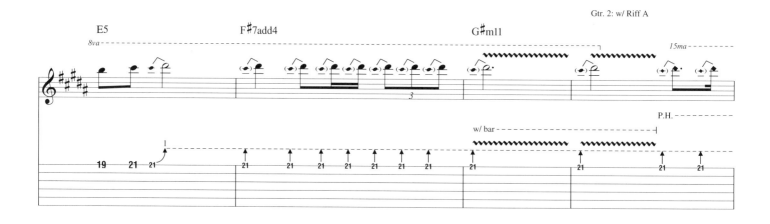

D.S. al Coda 2

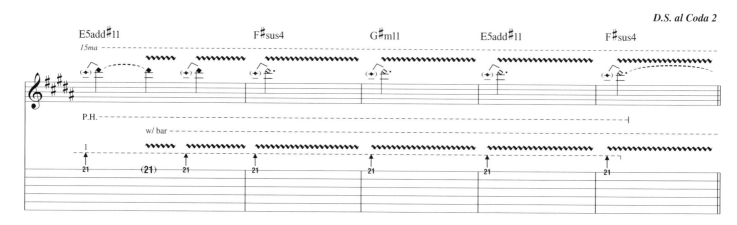

278

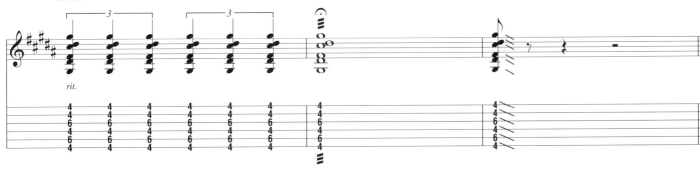

Misirlou

Music by Nicolas Roubanis

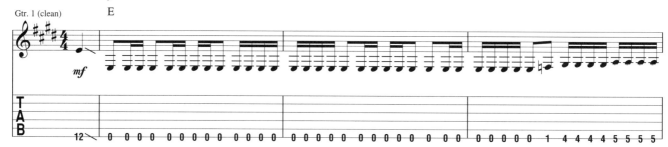

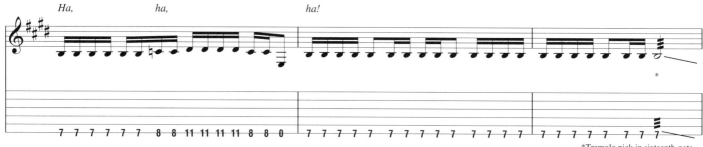

*Tremolo pick in sixteenth-note
pattern while sliding down string.

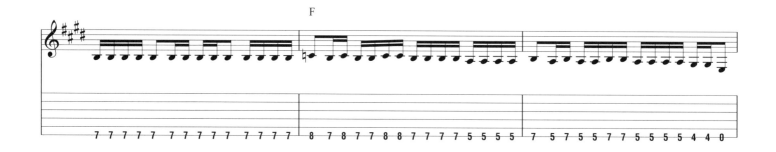

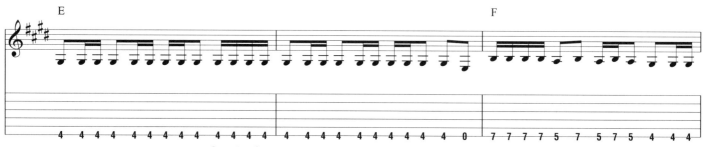

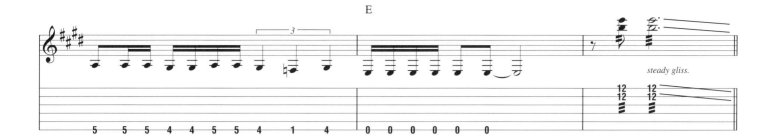

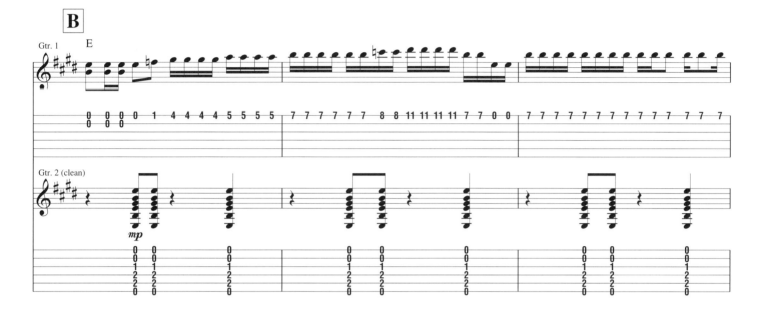

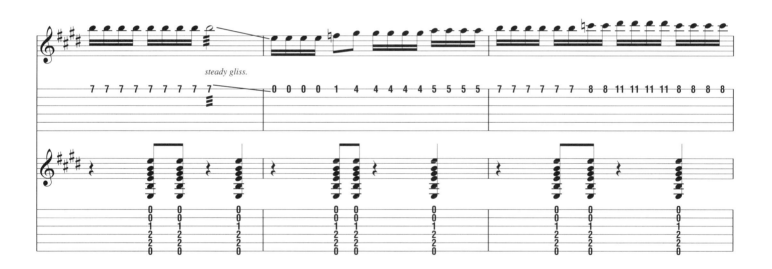

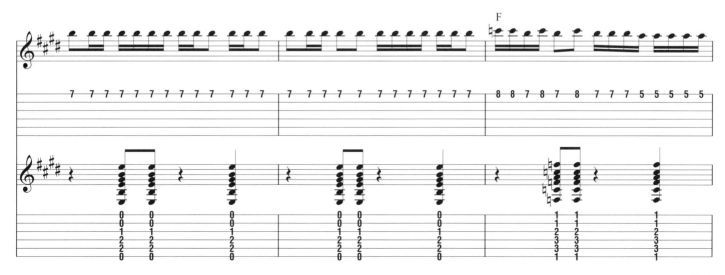

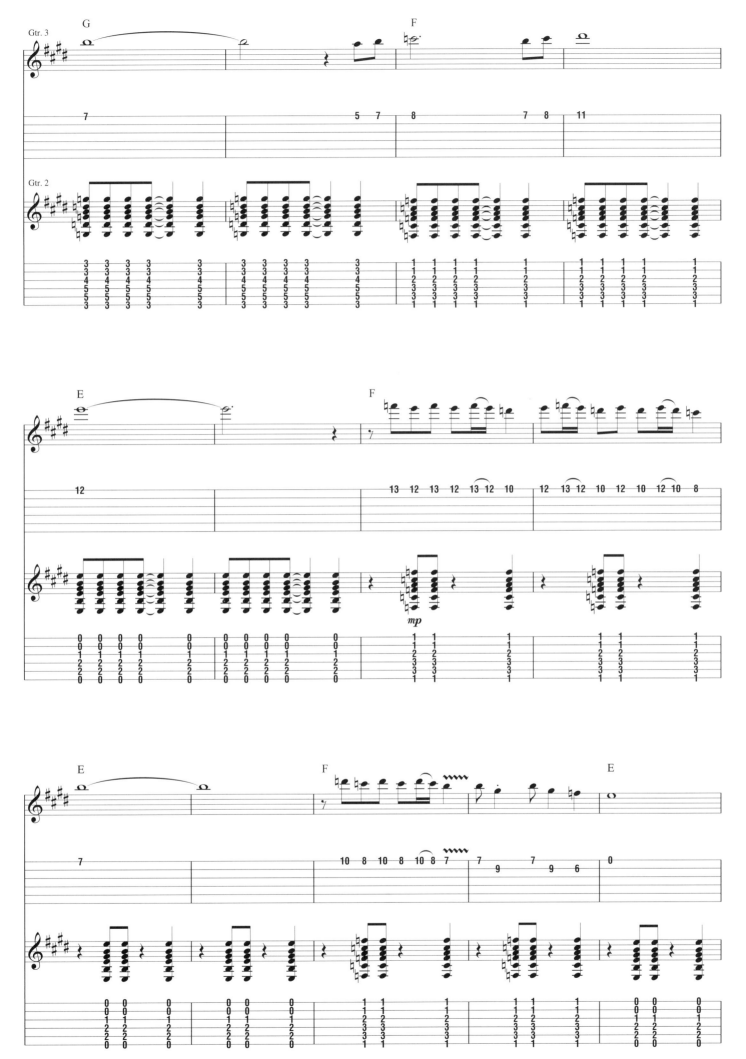

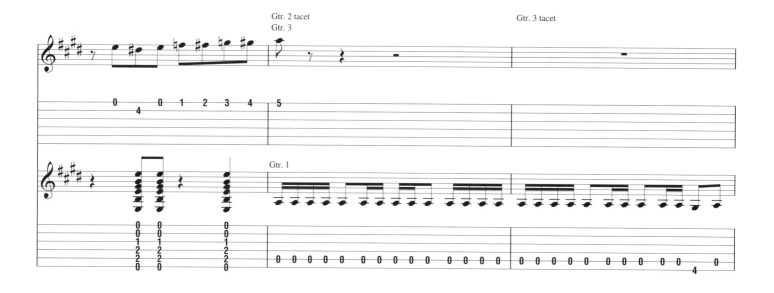

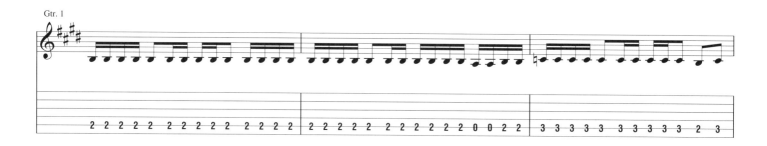

Play 5 times and fade

from Boston - *Boston*

Peace of Mind

Words and Music by Tom Scholz

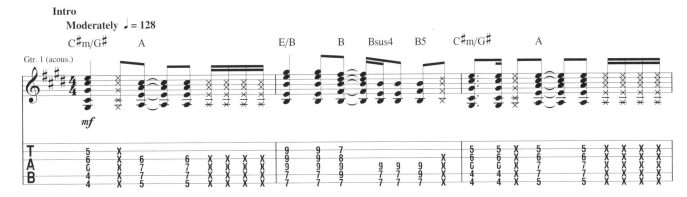

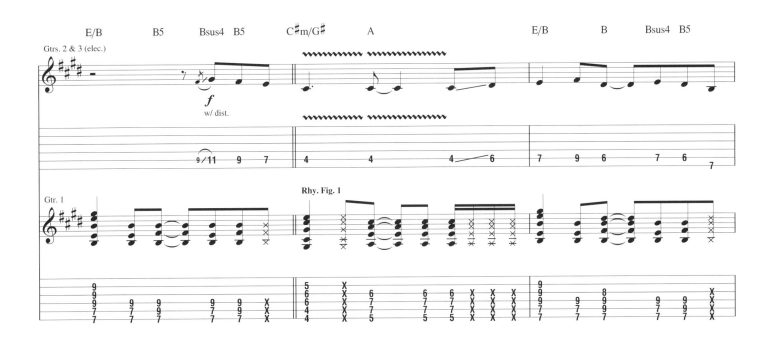

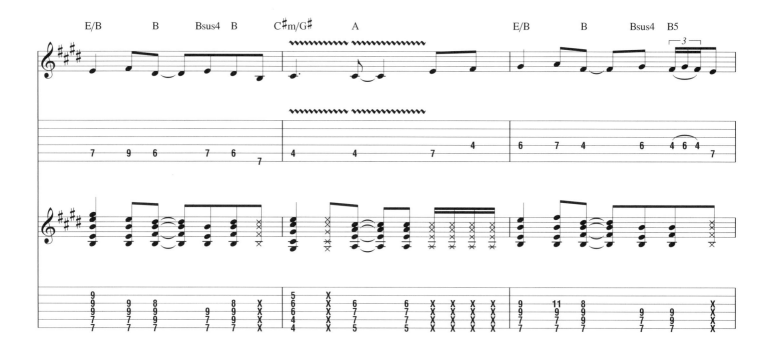

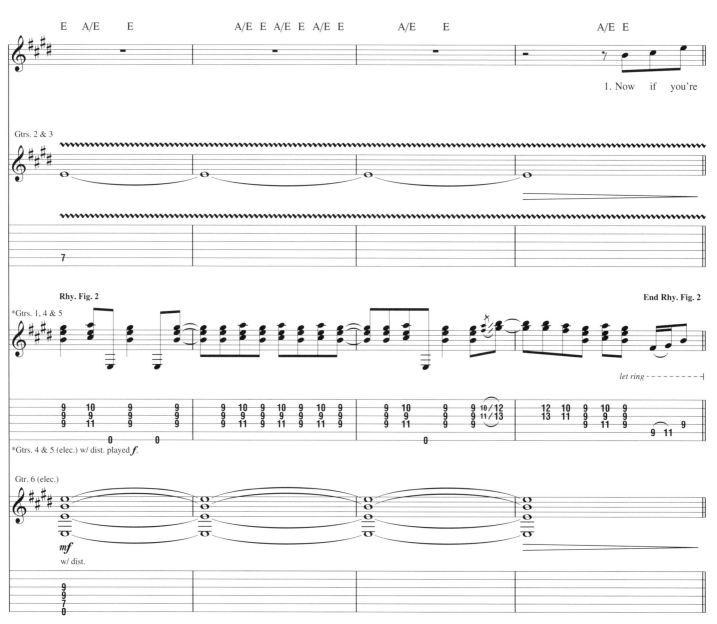

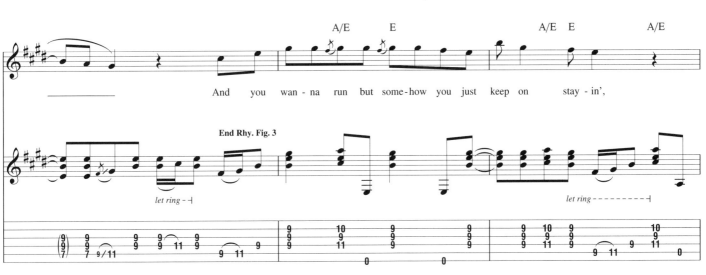

Bridge

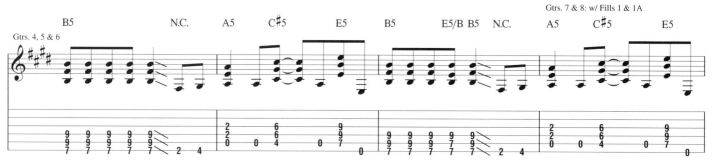

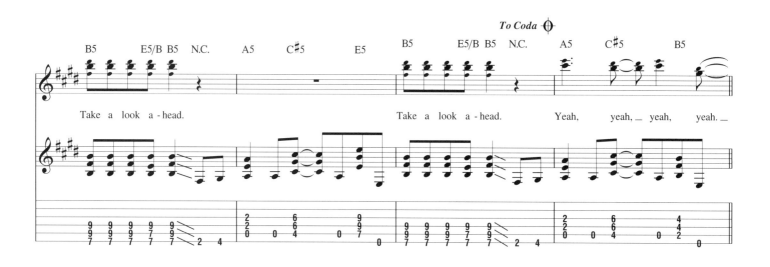

Interlude

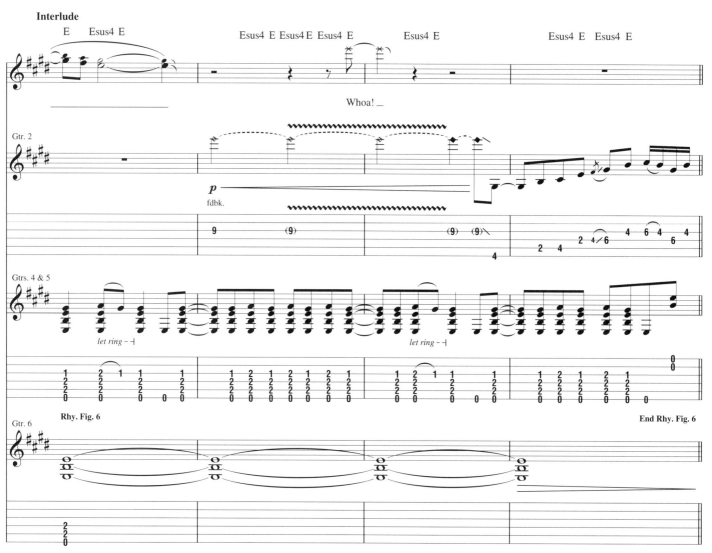

Guitar Solo

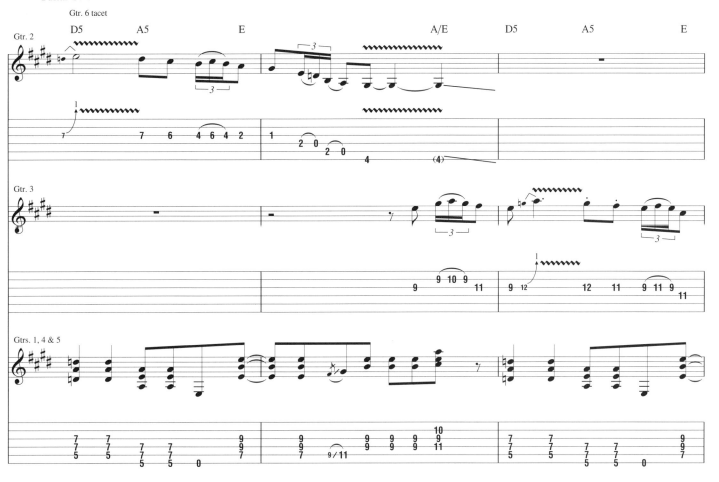

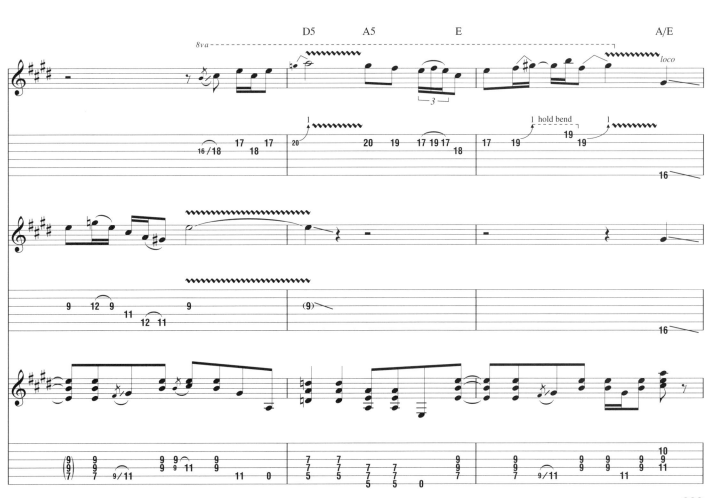

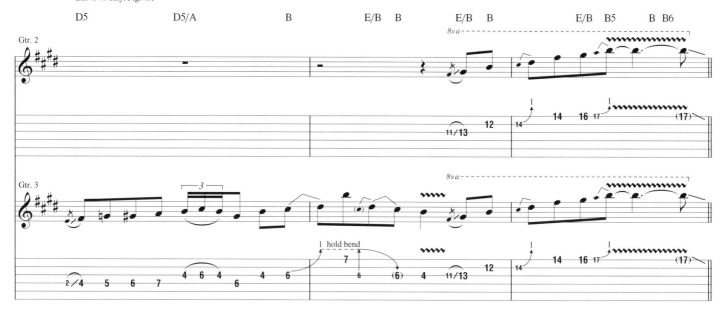

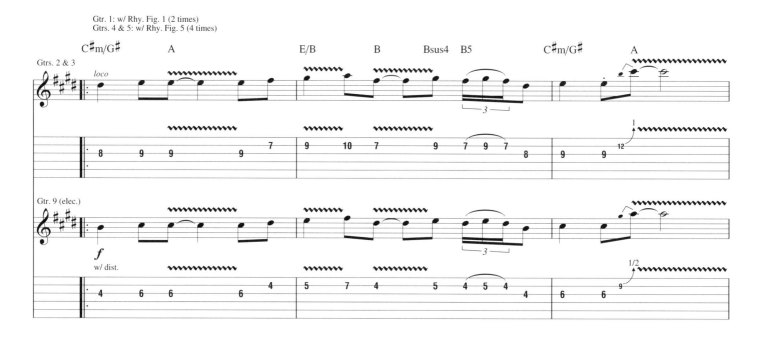

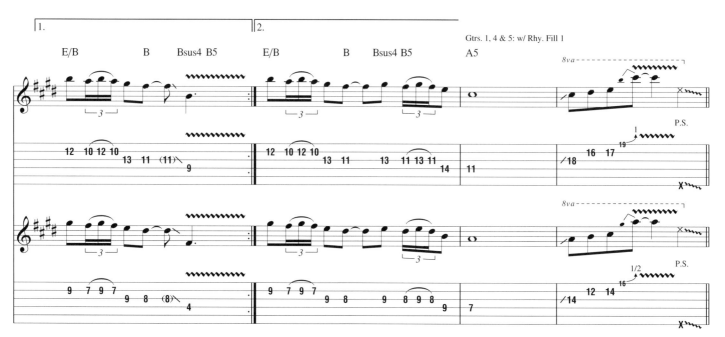

294

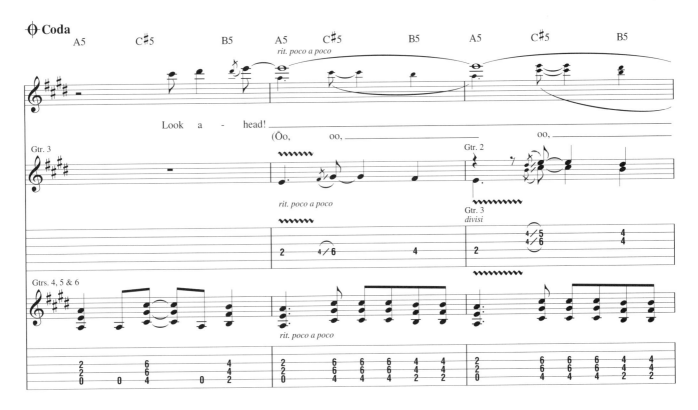

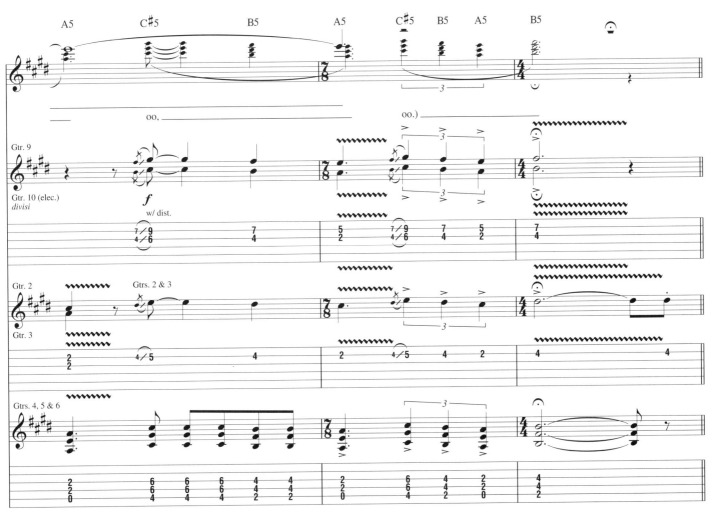

Breakdown
A tempo
Gtrs. 6, 9 & 10 tacet

Outro

Gtr. 1: w/ Rhy. Fig. 1 (till fade)
Gtrs. 4 & 5: w/ Rhy. Fig. 5 (till fade)

Gtr. 9: w/ Riff A (till fade)

Begin fade

3rd time, Fade out

Gtrs. 2 & 3: w/ Riff B (till fade)

from Def Leppard - *Pyromania*

Photograph

Words and Music by Joe Elliott, Steve Clark, Peter Willis, Richard Savage, Richard Allen and R.J. Lange

*Gtr. 1: w/ dist.

**Gtr. 1: w/ clean tone

Plush

Words and Music by Scott Weiland, Dean DeLeo, Robert DeLeo and Eric Kretz

feel it. Where you go - in' for to - mor-row?
feels it.

Where you go - in' with a mask I found? And I feel, and I feel when the

dogs be - gin to smell her, a, will she smell a - lone?

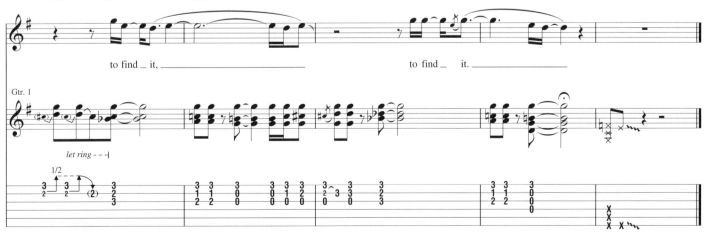

307

from Stevie Ray Vaughan and Double Trouble - *Texas Flood*

Pride and Joy

By Stevie Ray Vaughan

Tune down 1/2 step:
(low to high) E♭-A♭-D♭-G♭-B♭-E♭

Intro
Moderately ♩ = 122

3. Yeah, I love my la - dy, to be long and __ lean. __

You mess with her, you'll see a man get - tin' mean. __ She's my sweet __ lit - tle thang, __

she's my pride and joy. __ She's my

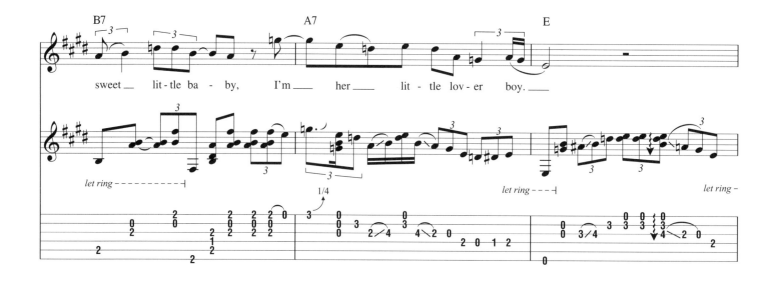

sweet___ lit-tle ba - by, I'm___ her___ lit-tle lov-er boy.___

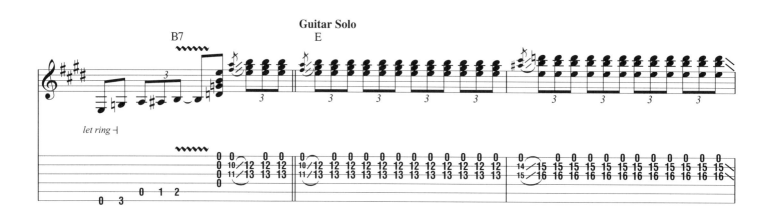

Guitar Solo

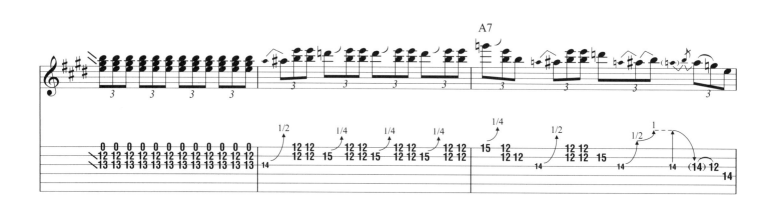

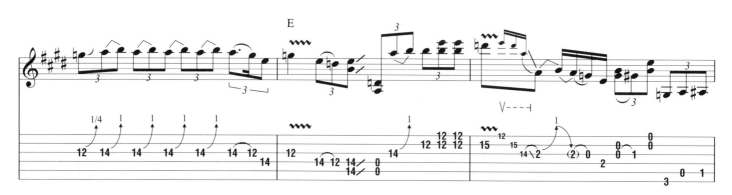

Verse

4. Well, I love my ba - by, like the fin - est w - wine.

Love like ___ ours, ah, won't ___ nev - er grow ___ old. ___ She's my sweet ___ lit - tle thang, ___

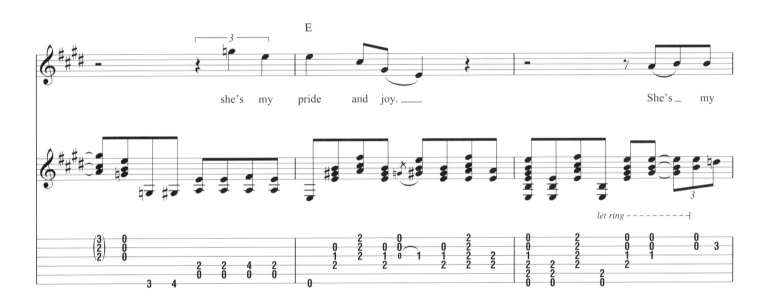

she's my pride and joy. ___ She's ___ my

sweet lit-tle ba - by, I'm ___ her ___ lit - tle lov - er boy. ___

Guitar Solo

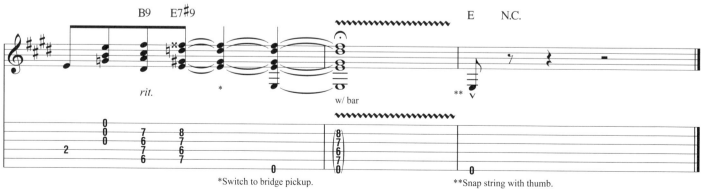

*Switch to bridge pickup.

**Snap string with thumb.

Purple Haze

Words and Music by Jimi Hendrix

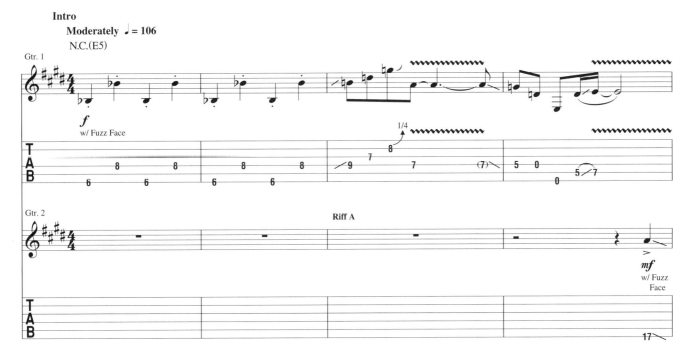

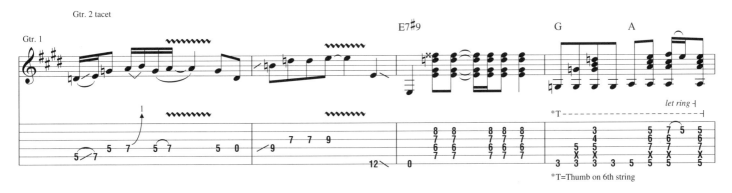

Guitar Solo
w/ voc. ad lib (next 8 meas.)
Gtr. 2: w/ misc. vibrato bar effects (next 8 meas.)

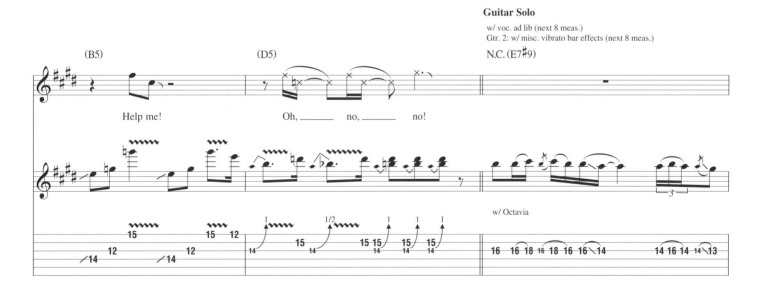

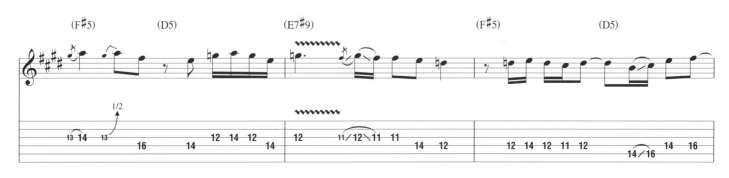

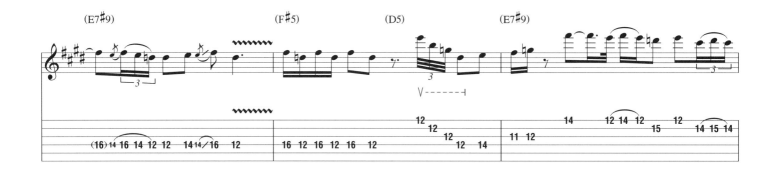

Interlude

Gtr. 2: w/ Riff A

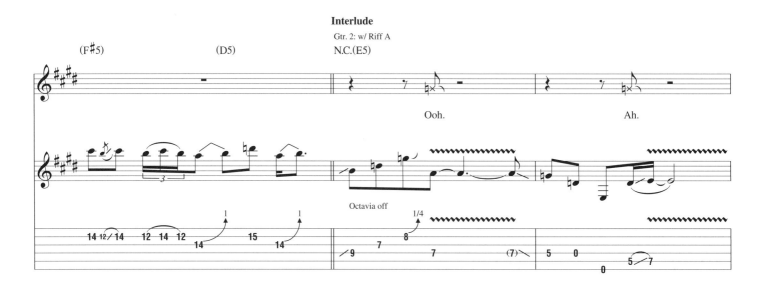

Ooh.　Ah.

Octavia off

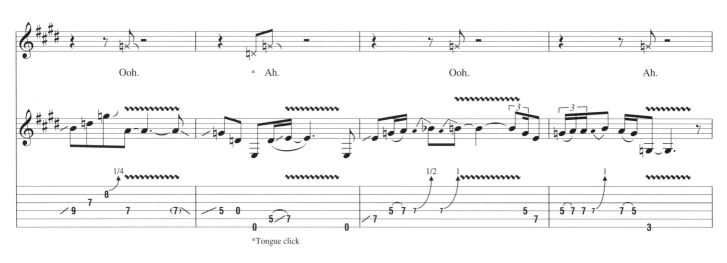

Ooh.　*　Ah.　Ooh.　Ah.

*Tongue click

Verse

E7#9　　　　　　　　G　　　A

Ooh.　Ah.　Yeah!　3. Pur-ple haze _____ all in my eyes, _____ uh,

let ring

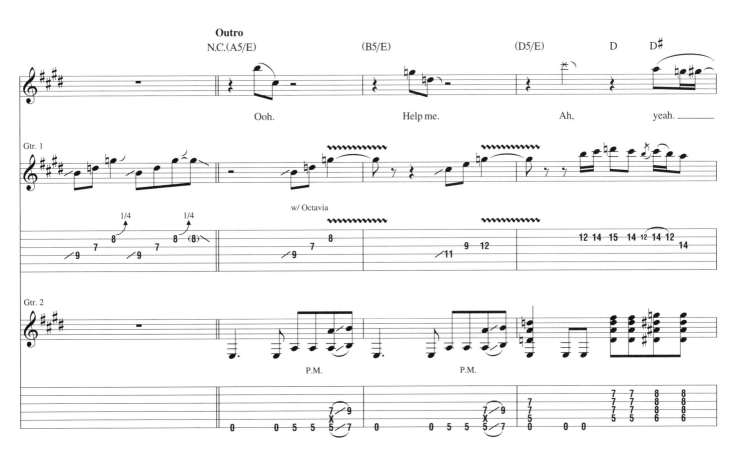

Rock Around the Clock

Words and Music by Max C. Freedman and Jimmy DeKnight

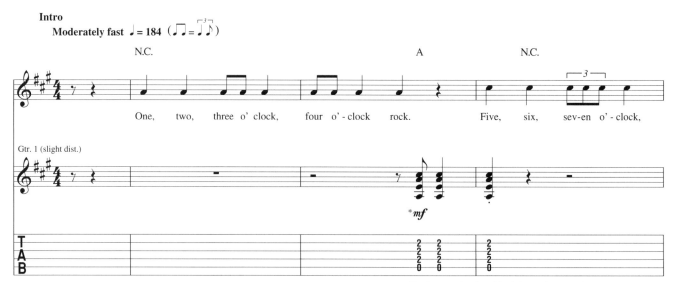

*Begin song w/ gtr.'s vol. knob lowered about halfway.

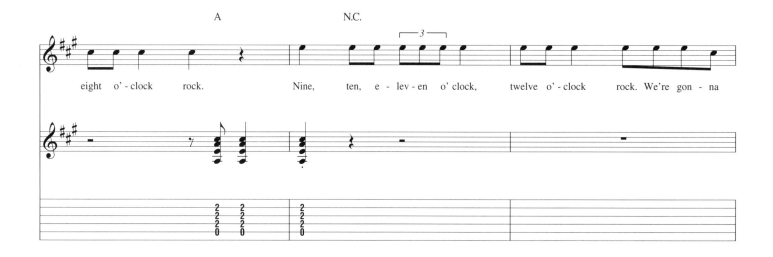

**Chord symbols reflect overall harmony.

*Raise gtr.'s vol. knob to full.

Guitar Solo

D.S. al Coda
(take repeat)

3. When the

Coda

Interlude

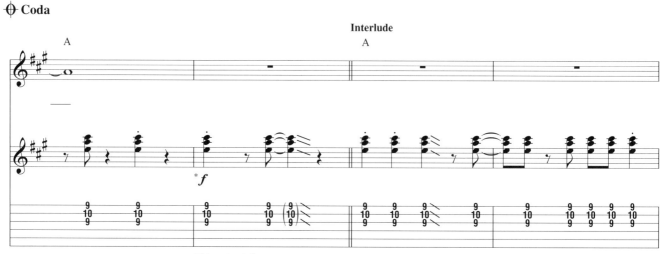

*Raise vol. as before.

326

Verse

5. When the clock strikes twelve, we'll cool off then, __ start, a,

rock - in' 'round the clock a - gain. __ We're gon - na rock a - round the

clock to - night. ___ We're gon - na rock, rock, rock till

broad day - light. ___ We're gon - na rock gon - na rock a - round ___ the clock ___ to - night. ___

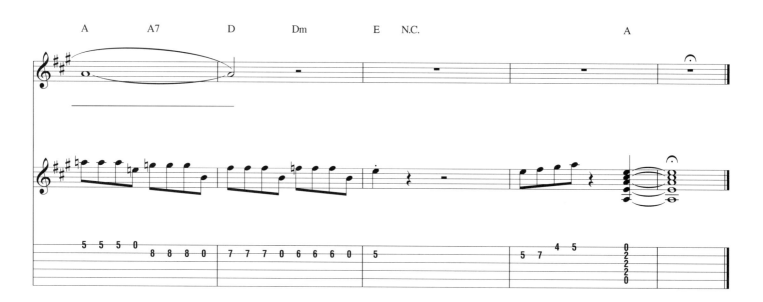

Additional Lyrics

3. When the chimes ring five, six and seven,
   We'll be right in seventh heaven.

4. When it's eight, nine, ten, eleven too,
   I'll be goin' strong and so will you.

Run to the Hills

Words and Music by Steven Harris

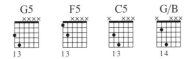

G5 F5 C5 G/B

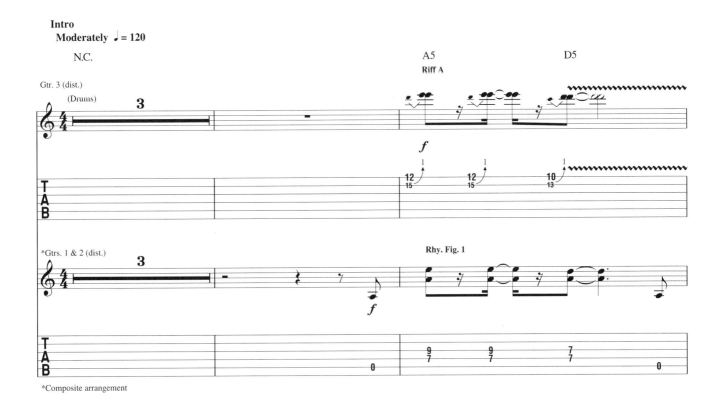

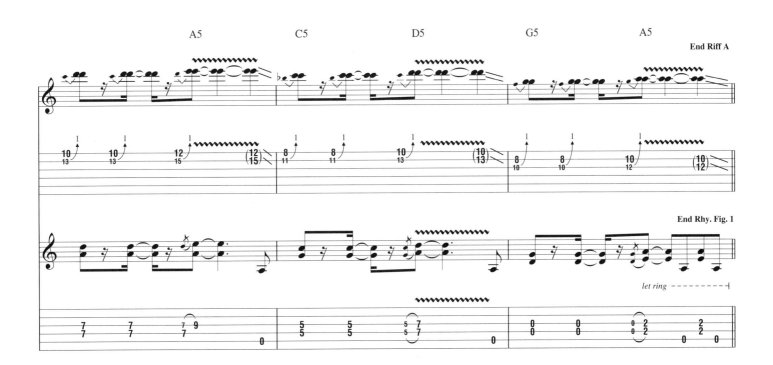

Verse

Gtrs. 1 & 2: w/ Rhy. Fig. 1 (3 3/4 times)
Gtr. 3: w/ Riff A (3 3/4 times)

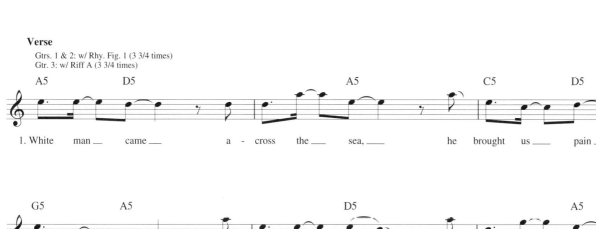

1. White man __ came __ a-cross the __ sea, __ he brought us __ pain __ and

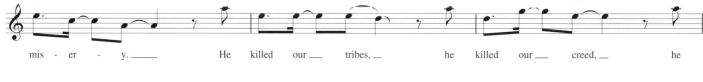

mis- er - y. __ He killed our __ tribes, __ he killed our __ creed, __ he

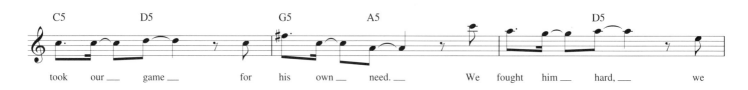

took our __ game __ for his own __ need. __ We fought him __ hard, __ we

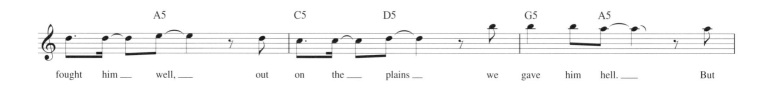

fought him __ well, __ out on the __ plains __ we gave him hell. __ But

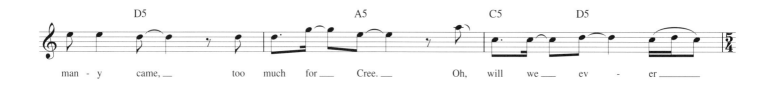

man - y came, __ too much for __ Cree. __ Oh, will we ev - er __

Interlude
Faster ♩ = 180

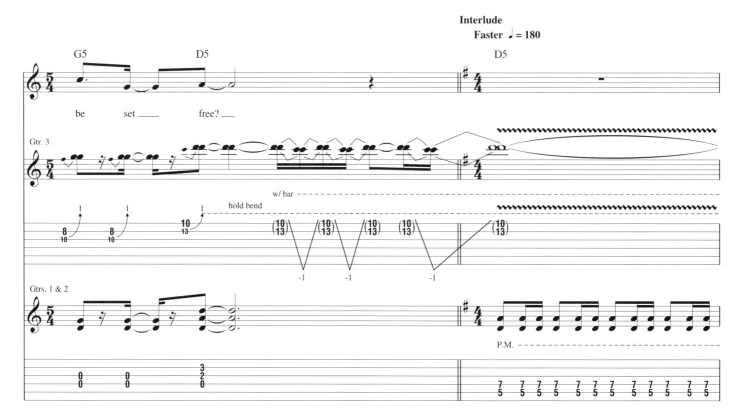

be set __ free? __

Gtr. 3

Gtrs. 1 & 2

Verse

1st time, Gtr. 3 tacet

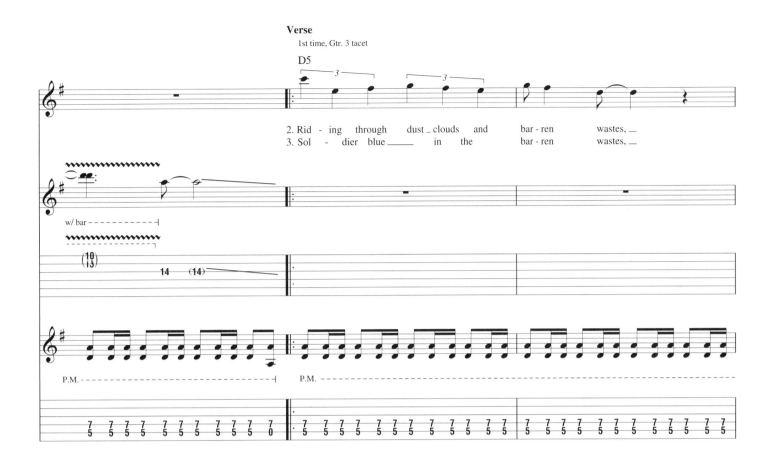

2. Rid - ing through dust _ clouds and bar - ren wastes, _
3. Sol - dier blue _ in the bar - ren wastes, _

w/ bar

P.M.

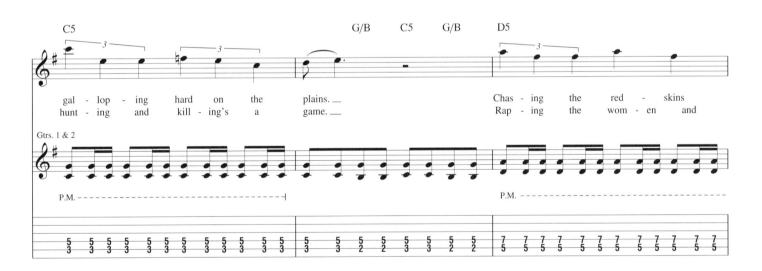

gal - lop - ing hard on the plains. _ Chas - ing the red - skins
hunt - ing and kill - ing's a game. _ Rap - ing the wom - en and

Gtrs. 1 & 2

P.M.

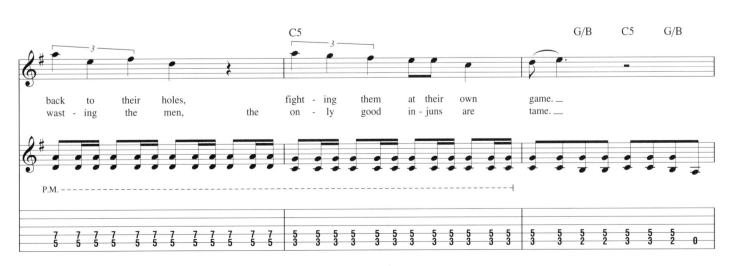

back to their holes, fight - ing them at their own game. _
wast - ing the men, the on - ly good in - juns are tame. _

P.M.

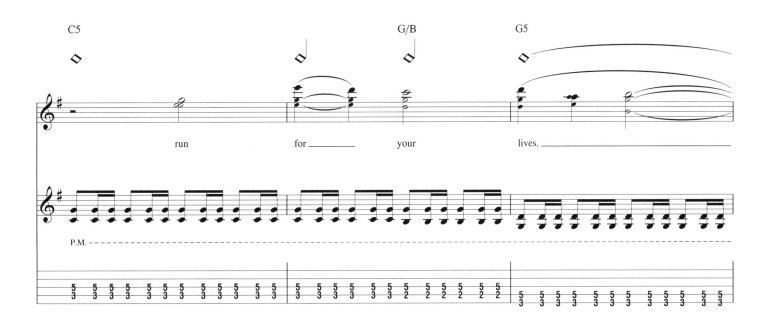

run   for _____   your   lives. _____

Gtrs. 1 & 2: w/ Rhy. Figs. 2 & 2A (1st 6 meas.)

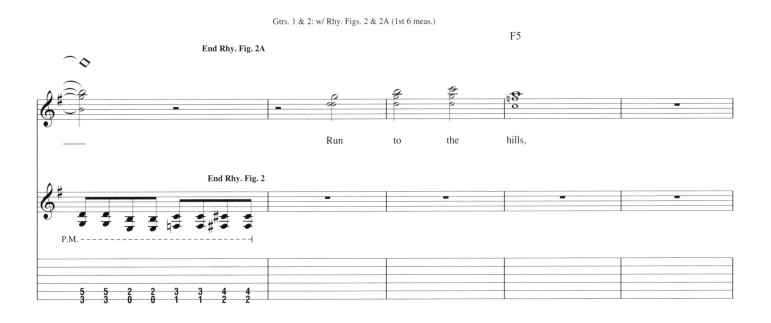

Run   to   the   hills,

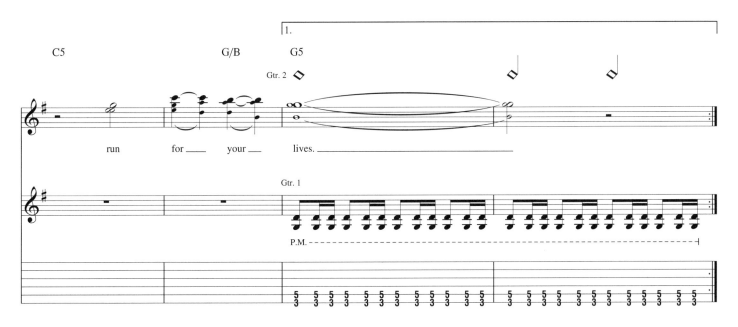

run   for ___   your ___   lives. _____

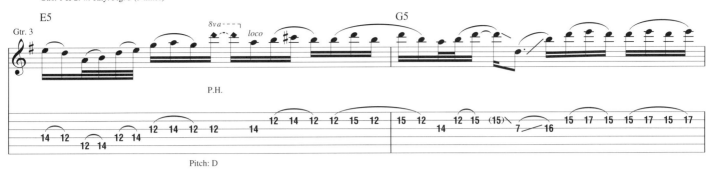

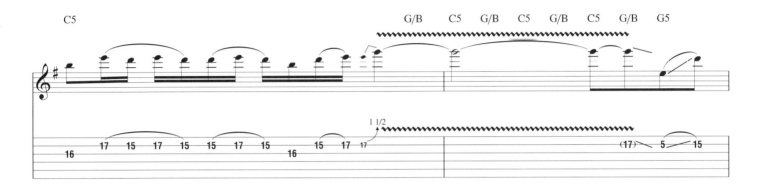

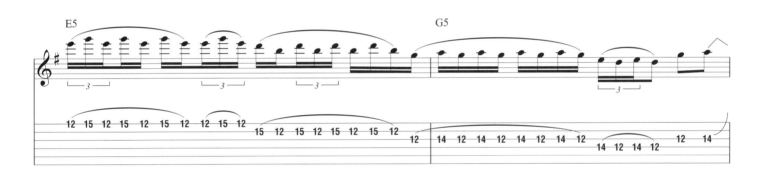

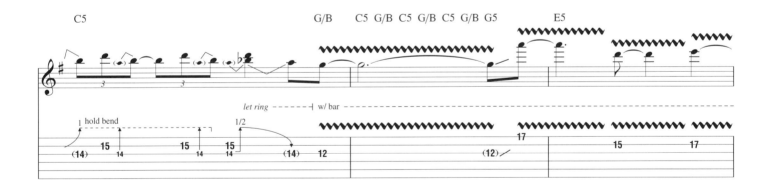

Interlude

1st time, Gtr. 3 tacet

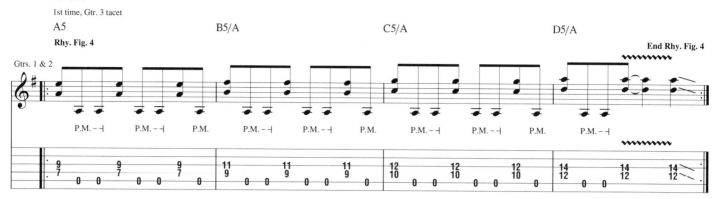

Gtrs. 1 & 2: w/ Rhy. Fig. 4

Yeah.

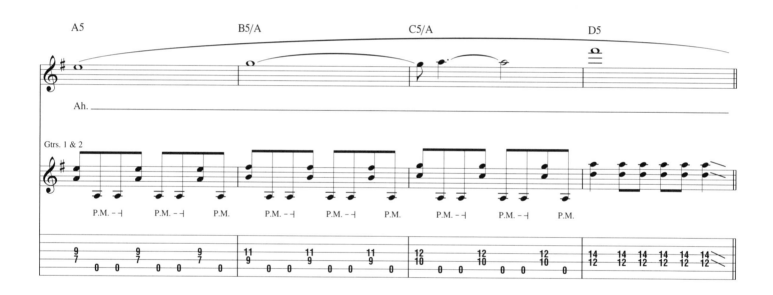

Ah.

Outro-Chorus

Gtrs. 1 & 2: w/ Rhy. Figs. 2 & 2A (3 1/2 times)

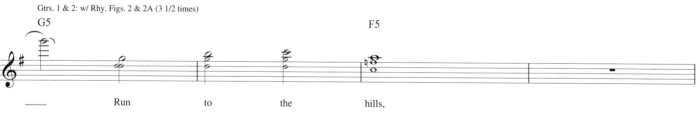

Run to the hills,

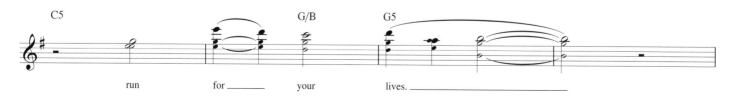

run for _____ your lives. _____

F5

Run to the hills,

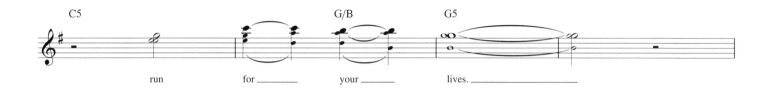

C5 G/B G5

run for _____ your _____ lives. _____

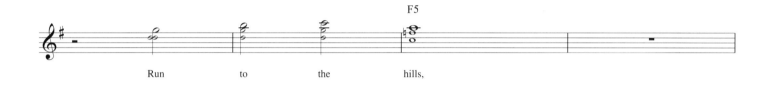

F5

Run to the hills,

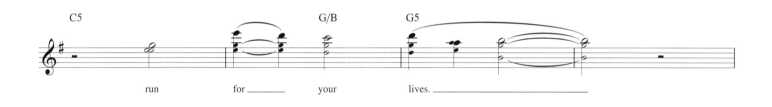

C5 G/B G5

run for _____ your lives. _____

F5

Run to the hills,

Free time

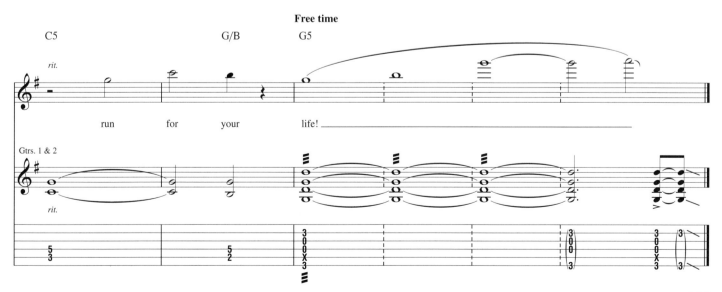

C5 G/B G5

run for your life! _____

Gtrs. 1 & 2

from Alice Cooper - *School's Out*

School's Out

Words and Music by Alice Cooper and Michael Bruce

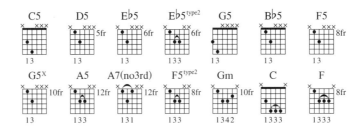

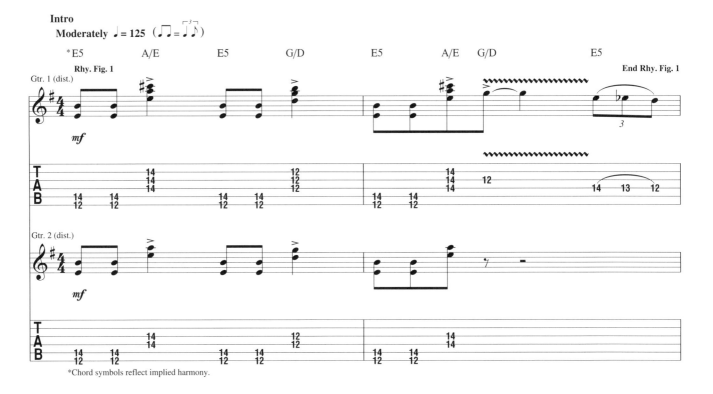

*Chord symbols reflect implied harmony.

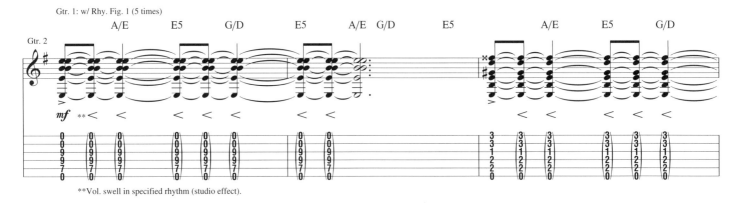

**Vol. swell in specified rhythm (studio effect).

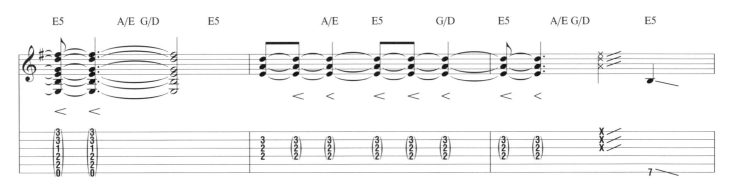

Pre-Chorus

can't sa - lute __ ya, can't find a flag. __ If that don't suit ya, that's a drag. __

*See top of first page of song for chord diagrams pertaining to rhythm slashes.

Chorus

School's out for sum - mer!

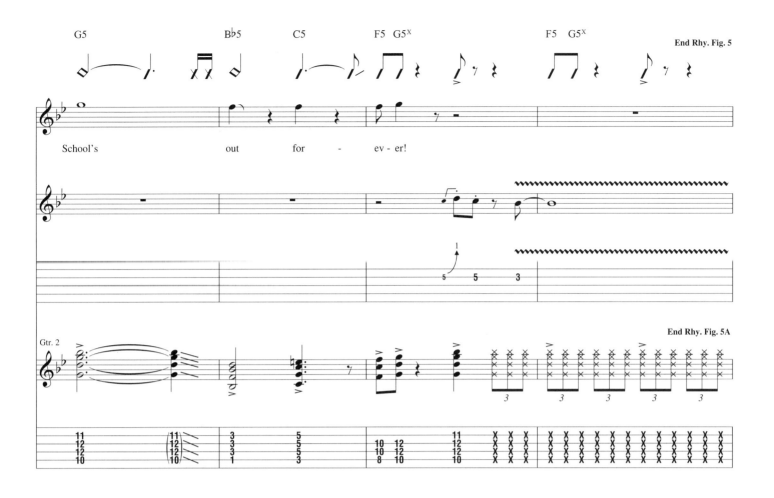

School's ... out ... for - ev - er!

Gtr. 2

Gtrs. 1 & 2: w/ Rhy. Figs. 5 & 5A (1st 4 meas.)

School's ... been blown ... to ... piec - es!

Gtr. 3

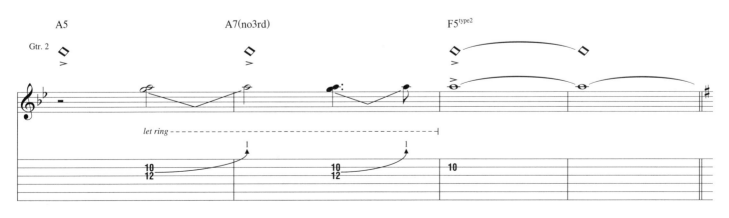

Gtr. 2

let ring

Bridge

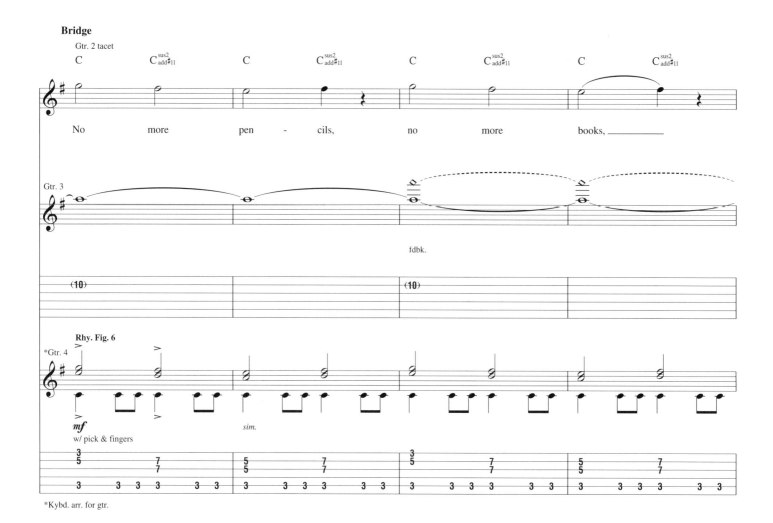

No more pen - cils, no more books,

*Kybd. arr. for gtr.

no more teach - er's dirt - y looks. Yeah! (Looks.)

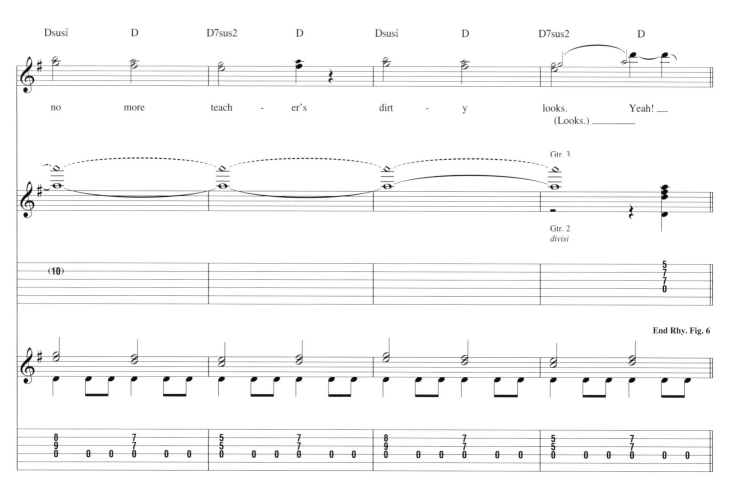

Guitar Solo

Gtr. 2: w/ Rhy. Fig. 2 (2 times)
Gtr. 4 tacet

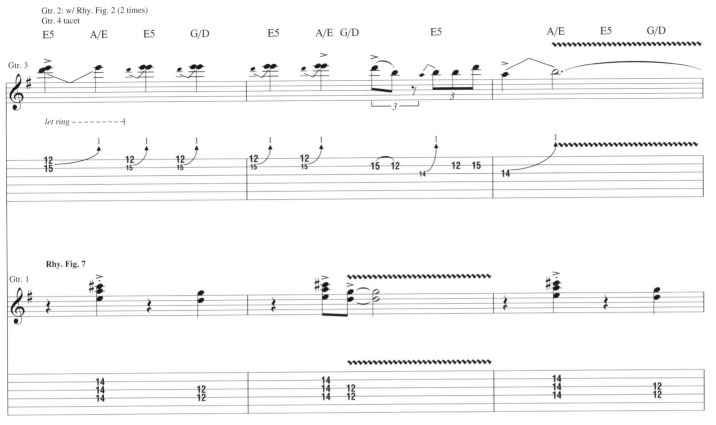

Rhy. Fig. 7

Gtr. 1: w/ Rhy. Fig. 7

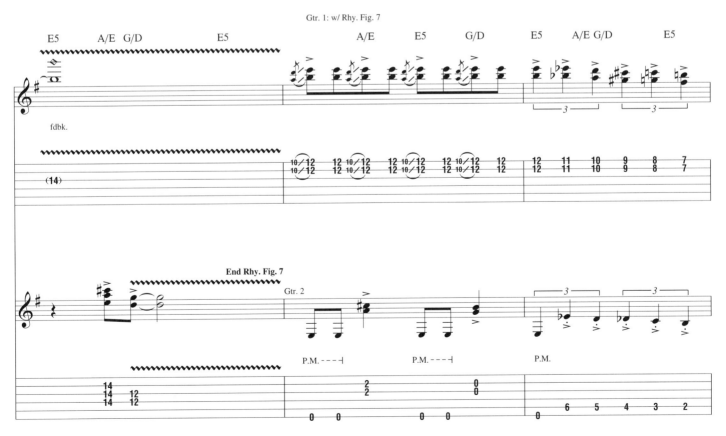

344

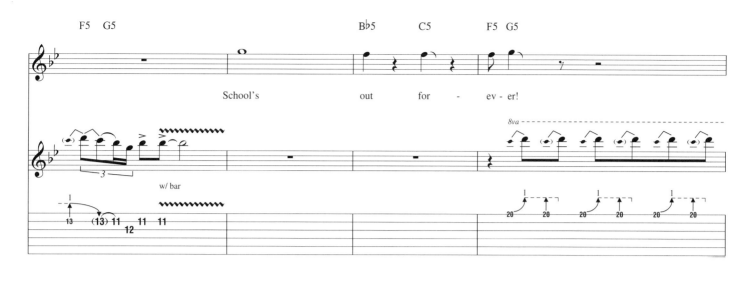

School's out for - ev - er!

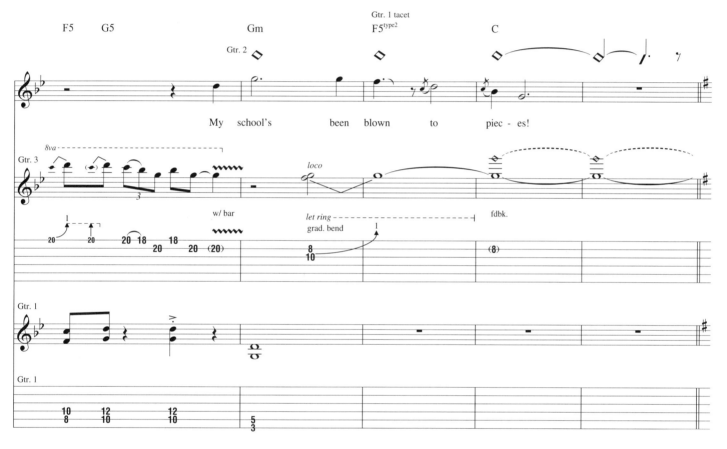

My school's been blown to piec - es!

Bridge

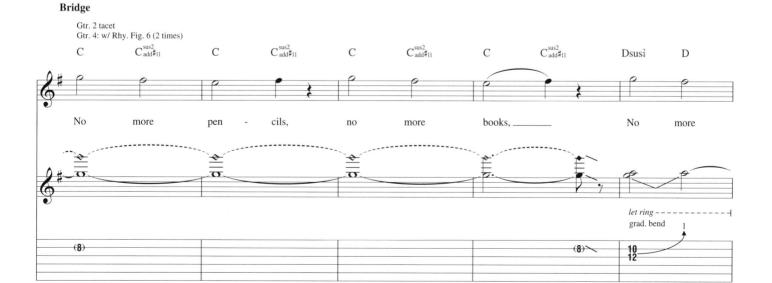

No more pen - cils, no more books, _____ No more

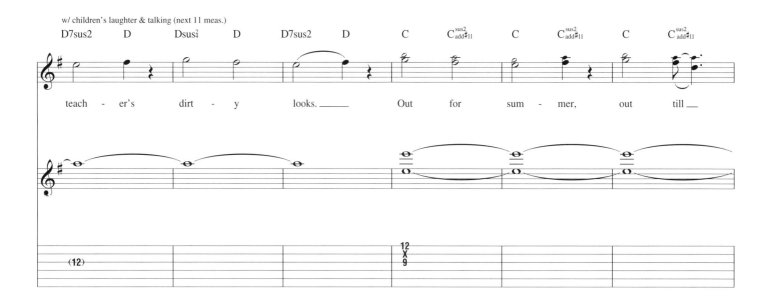

w/ children's laughter & talking (next 11 meas.)

teach - er's dirt - y looks. _____ Out for sum - mer, out till ___

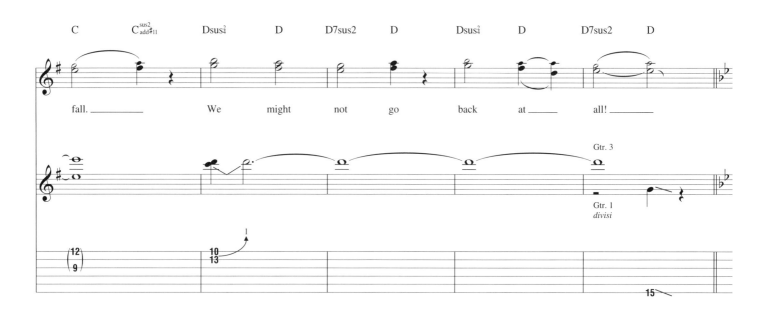

fall. _____ We might not go back at _____ all! _____

Outro-Chorus

Gtrs. 1 & 2: w/ Rhy. Figs. 5 & 5A (1 1/2 times)

School's out for - ev - er!
(Out for...)

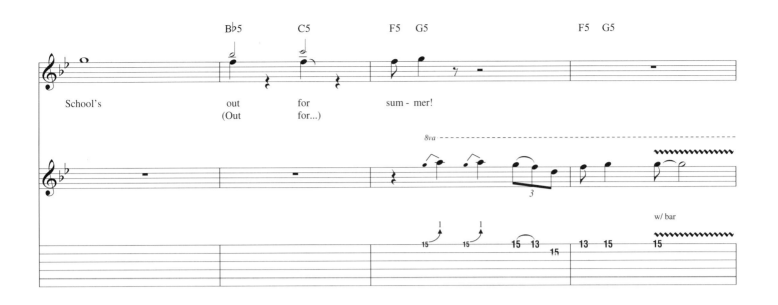

School's   out   for   sum - mer!
(Out   for...)

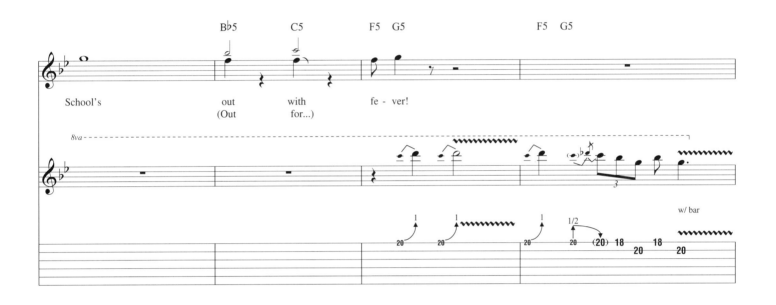

School's   out   with   fe - ver!
(Out   for...)

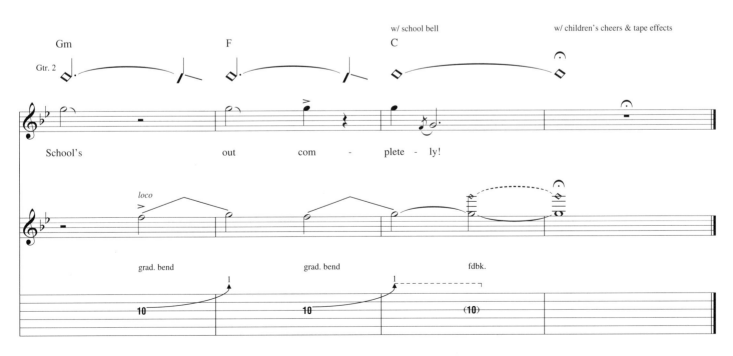

School's   out   com -   plete - ly!

from Nirvana - *Nevermind*

Smells Like Teen Spirit

Words and Music by Kurt Cobain, Krist Novoselic and Dave Grohl

Guitar Solo

351

from Deep Purple - *Machine Head*

Smoke on the Water

Words and Music by Ritchie Blackmore, Ian Gillan, Roger Glover, Jon Lord and Ian Paice

*Chord symbols reflect implied harmony.

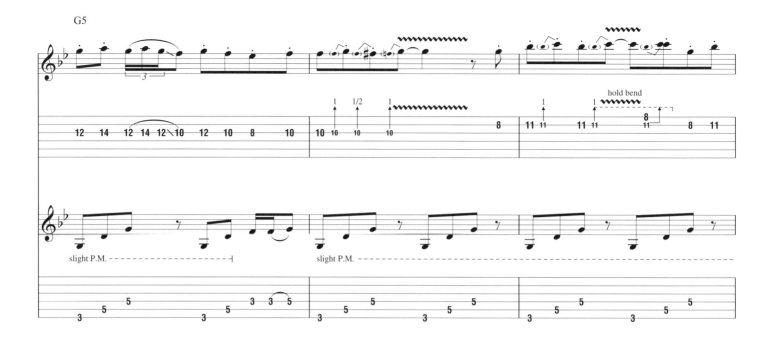

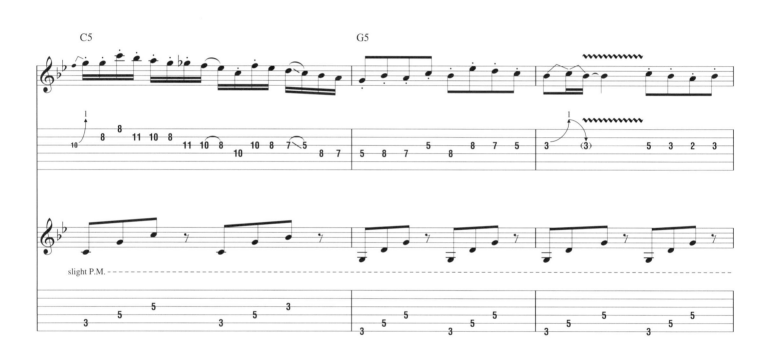

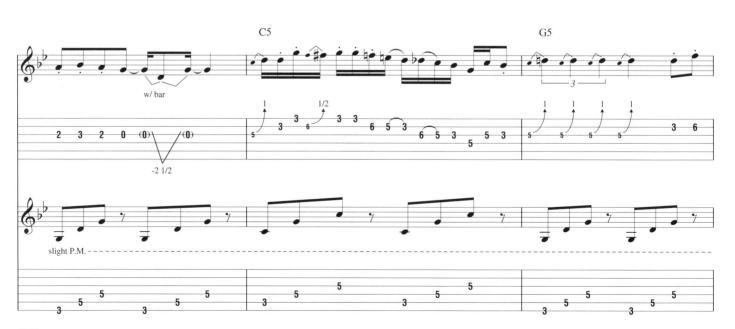

Gtr. 1: w/ Riff A (1 3/4 times)

N.C. (G5)

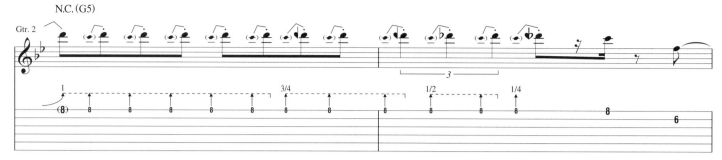

D.S. al Coda

Gtr. 2 tacet   Gtr. 1: w/ Fill 1

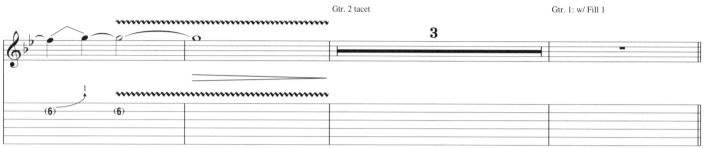

$\oplus$ Coda

Interlude

Gtr. 1: w/ Riff A (4 times)

N.C. (G5)

Outro-Organ Solo

N.C. (G5)

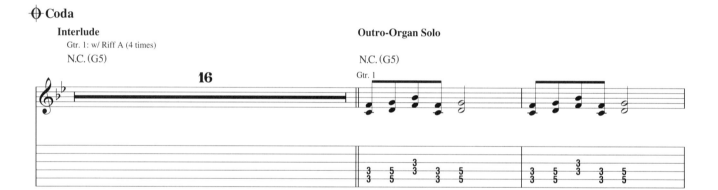

Begin fade

Fade out

Fmaj7   Am   Am7/G   Fmaj7

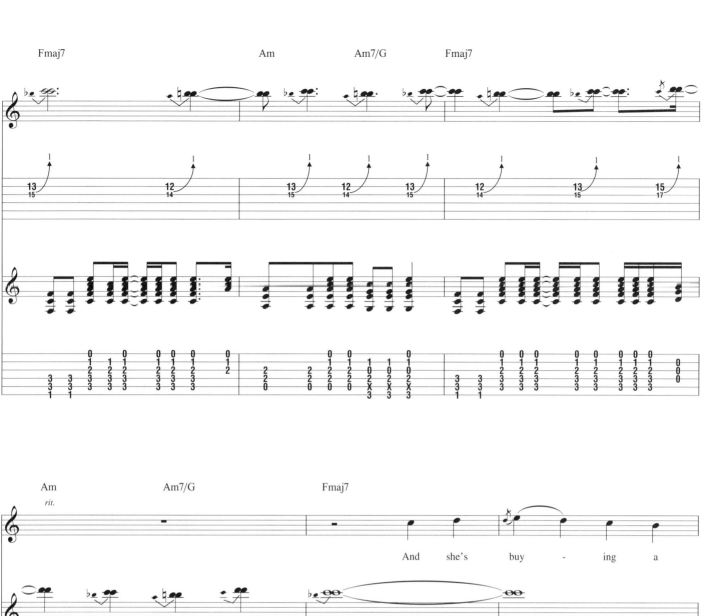

Am   Am7/G   Fmaj7

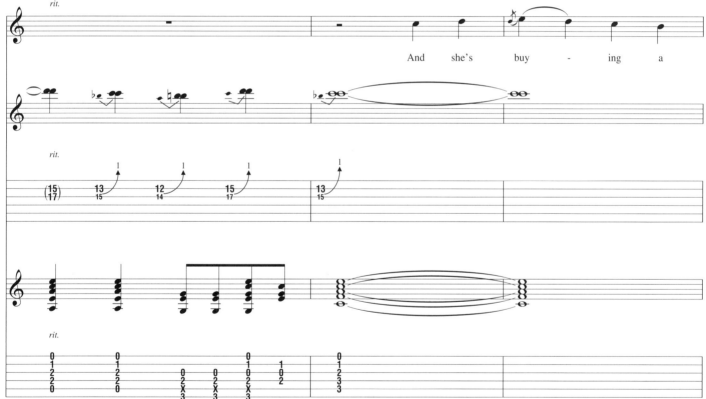

And   she's   buy -   ing   a

Gtrs. 3 & 4 tacet

N.C.

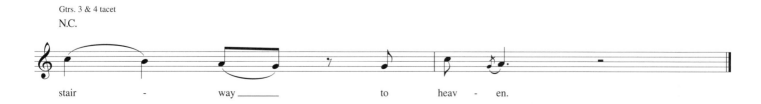

stair -   way _____   to   heav -   en.

from Crosby, Stills & Nash - *Crosby, Stills & Nash*

Suite: Judy Blue Eyes

Words and Music by Stephen Stills

Gtrs. 1, 2 & 4: Open E5 tuning:
(low to high) E-E♭-E-E-B-E

Intro

Moderately fast ♩ = 152

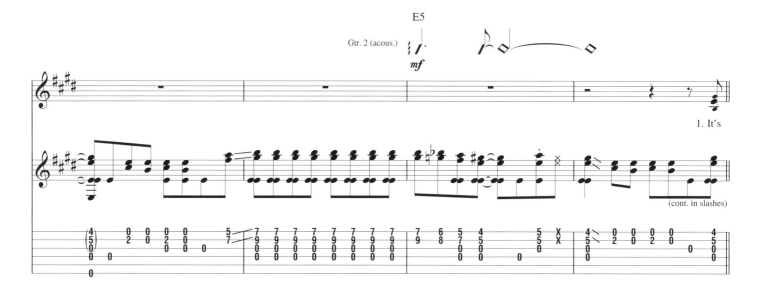

(cont. in slashes)

1. It's

Verse

1st time, Gtr. 2 tacet
2nd time, Gtrs. 1, 2 & 3: w/ Rhy. Fills 2 & 2A

get - ting   to   the   point ___   where   I'm   no   and
mem - ber   what ___   we've   said ___   and   done   and

* Composite arrangement
**T = Thumb on 6th string

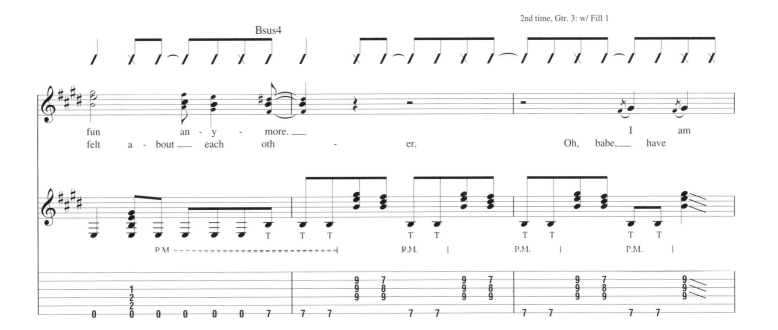

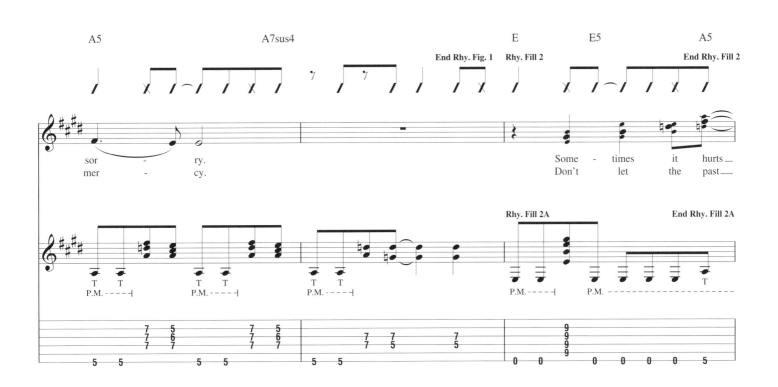

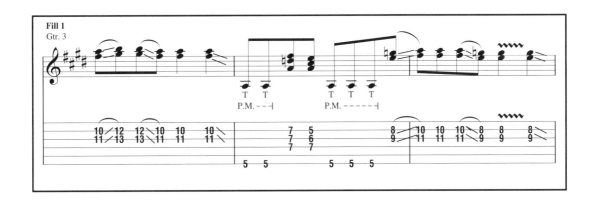

Interlude

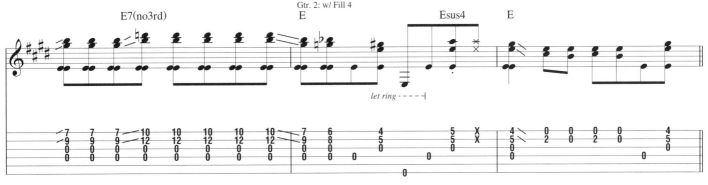

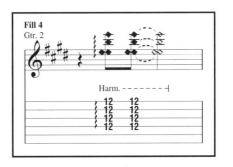

374

Bridge

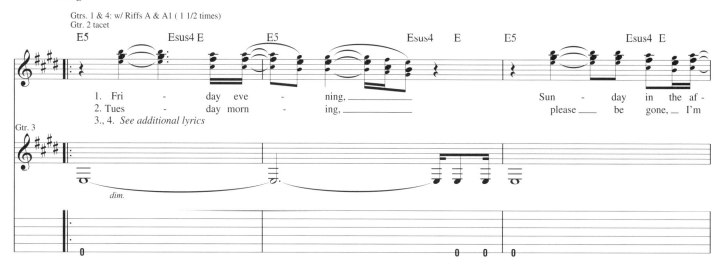

Gtrs. 1 & 4: w/ Riffs A & A1 (1 1/2 times)
Gtr. 2 tacet

E5   Esus4 E   E5   Esus4 E   E5   Esus4 E

1. Fri - day eve - ning,_____ Sun - day in the af -
2. Tues - day morn - ing,_____ please ___ be gone, ___ I'm
3., 4. *See additional lyrics*

Gtr. 3

dim.

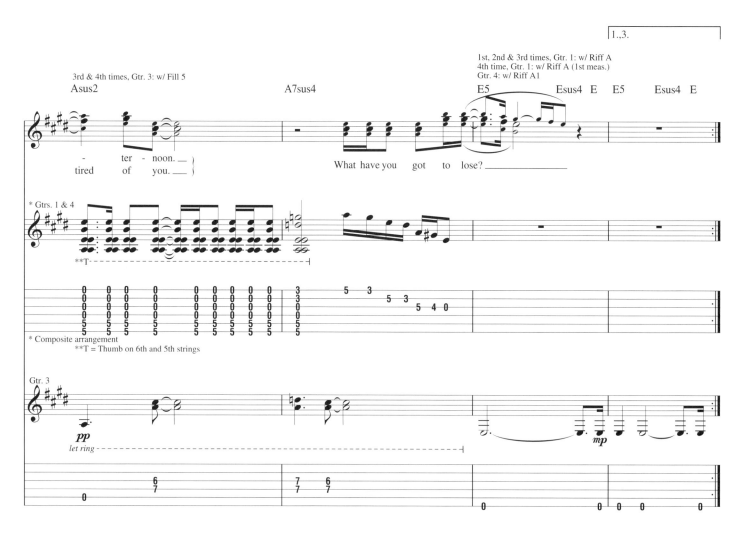

1.,3.

3rd & 4th times, Gtr. 3: w/ Fill 5

1st, 2nd & 3rd times, Gtr. 1: w/ Riff A
4th time, Gtr. 1: w/ Riff A (1st meas.)
Gtr. 4: w/ Riff A1

Asus2   A7sus4   E5   Esus4 E   E5   Esus4 E

- ter - noon. ___ }
tired of you. ___ }

What have you got to lose? _____

* Gtrs. 1 & 4

**T -

* Composite arrangement
**T = Thumb on 6th and 5th strings

Gtr. 3

pp

let ring -

mp

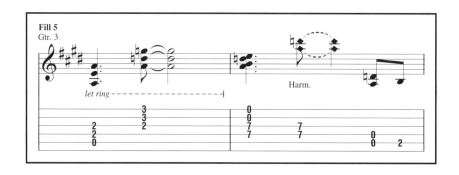

Fill 5
Gtr. 3

let ring - - - - - - - - - - - - - - - -

Harm.

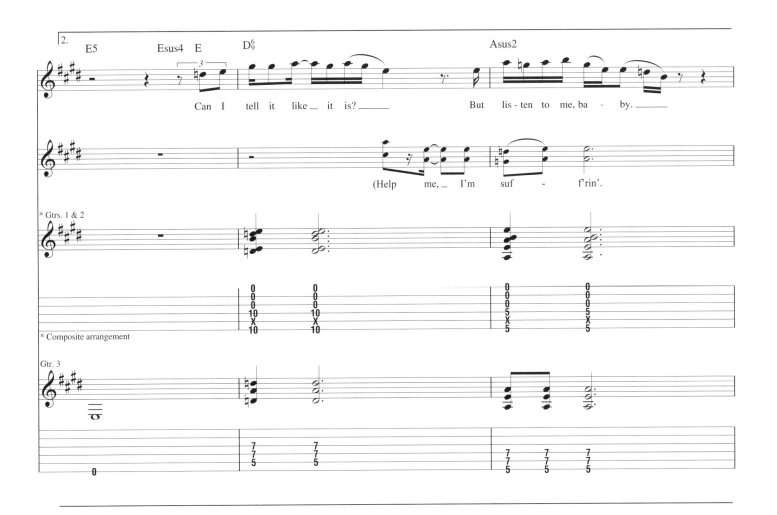

Can I tell it like _ it is? _____ But lis - ten to me, ba - by. _____

(Help me, _ I'm suf - f'rin'.

* Gtrs. 1 & 2

* Composite arrangement

Gtr. 3

It's _ my heart _ that's a suf - f'rin', it's a dy - in'. That's _ what I _____ have to

Help me, _____ I'm dy - in'. _____ ...to

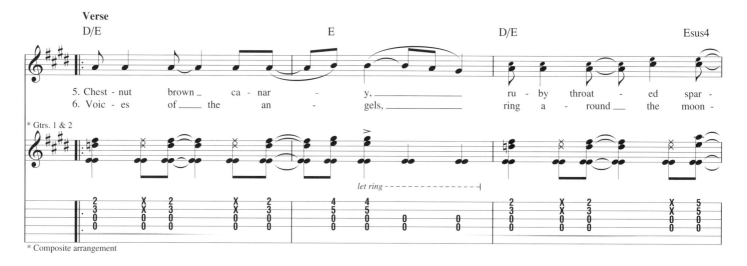

Verse

5. Chest - nut brown__ ca - nar - y,_____ ru - by throat - ed spar -
6. Voic - es of __ the an - gels,_____ ring a - round__ the moon -

* Gtrs. 1 & 2

let ring - - - - - - - - - - - - - - -|

* Composite arrangement

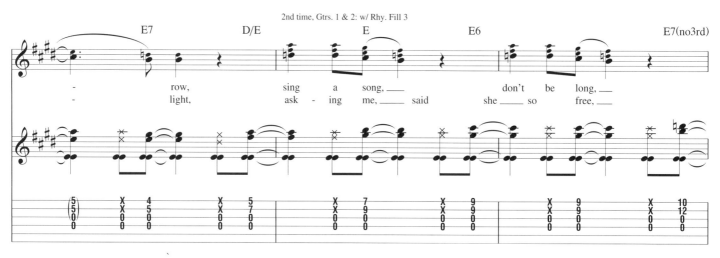

2nd time, Gtrs. 1 & 2: w/ Rhy. Fill 3

- row, sing a song,_____ don't be long,_____
- light, ask - ing me,_____ said she __ so free,_____

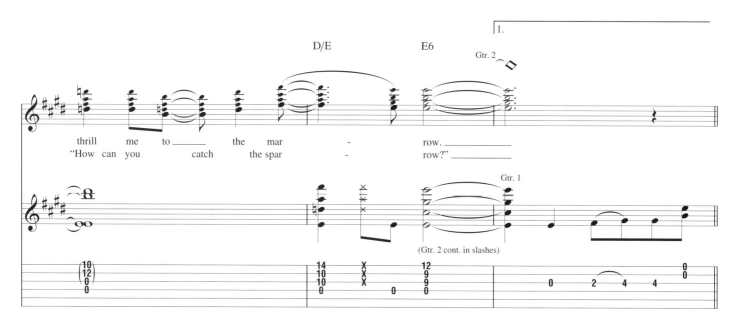

| 1.

thrill me to _____ the mar - row.
"How can you catch the spar - row?" _____

(Gtr. 2 cont. in slashes)

Rhy. Fill 3
Gtrs. 1 & 2

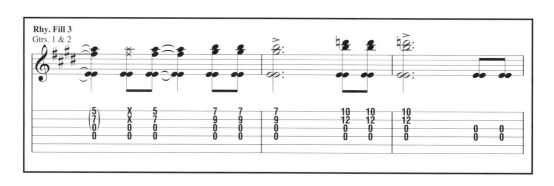

Verse

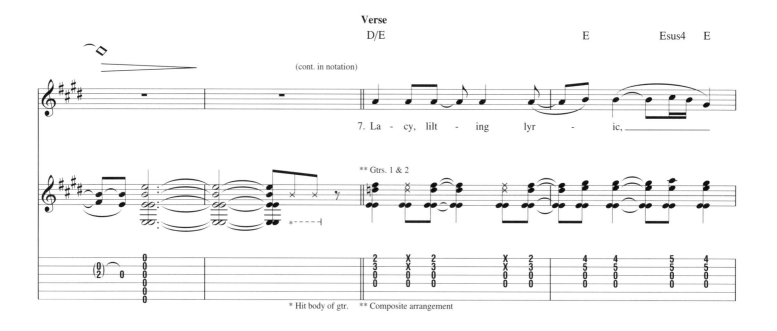

(cont. in notation)

7. La - cy, lilt - ing lyr - ic, _____

** Gtrs. 1 & 2

* Hit body of gtr.   ** Composite arrangement

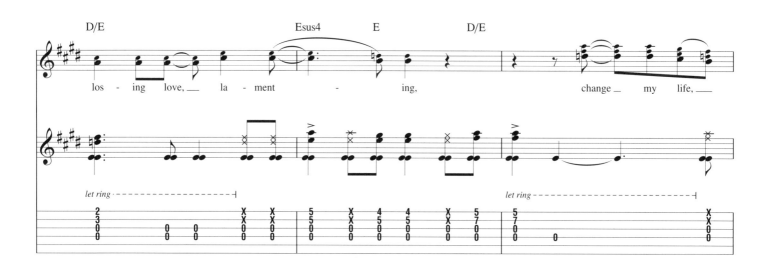

los - ing love, _____ la - ment - ing, _____ change _____ my life, _____

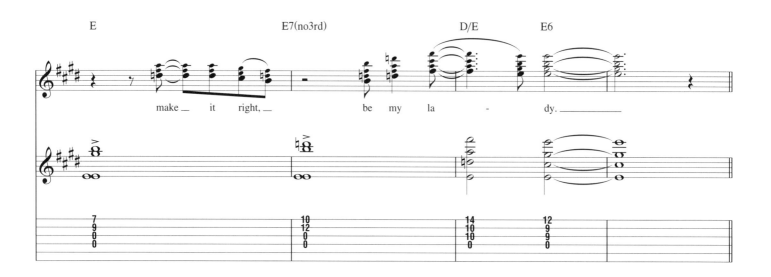

make _____ it right, _____ be my la - dy. _____

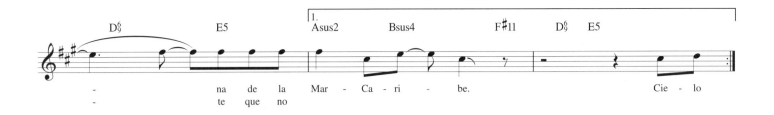

na de la Mar Ca - ri - be.   Cie - lo
te que no

pue - do va - ya.   Oh, ____ va! Oh, va!   Do, do, do, do, do,   do,   do,   do, do, do, do.

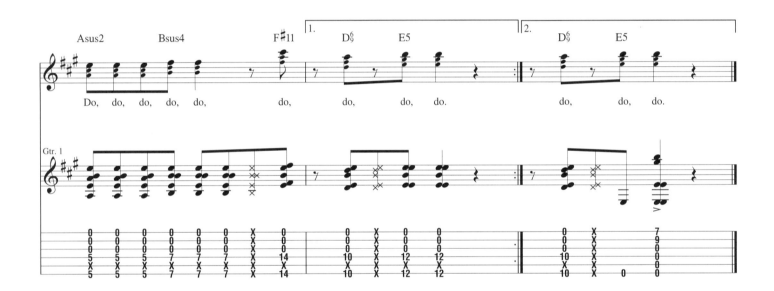

Do, do, do, do, do,   do,   do,   do,   do.   do,   do,   do.

Additional Lyrics

Bridge:

3. I've got an answer,
I'm going to fly away.
What have I got to lose?

4. Will you come see me
Thursdays and Saturdays? Hey, (hey,) hey.
What have you got to lose?

Outro translation:
How happy it makes me to think of Cuba,
The smiles of the Caribbean Sea.
Sunny sky has no blood,
And how sad that I'm not able to go.
Oh, go! Oh, go!

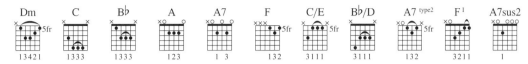

Sultans of Swing

Words and Music by Mark Knopfler

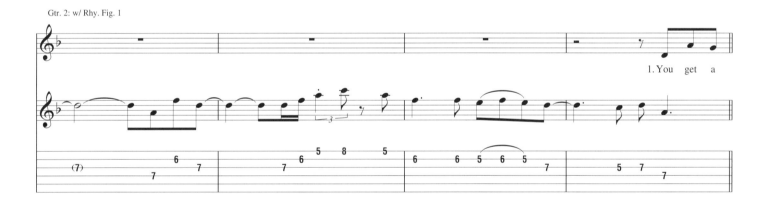

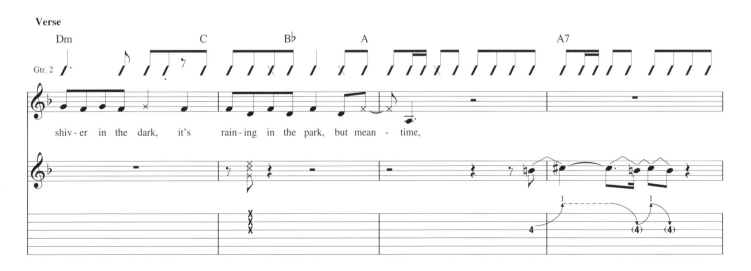

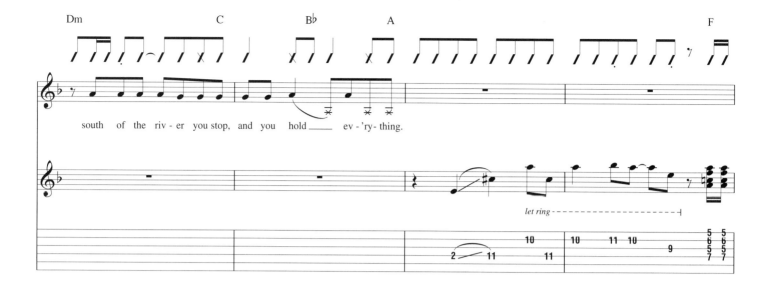

south of the riv - er you stop, and you hold _____ ev - 'ry - thing.

A band is blow-ing Dix - ie dou - ble four _____ time,

you feel al - right when you hear the mu - sic _____ ring.

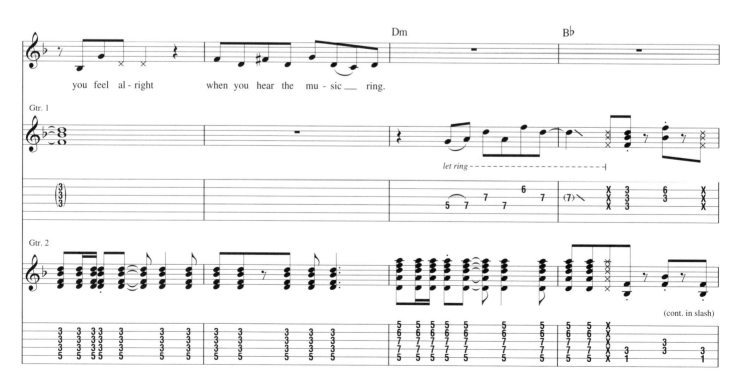

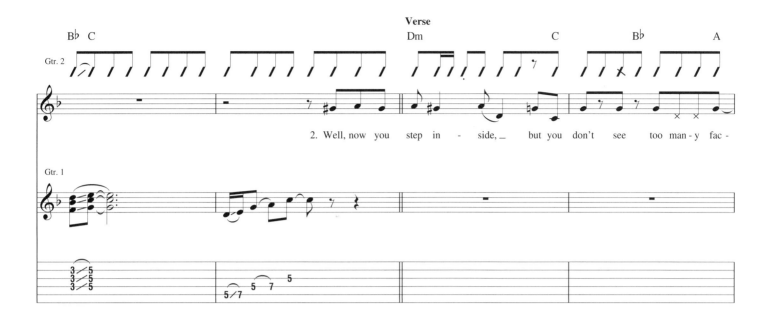

2. Well, now you step in - side, __ but you don't see too man - y fac -

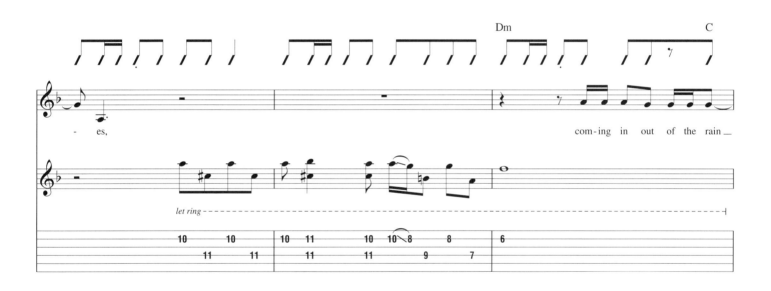

- es, __ com - ing in out of the rain __

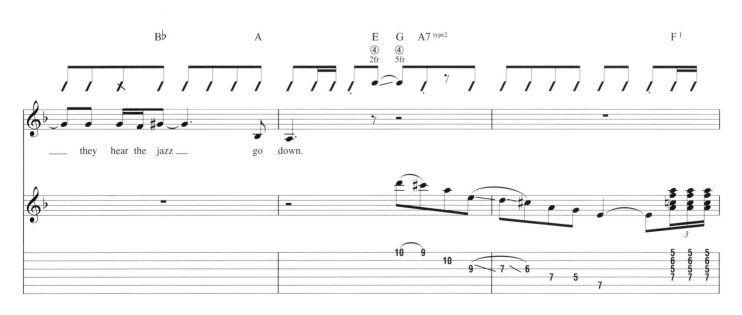

__ they hear the jazz __ go down.

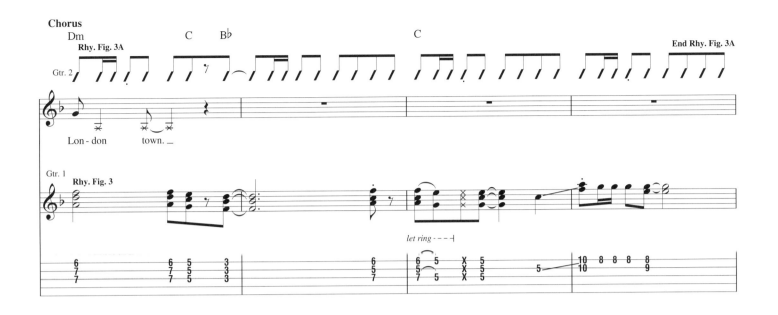

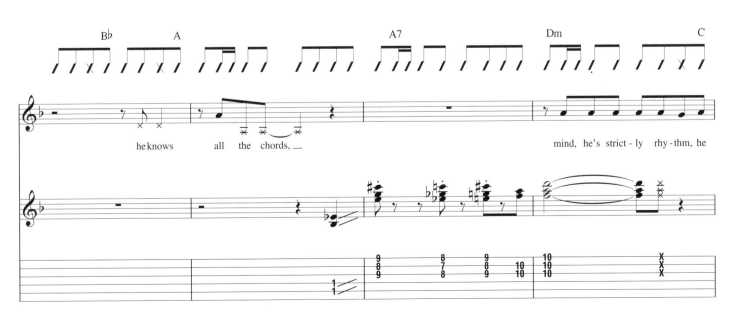

does-n't want to make it cry or sing. ___

Yes, and an old gui - tar ___ is all ___ he can af - ford ___

when he gets up un - der the lights ___ to play his thing. ___

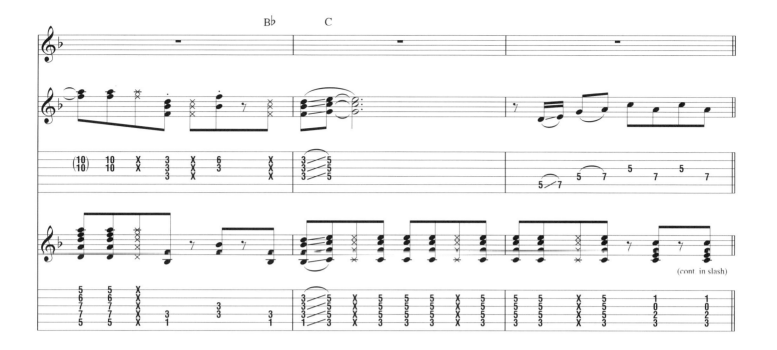

Verse

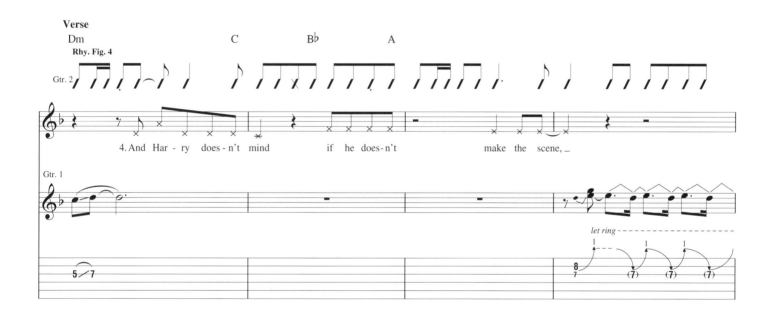

4. And Har-ry does-n't mind if he does-n't make the scene, _

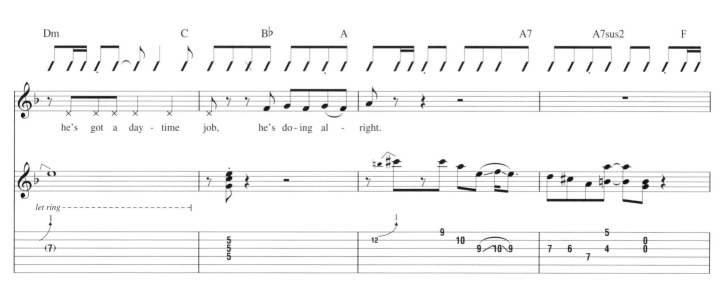

he's got a day - time job, he's do-ing al - right.

And the Sul - tans, ___ yeah, the Sul - tans ___ are play-ing

Chorus

Cre - ole, Cre - ole, ba - by. Ah ah.

Guitar Solo

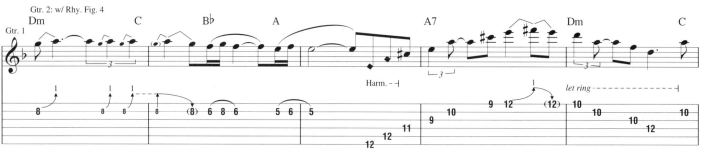

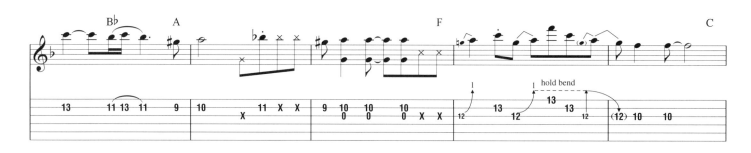

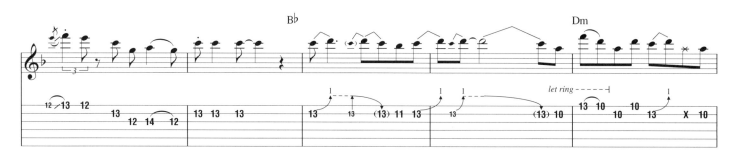

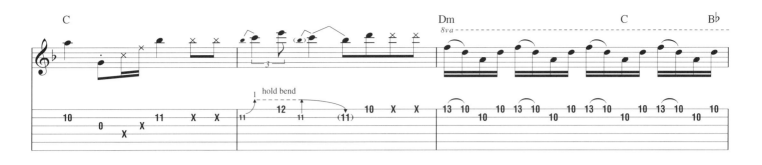
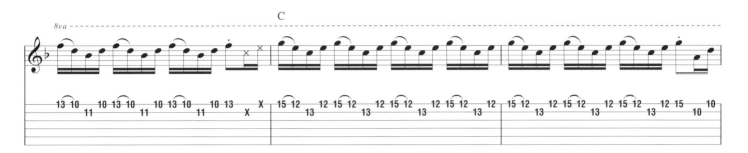
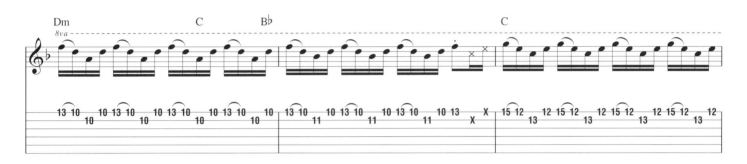
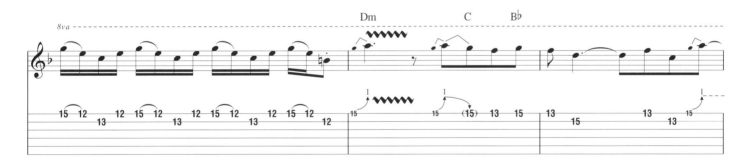
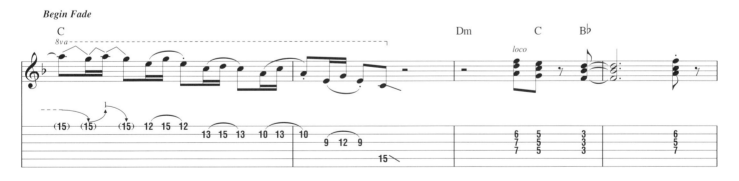
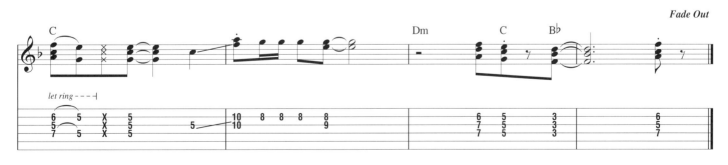

from Cheap Trick - *Heaven Tonight*

Surrender

Words and Music by Rick Nielsen

Verse lyrics:

1. Moth-er told me, yes, she told me I meet girls like you.
2. Fa-ther says, "Your moth-er's right, she's real-ly up on things."

She al-so told me, "Stay a-way, you'll nev-er know what you'll catch."
"Be-fore we mar-ried, Mom-my served in the WACS in the Phil-ip-pines."

*See top of page for chord diagrams pertaining to rhythm slashes.

**Gtrs. 1 & 2

**Composite arrangement

Bridge

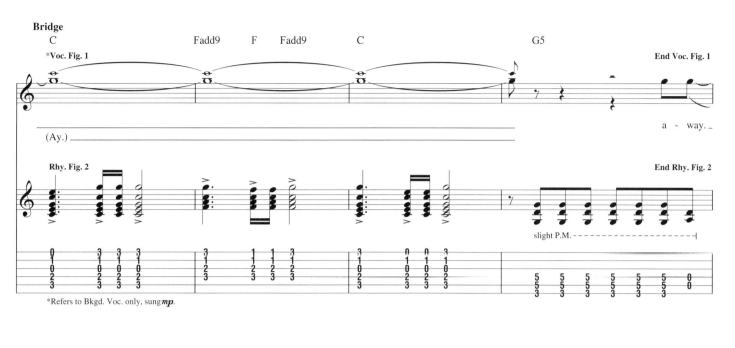

*Refers to Bkgd. Voc. only, sung **mp**.

(Ay.)

a - way.

Bkgd. Voc.: w/ Voc. Fig. 1
Gtrs. 1 & 2: w/ Rhy. Fig. 2

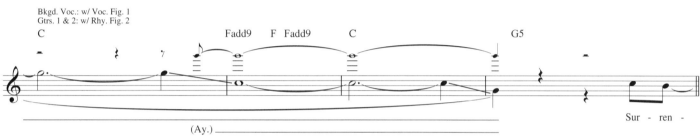

(Ay.)

Sur - ren -

Outro-Chorus

Gtrs. 1 & 2: w/ Rhy. Fig. 1 (till fade)

Play 3 times

- der, sur-ren - der, but don't __ give your-self a - way. __ Sur-ren -
(Mom-my's al - right, Dad - dy's al - right.

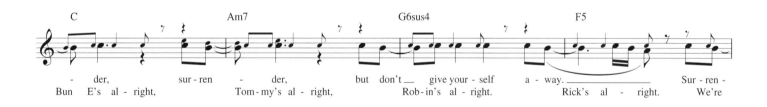

- der, sur-ren - der, but don't __ give your-self a - way. __ Sur-ren -
Bun E's al - right, Tom-my's al - right, Rob-in's al - right. Rick's al - right. We're

- der, sur-ren - der, but don't __ give your-self a - way. Sur-ren -
all al - right, we're all al - right, we're all al - right, we're all al - right!

Begin fade   ***2nd time, Fade out***

- der, sur-ren - der, but don't __ give your-self a - way. __ Sur-ren -
Mom-my's al - right, Dad - dy's al - right.)

405

from Guns N' Roses - *Appetite for Destruction*

Sweet Child o' Mine

Words and Music by W. Axl Rose, Slash, Izzy Stradlin', Duff McKagan and Steven Adler

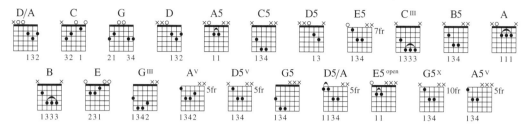

Tune down 1/2 step:
(low to high) Eb-Ab-Db-Gb-Bb-Eb

Intro

Moderately fast ♩ = 128

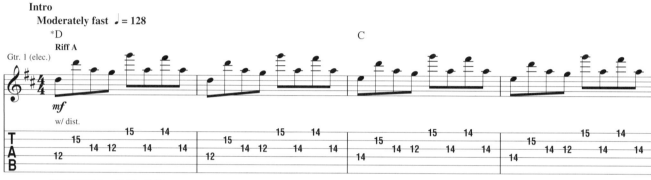

*Chord symbols reflect implied harmony.

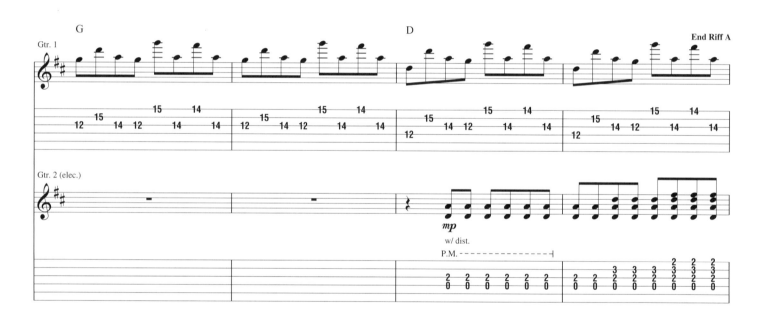

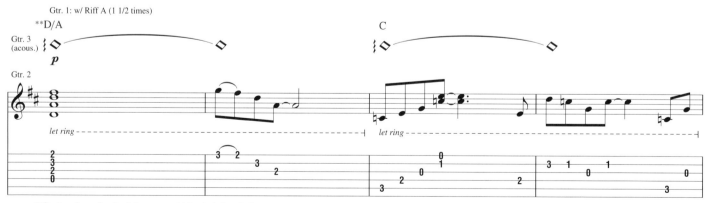

**See top of page for chord diagrams pertaining to rhythm slashes.

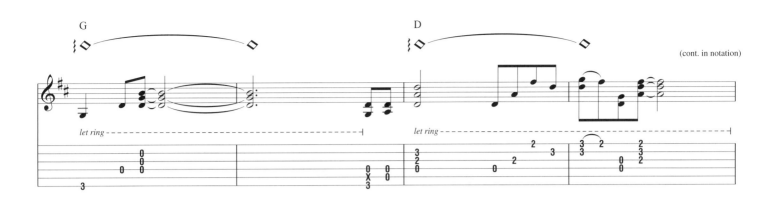

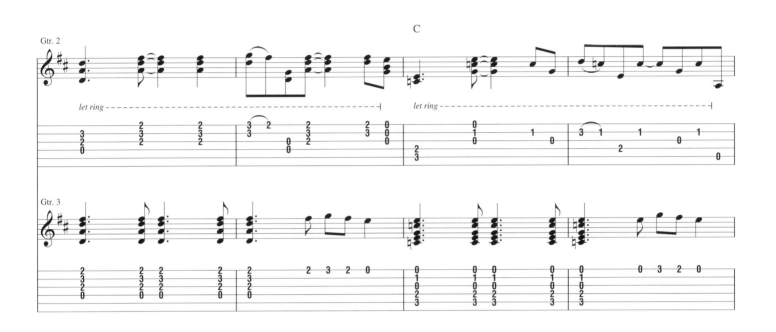

Now and then _ when I see her face _ she takes me a - way _ to that spe - cial place, _ and if I

stared _ too _ long, I'll prob-'ly break down and cry. _____

Interlude

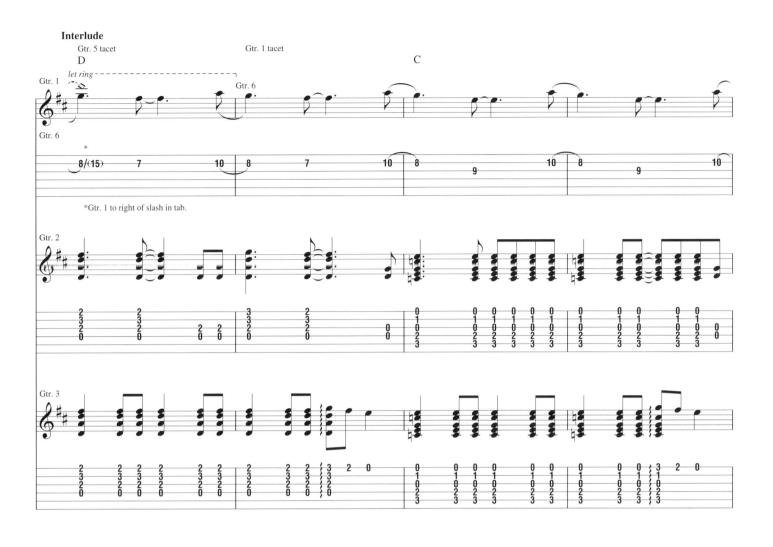

*Gtr. 1 to right of slash in tab.

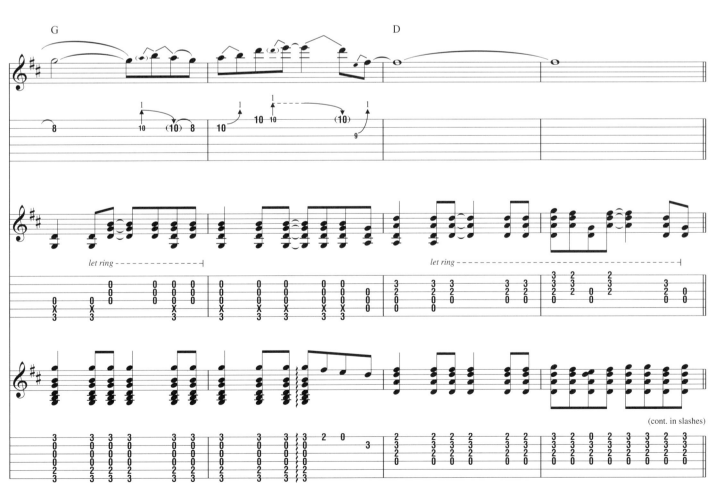

(cont. in slashes)

Verse

pray for the thun - der and the rain___ to qui - et - ly pass___ me by.___

Chorus

Gtr. 1: w/ Riff C
Gtr. 4 tacet

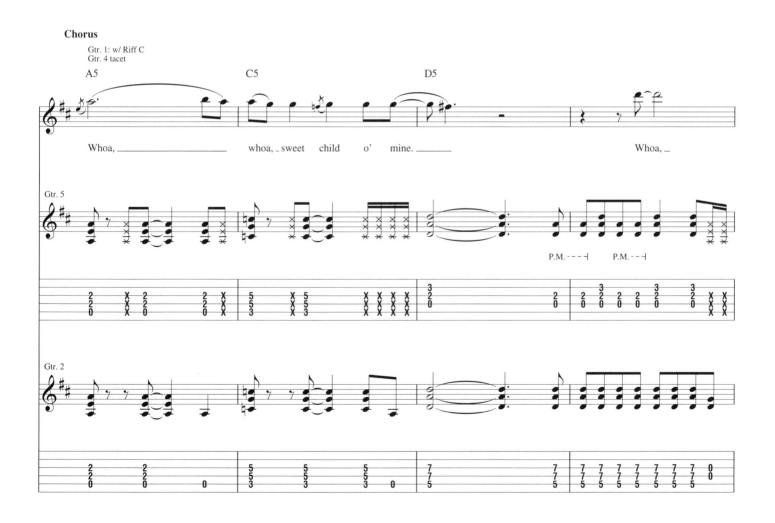

Whoa,_____ whoa,_ sweet child o' mine._____ Whoa,_

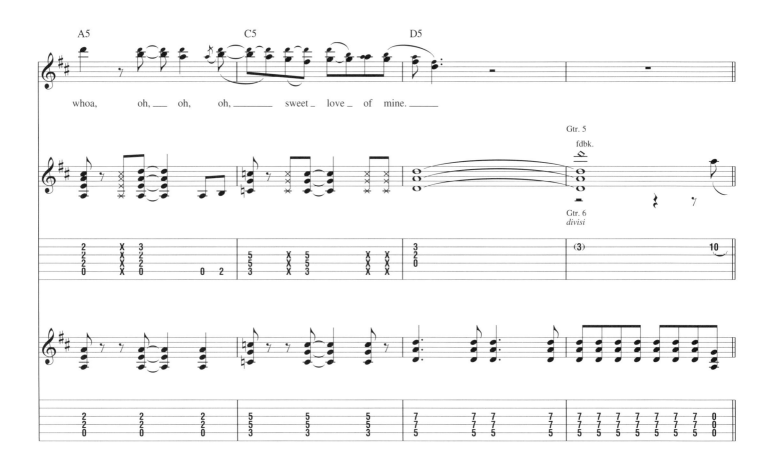

whoa, oh, __ oh, oh, _____ sweet _ love _ of mine. _____

Interlude

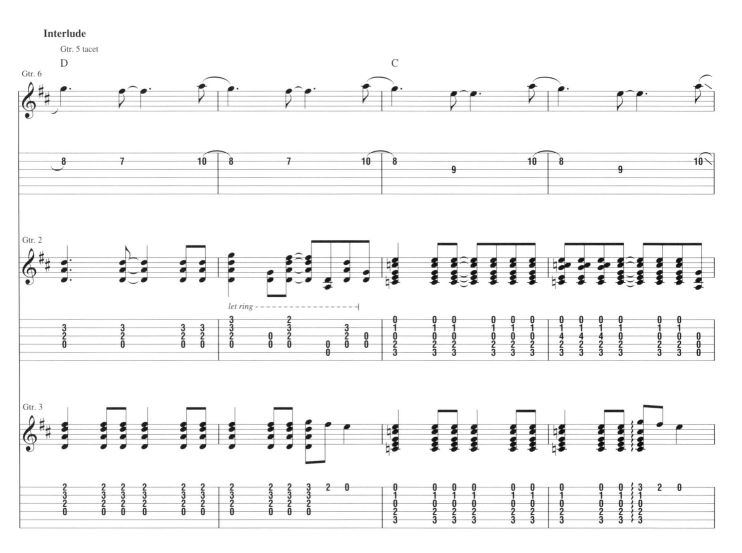

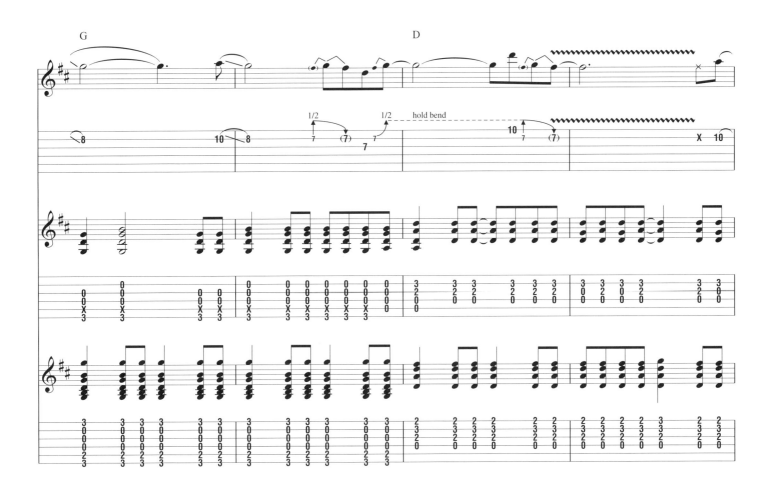

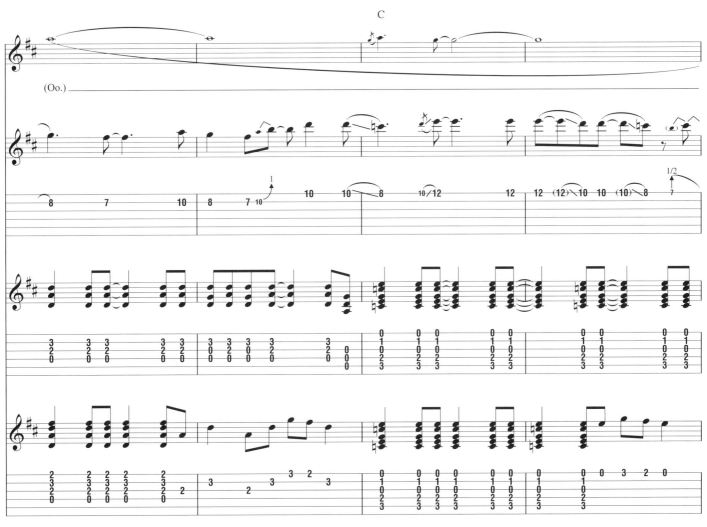

Ah, oh, ___ yeah. ___

let ring -

Chorus

Gtrs. 3 & 6 tacet

A5   C5   D

Whoa, oh, ___ oh, oh, ___ sweet _ child o' mine. ___   Oo, ___

Rhy. Fig. 2   **End Rhy. Fig. 2**

Gtr. 5

(cont. in slashes)

1/2

Gtr. 2

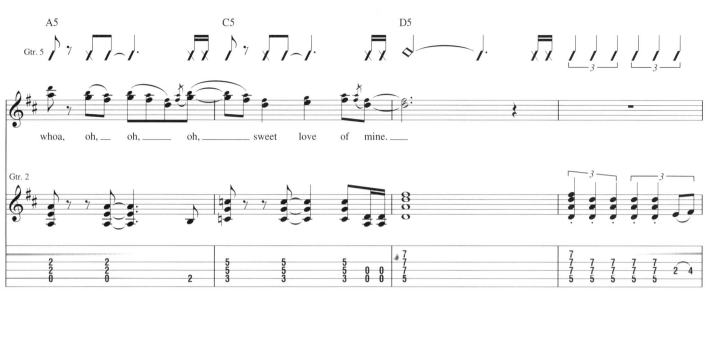

whoa, oh,__ oh,__ oh,___ sweet love of mine.__

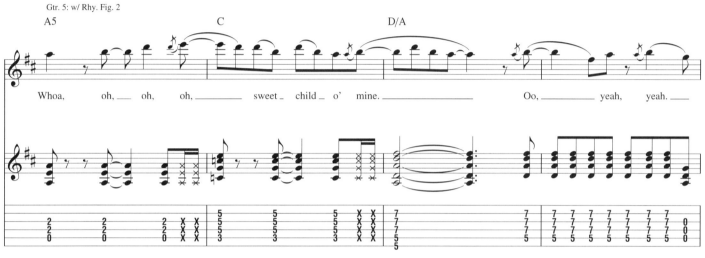

Gtr. 5: w/ Rhy. Fig. 2

Whoa, oh,__ oh, oh,___ sweet_ child_ o' mine._____ Oo,_____ yeah, yeah.__

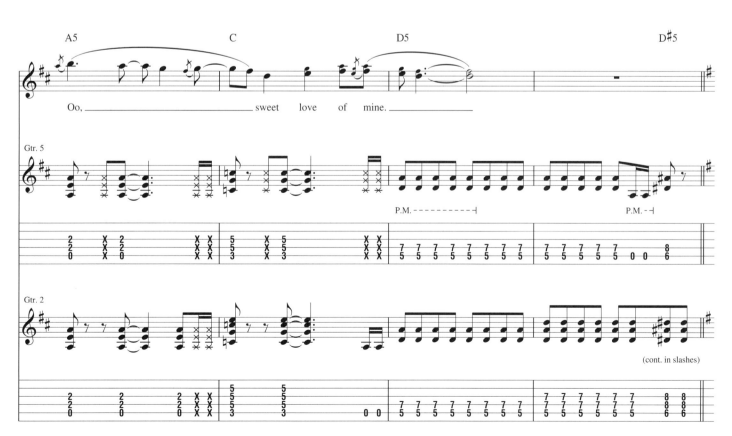

Oo,_____ sweet love of mine._____

(cont. in slashes)

Guitar Solo

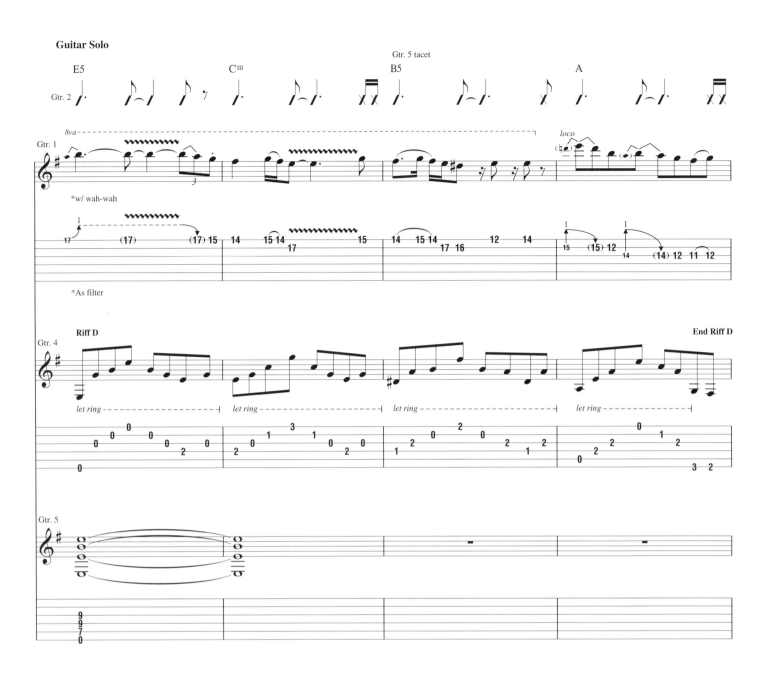

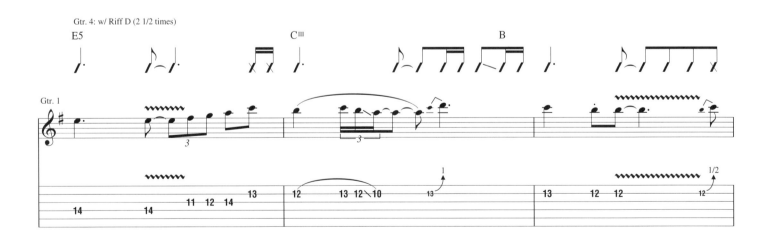

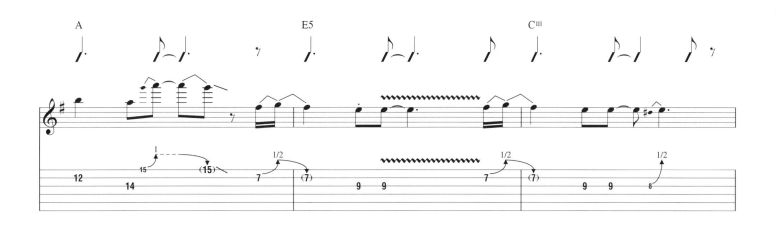

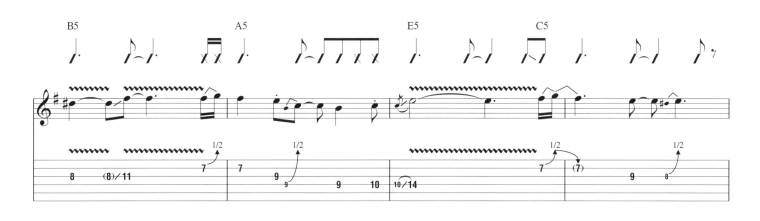

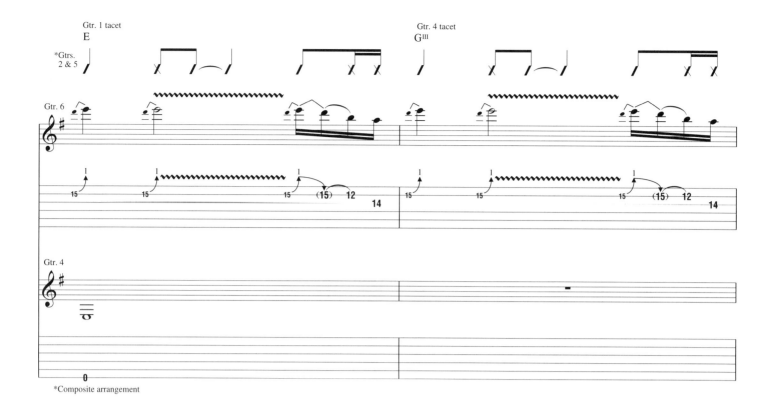

*Composite arrangement

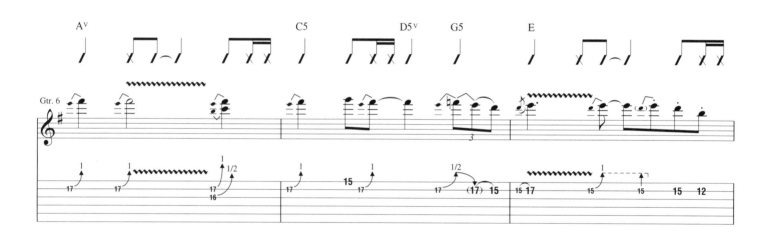

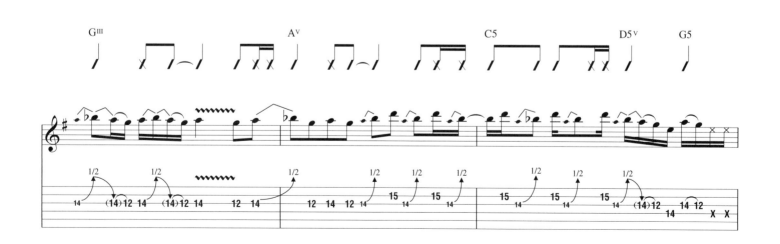

421

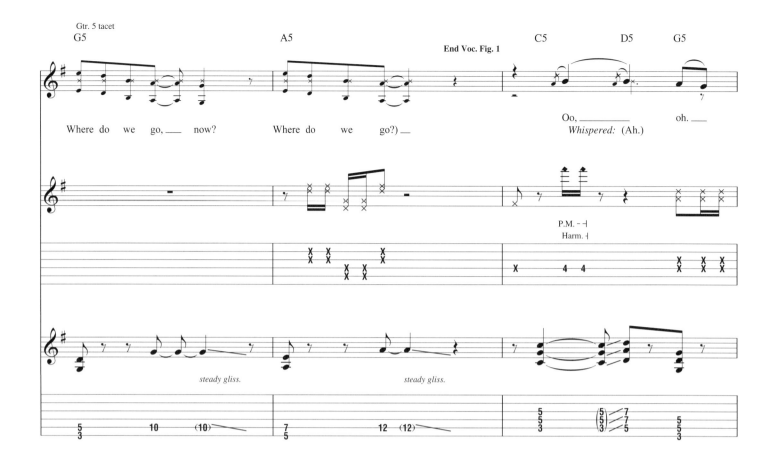

Where do we go? ___

Oo, _____ oh,

Whispered: (Sweet child o' mine.) ___

where do we go, ___ now?

Bkgd. Voc.: w/ Voc. Fig. 1

I, I, I, I,

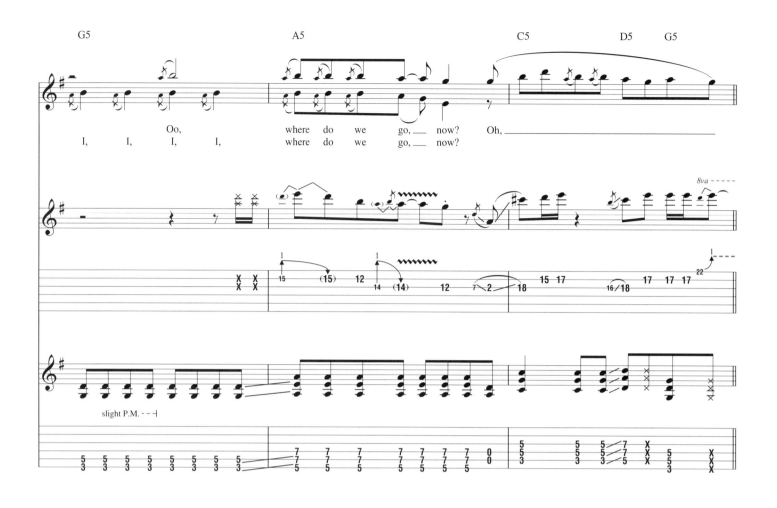

Outro-Guitar Solo

Gtr. 5: w/ Rhy. Fig. 3 (2 1/2 times)

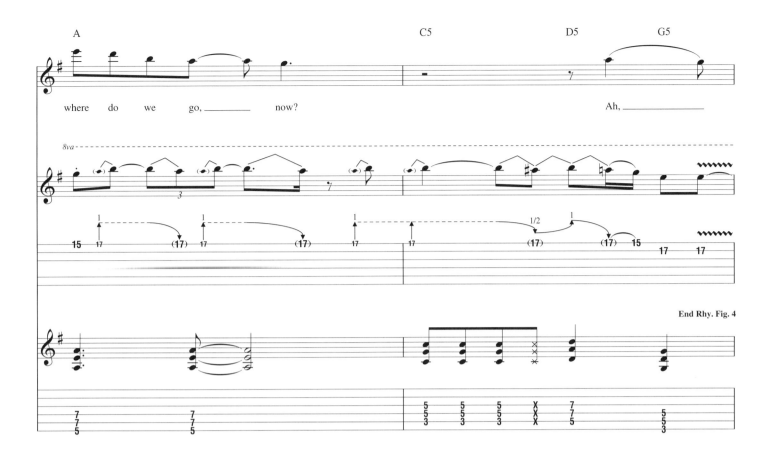

where do we go, _____ now?   Ah, _____

End Rhy. Fig. 4

Gtr. 2: w/ Rhy. Fig. 4 (1 1/2 times)

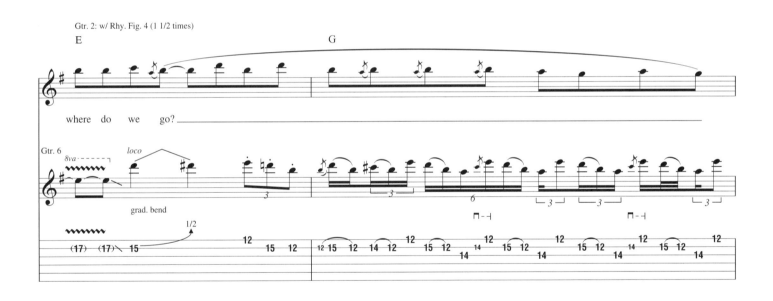

where do we go? _____

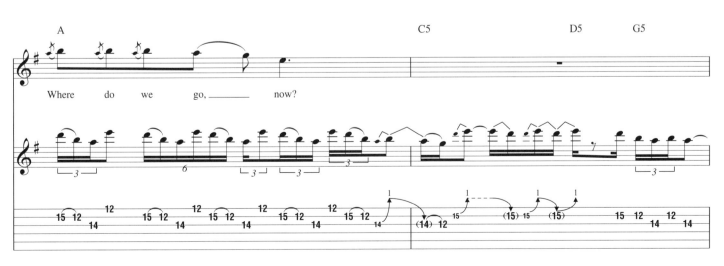

Where do we go, _____ now?

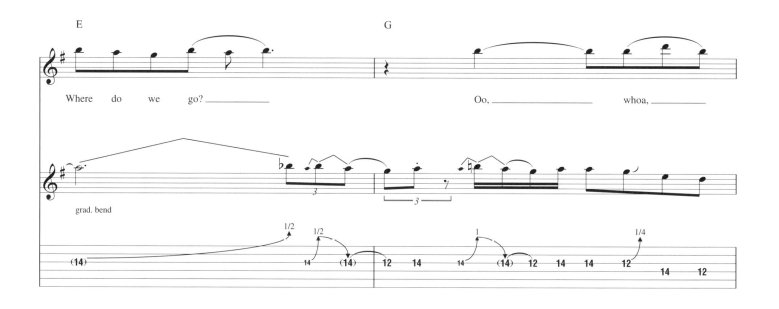

Where do we go? _____ Oo, _____ whoa, _____

grad. bend

where do we go, ___ now? No, no, no, no, no, no, no. Sweet child. ___

(cont. in slashes)

Sweet _____ child _____ of

mine. _____

*Hold body of guitar firmly with pick-hand and push on
back of headstock to lower the pitch of the open 6th string.

let ring - - - - - - - - - - - - - - - - - - -

from ZZ Top - *Fandango!*

Tush

Words and Music by Billy F Gibbons, Dusty Hill and Frank Lee Beard

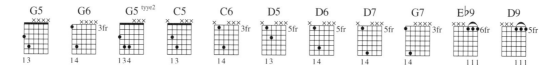

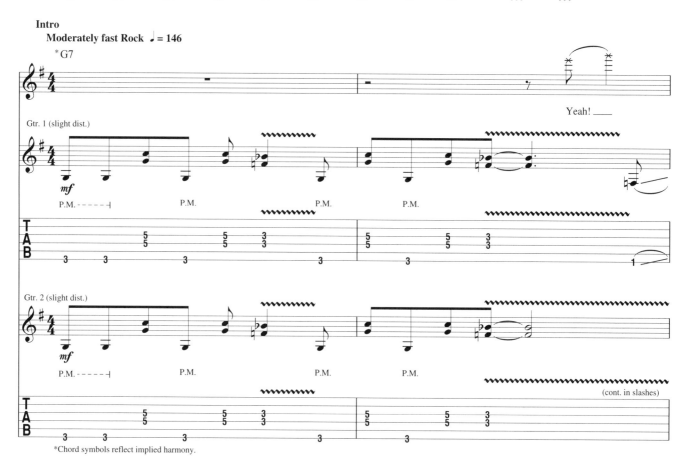

*Chord symbols reflect implied harmony.

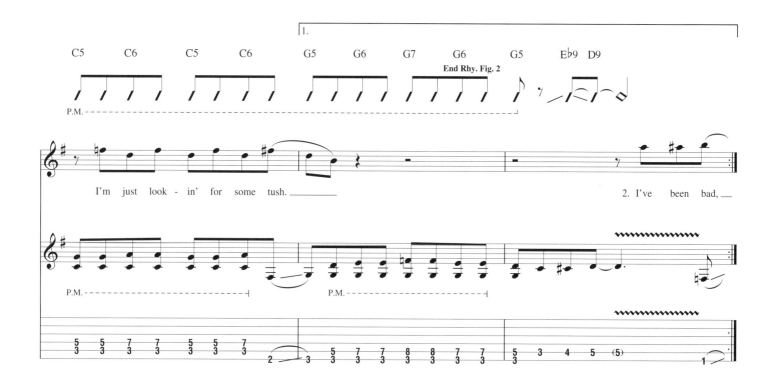

I'm just look - in' for some tush. _____

2. I've been bad, _____

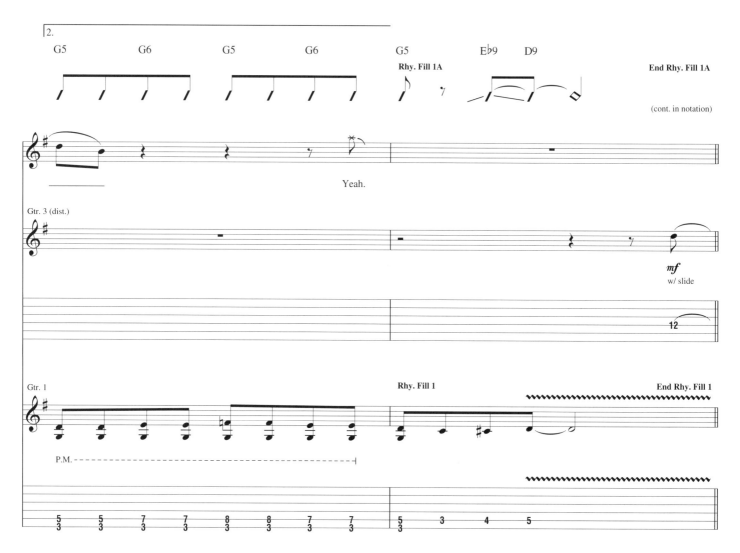

Yeah.

I'm just look-in' for some tush.

Outro-Guitar Solo

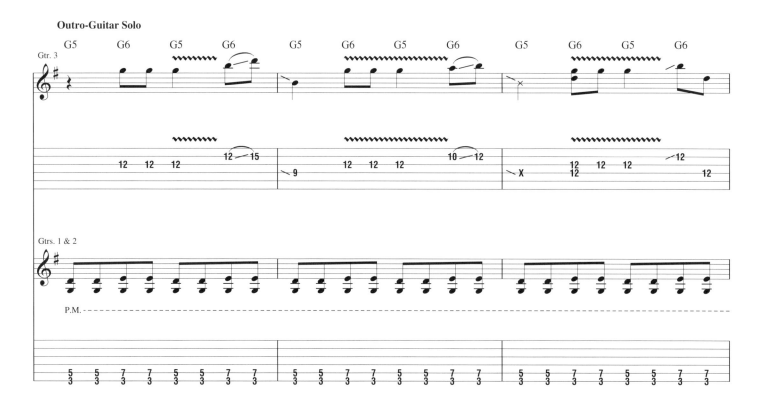

from Aerosmith - *Toys in the Attic*

Walk This Way

Words and Music by Steven Tyler and Joe Perry

*Chord symbols reflect basic harmony.
**Joe Perry

***Brad Whitford

ain't seen noth-in' till you're down on a muf-fin, then you're sure to be, a, chang-in' your ways." _ I met a

cheer - lead - er, was a real young bleed-er, oh, the times I could rem - i - nisce, _ 'cause the

best things in lov-in' with a sis-ter and a cou-sin on - ly start-ed with a lit-tle kiss, _ a, like _ this!

440

Outro-Guitar Solo

Gtrs. 1 & 2: w/ Riff A

Gtrs. 1 & 2: w/ Riff B

Gtr. 1: w/ Riff E (3 times)
Gtr. 2: w/ Riff E1 (till fade)

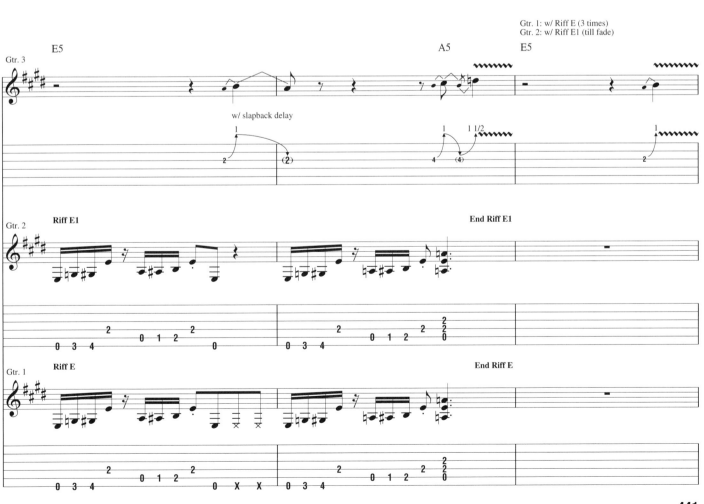

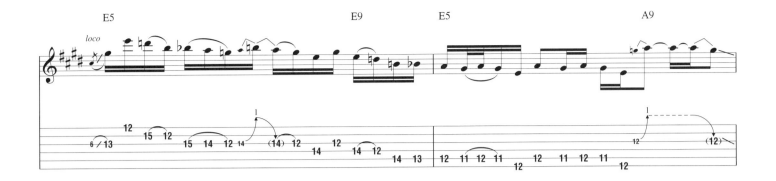

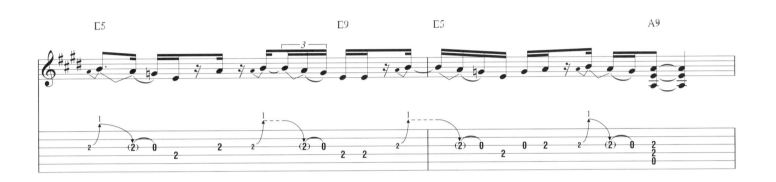

Begin fade

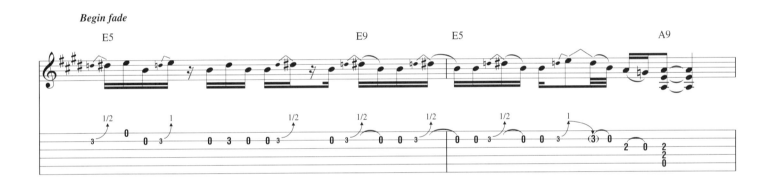

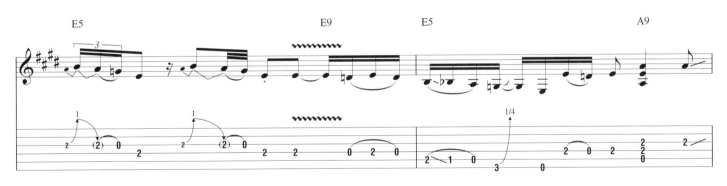

Fade out

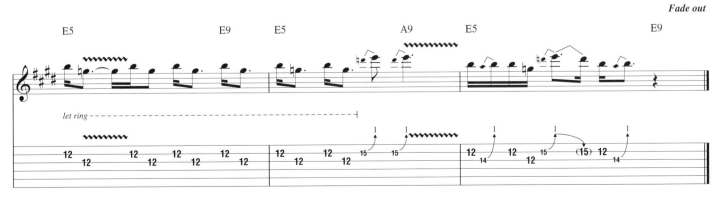

from Guns N' Roses - *Appetite for Destruction*

Welcome to the Jungle

Words and Music by W. Axl Rose, Slash, Izzy Stradlin', Duff McKagan and Steven Adler

Tune down 1/2 step:
(low to high) Eb-Ab-Db-Gb-Bb-Eb

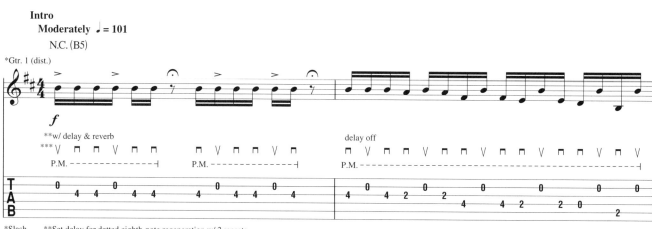

†††Second string open is played with an upstroke, other notes are played with downstrokes.

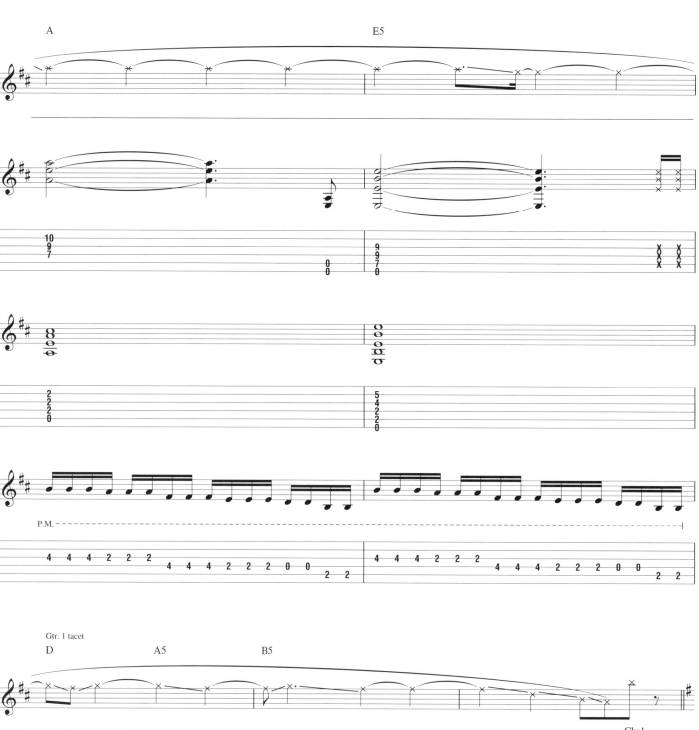

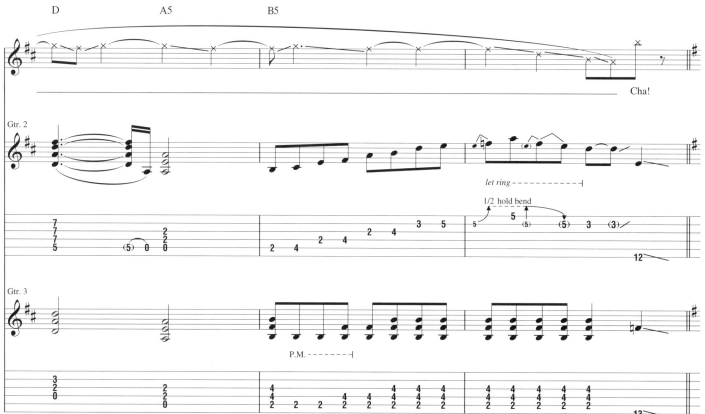

Faster ♩ = 122

*Chord symbols reflect overall harmony.

Pitch: A

Verse

1. Wel-come   to the   jun - gle,   we got   fun 'n'   games. _____

Rhy. Fig. 1

We got ev - 'ry - thing you want, ___ hon - ey, we know the names. ___ We are the

peo - ple that ___ can find ___ what - ev - er you ___ may need.

448

Guitar Solo

E7

Gtr. 3: w/ Rhy. Fig. 3 (2 times)

Oh, _____ oh. _____

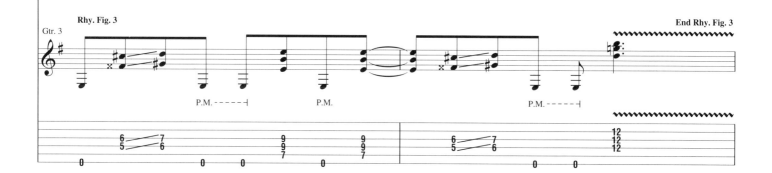

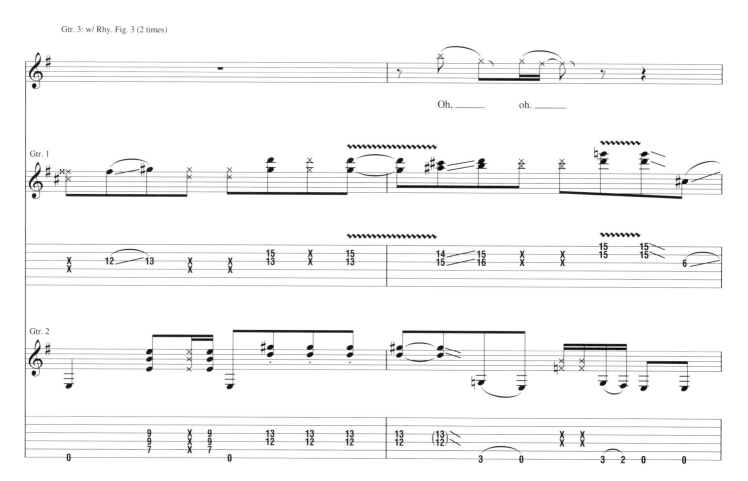

Interlude

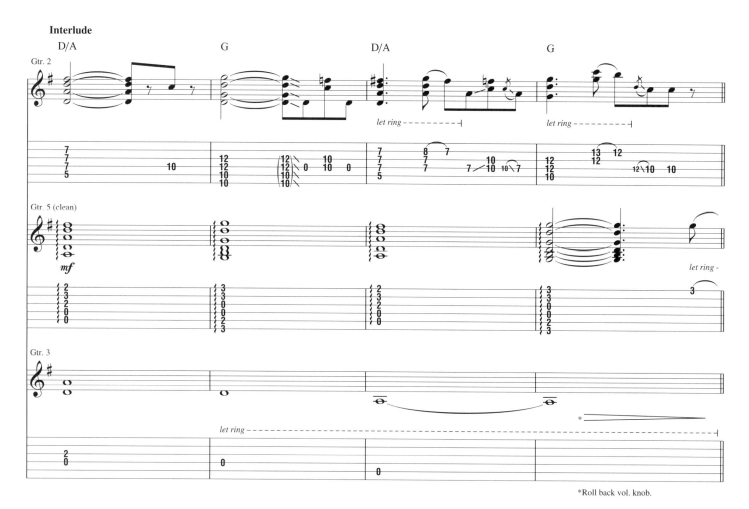

*Roll back vol. knob.

Bridge

And when you're high, ____ you nev - er, ev - er wan-na come down, ___

**Vol. swell

456

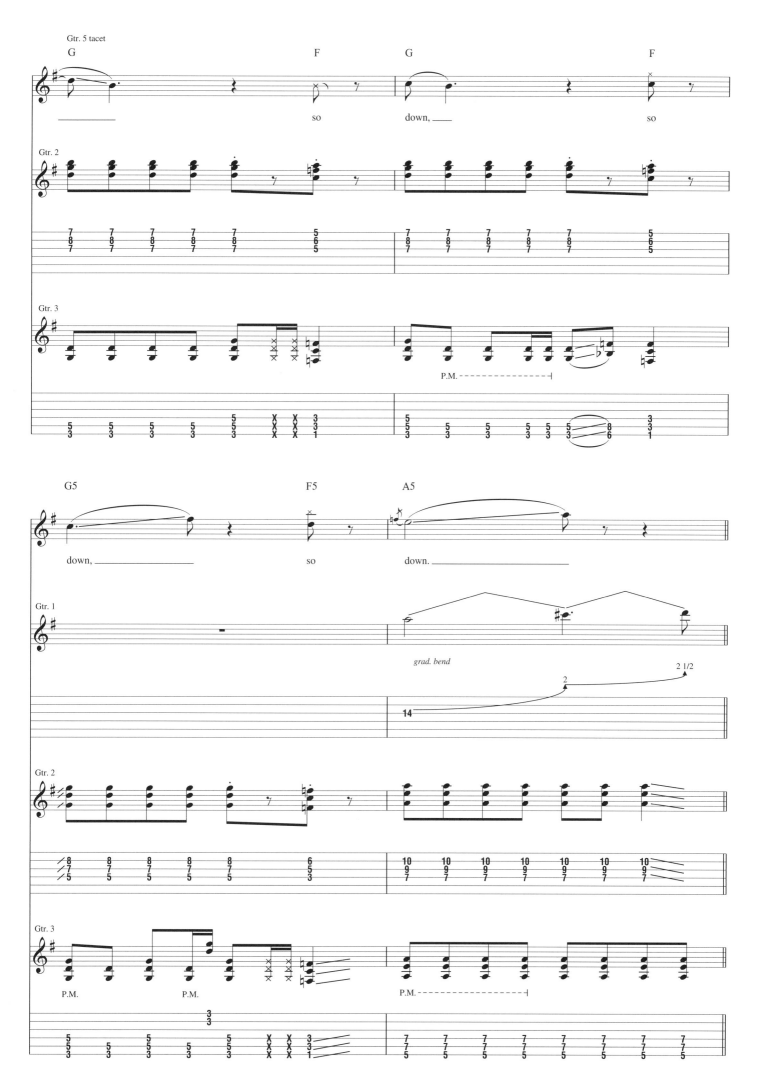

Guitar Solo

Gtr. 3: w/ Rhy. Fig. 3

E7

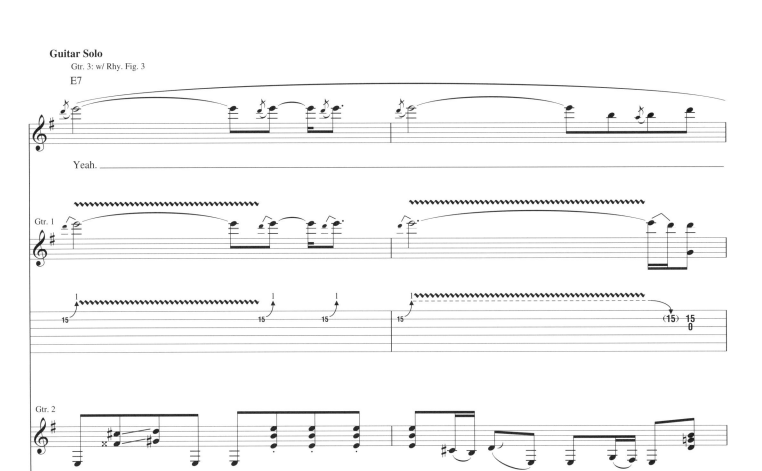

Yeah. _____

Gtr. 3: w/ Rhy. Fig. 4

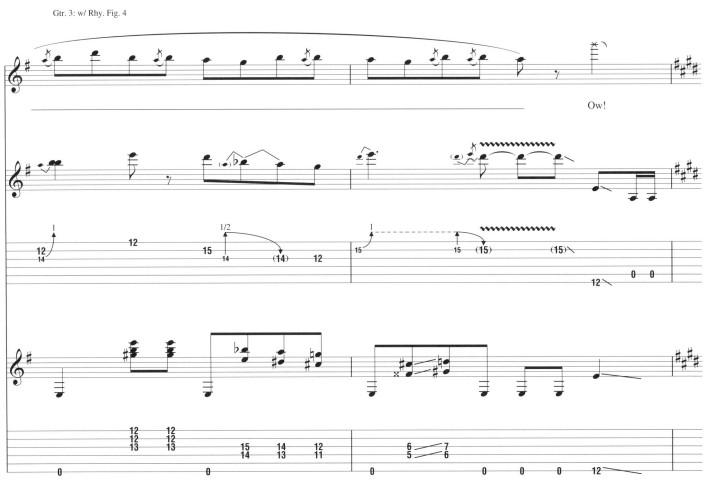

Ow!

*Hypothetical frets; located over pickups

You know_ where you are? _____

You're in the jun - gle, ba - by.

462

It's — gon - na — bring you down! — Huh!

from The Allman Brothers Band - *The Allman Brothers Band*

Whipping Post

Words and Music by Gregg Allman

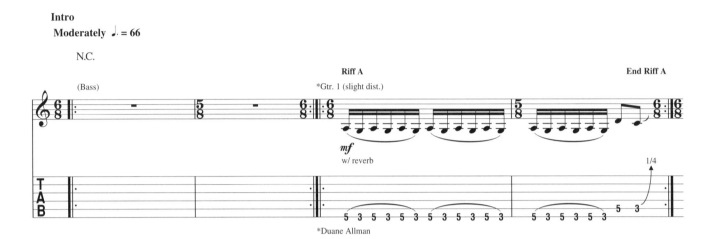

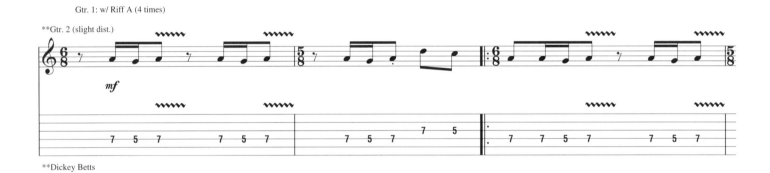

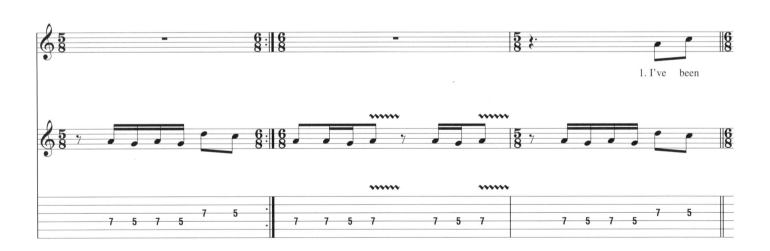

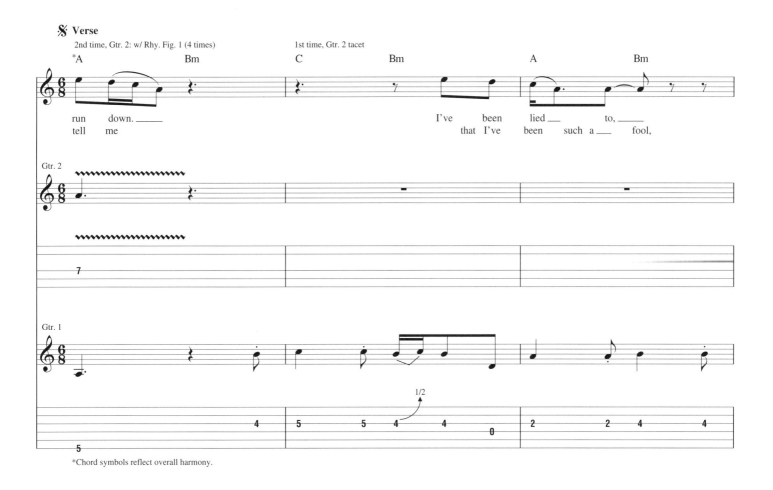

*Chord symbols reflect overall harmony.

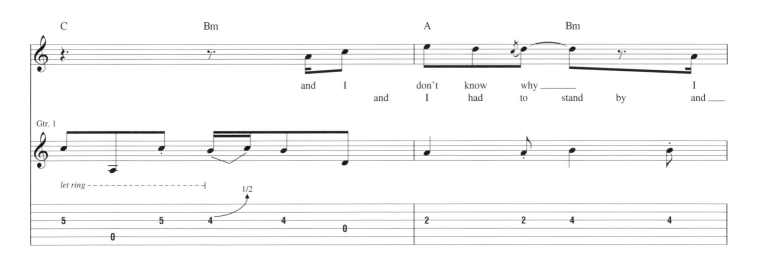

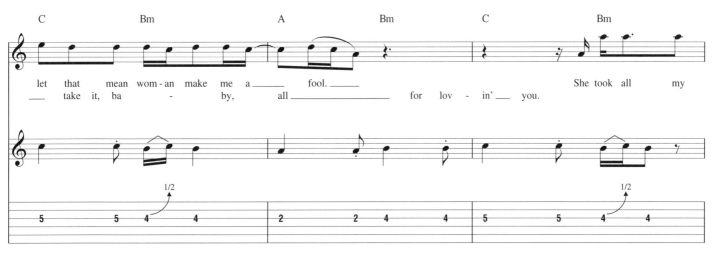

467

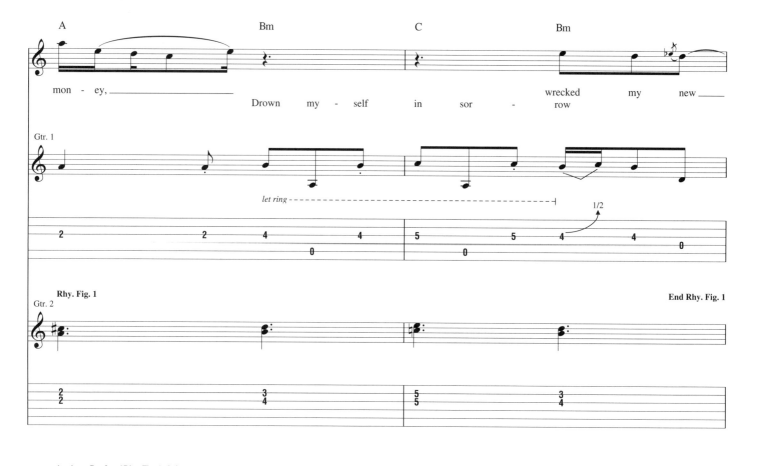

1st time, Gtr. 2: w/ Rhy. Fig. 1 (3 times)
2nd time, Gtr. 2: w/ Rhy. Fig. 1 (2 1/2 times)

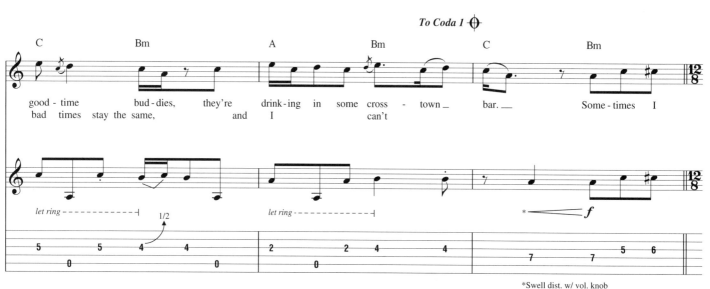

*Swell dist. w/ vol. knob

tied _____ to the whip-ping _ post. _ Good Lord, I feel_ like I'm dy - in'. _

Interlude

N.C.

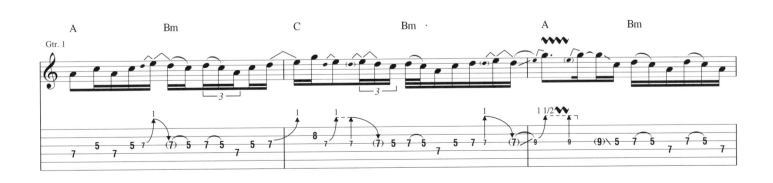

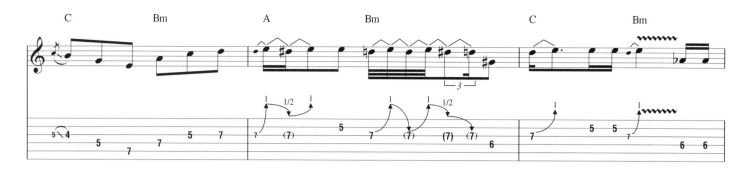

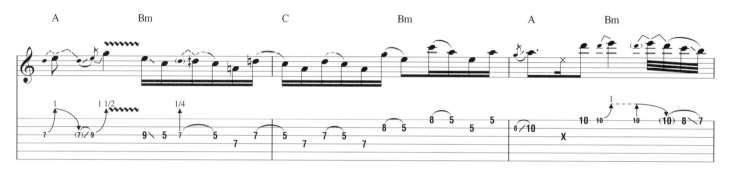

D.S. al Coda 1

2. My ____ friends

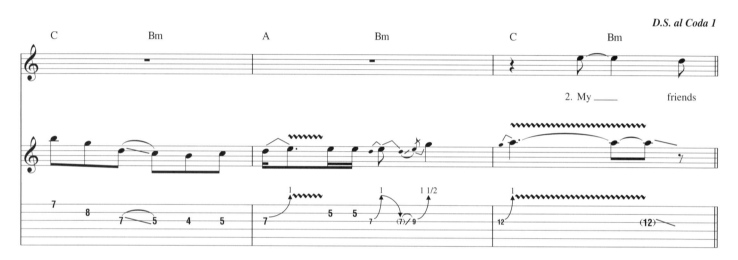

Coda 1

Pre-Chorus

run. ____ Some-times I feel, ____ some - times ____

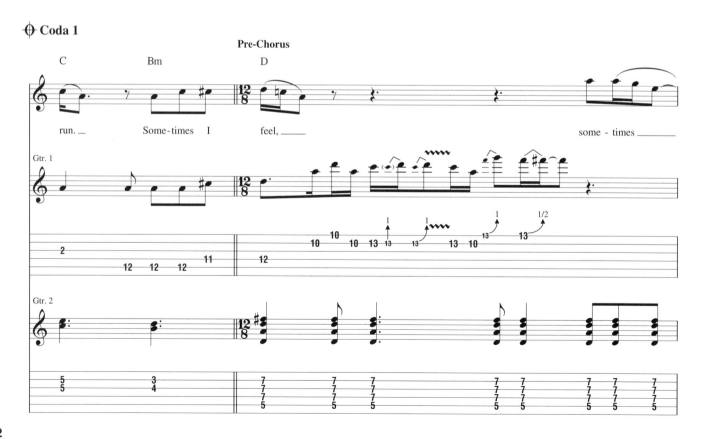

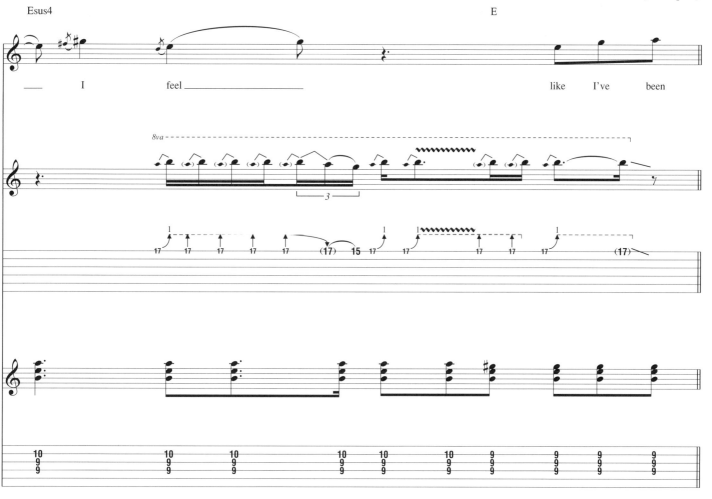

I feel _____

like I've been

⊕ Coda 2

Guitar Solo

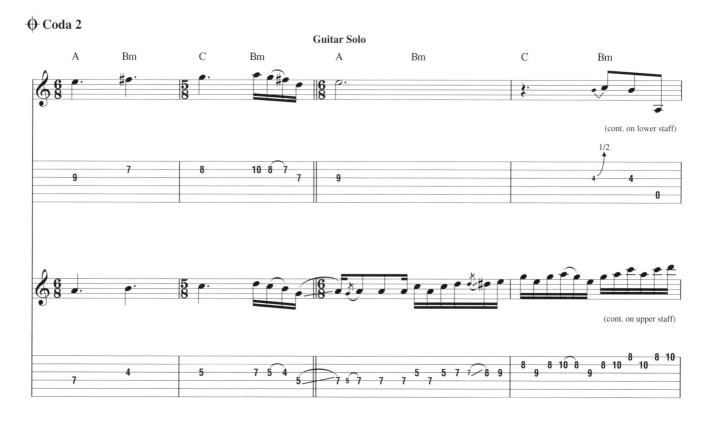

(cont. on lower staff)

(cont. on upper staff)

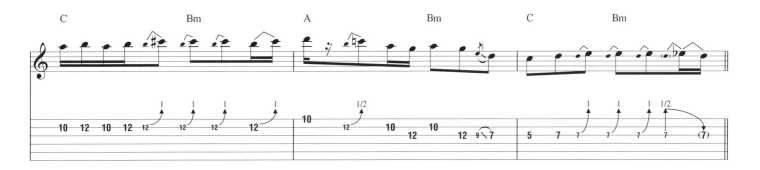

Interlude

Gtr. 2 tacet

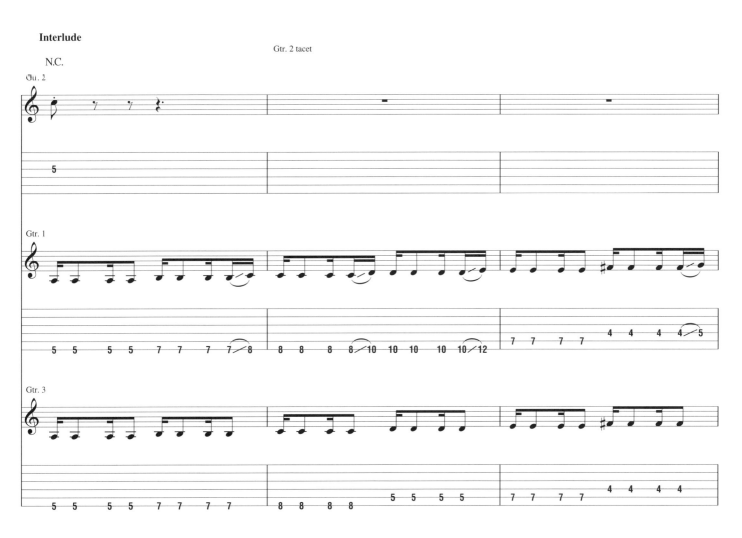

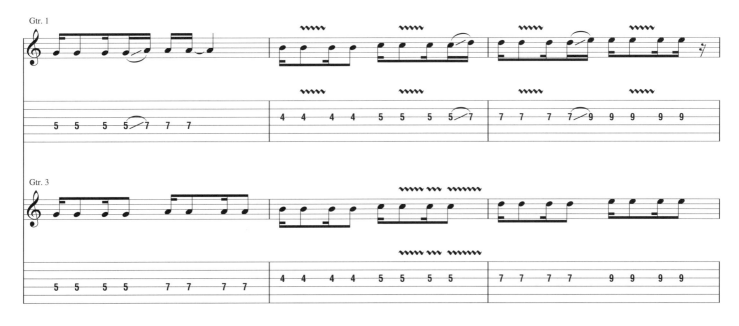

476

Pre-Chorus

Slower ♩. = 54

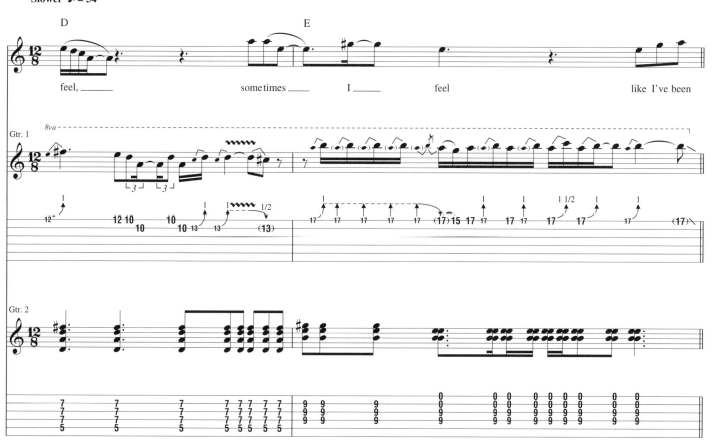

feel, _____ sometimes _____ I _____ feel like I've been

Outro-Chorus

Gtr. 3: w/ Riff B (3 times)

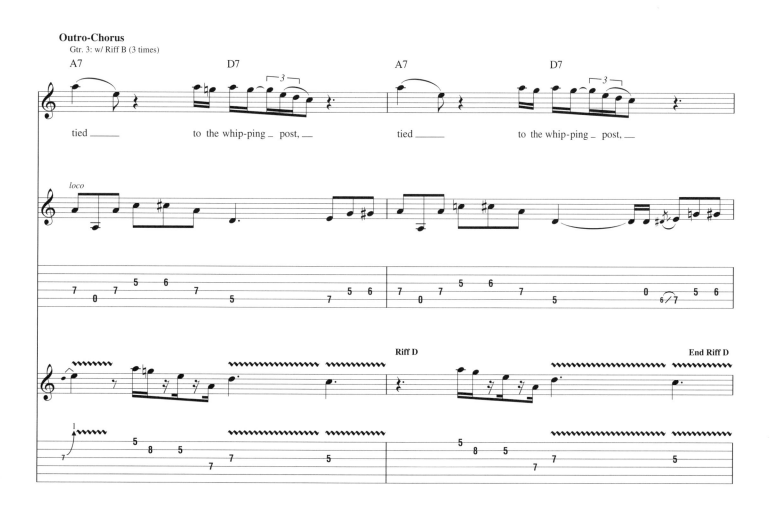

tied _____ to the whip-ping _ post, _____ tied _____ to the whip-ping _ post, _____

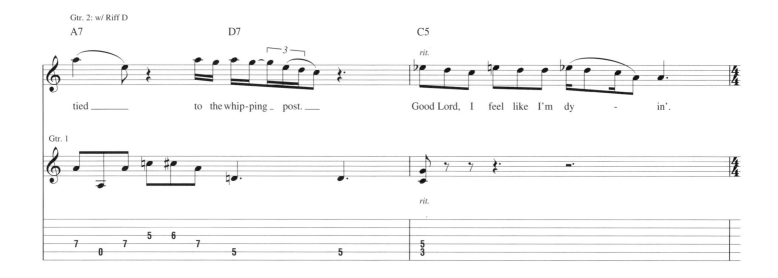

tied _____ to the whip-ping _ post. _____ Good Lord, I feel like I'm dy - in'.

Free time (♩ = ♪)

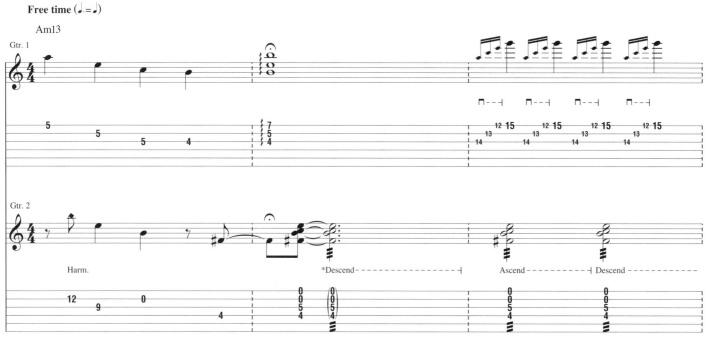

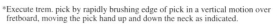

*Execute trem. pick by rapidly brushing edge of pick in a vertical motion over fretboard, moving the pick hand up and down the neck as indicated.

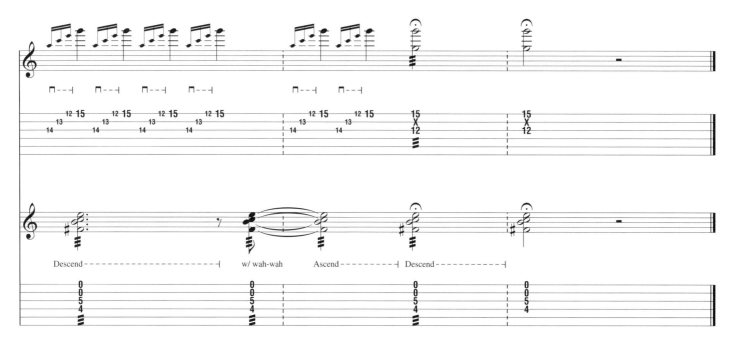

478

from Led Zeppelin - *Led Zeppelin II*

Whole Lotta Love

Words and Music by Jimmy Page, Robert Plant, John Paul Jones, John Bonham and Willie Dixon

Intro
Moderately slow ♩ = 89

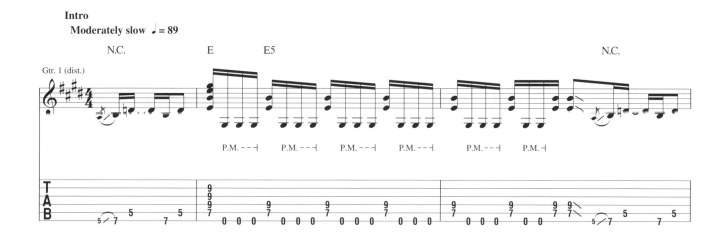

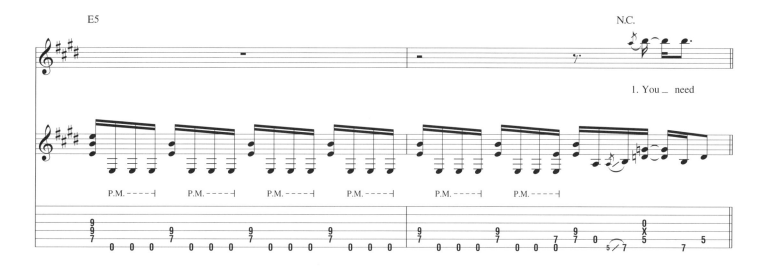

1. You ___ need

Verse

cool - in', ___ ba - by, I'm not fool - in', I'm ___ gon-na
___ learn - in' and, ba - by, I've been ___ learn - in', all them

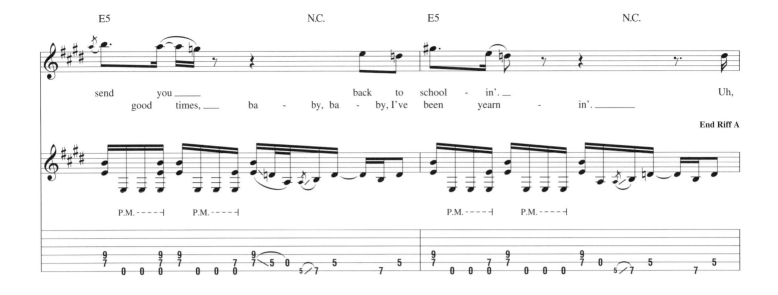

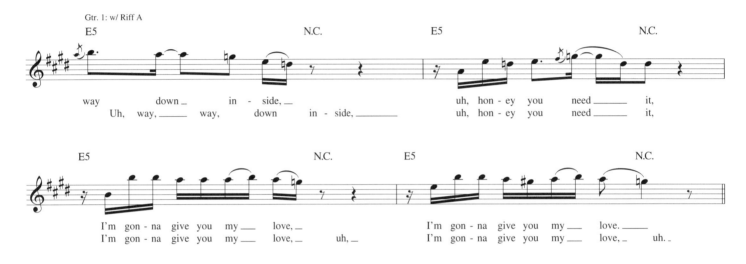

Chorus

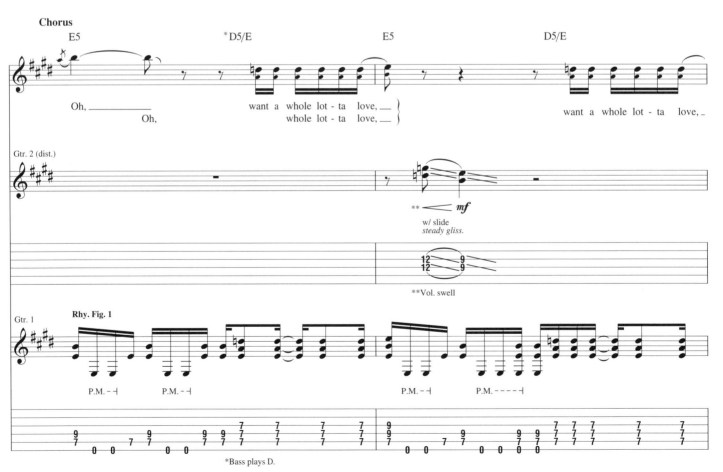

480

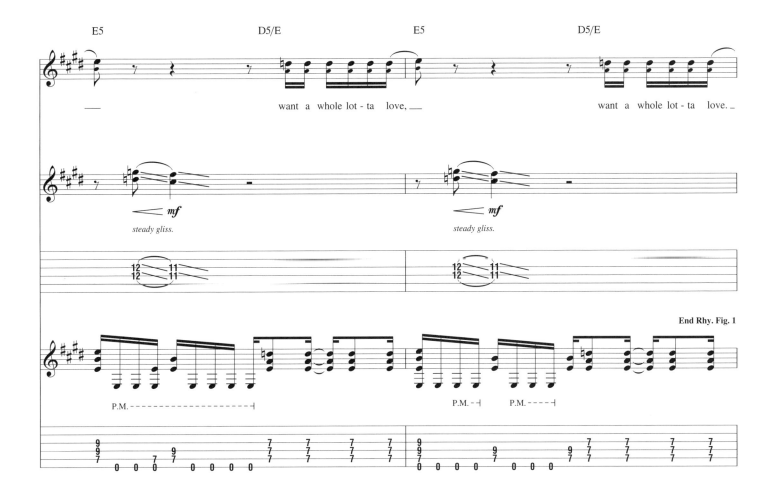

want a whole lot-ta love, ___

want a whole lot-ta love. ___

steady gliss.

steady gliss.

End Rhy. Fig. 1

P.M. --------------------

P.M. -| P.M. ----|

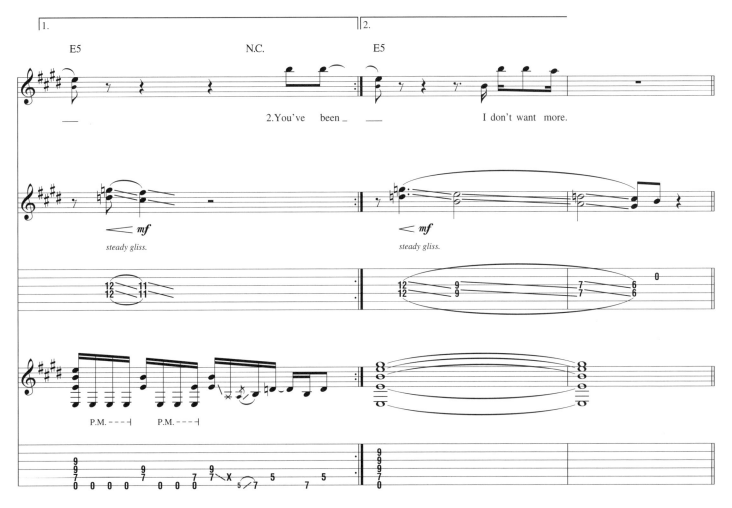

1.

2.

2.You've been ___ ___

I don't want more.

steady gliss.

steady gliss.

P.M. ----| P.M. ----|

Interlude

Gtrs. 1 & 2 tacet
w/ misc. gtr. effects, theremin & voc. ad libs.
N.C.
(drums & perc.)
7
29
(drum fill)

Guitar Solo

E
N.C.
E
N.C.
Gtr. 3 (dist.)
f
*w/ wah-wah & delay
*Delay set for dotted quarter-note regeneration w/ 1 repeat.
Gtr. 1

E
N.C.
E
N.C.
8va
p
f

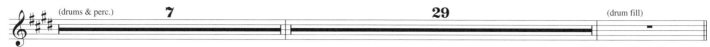

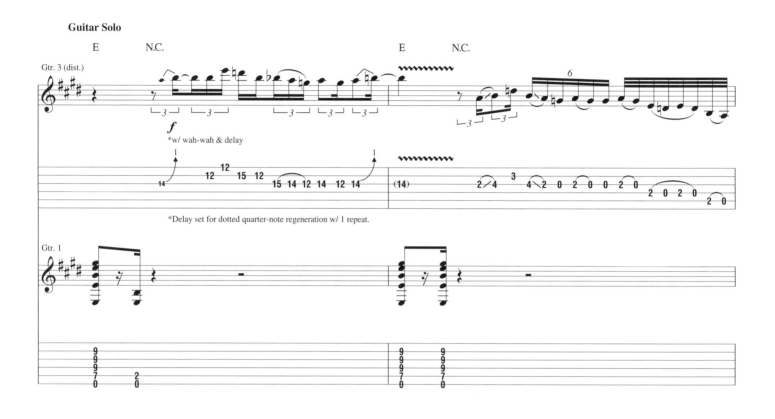

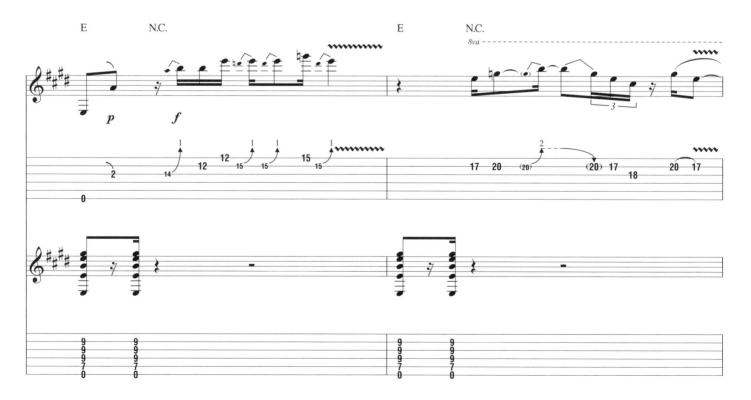

I'm gon-na give you ev-'ry inch of my __ love, __

I'm gon-na give you my __ love. __

(Ah, _____ ah.)

Yeah, __

al - right, __ let's go!

Gtr. 1

P.M. - - - - ┤   P.M. - - - - ┤   P.M. - ┤   P.M.

Chorus

Gtr. 1: w/ Rhy. Fig. 1

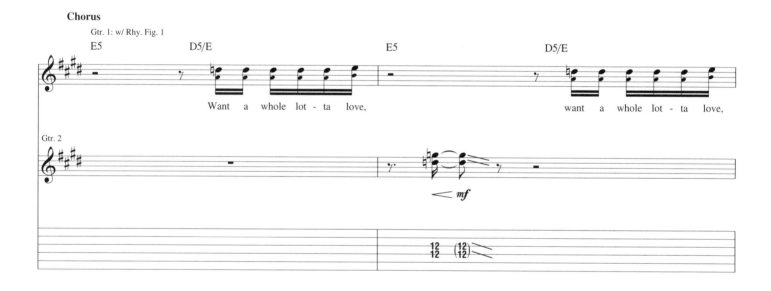

Want a whole lot - ta love,

want a whole lot - ta love,

Gtr. 2

mf

want a whole lot - ta love,

want a whole lot - ta love.

mf

mf

steady gliss.

*w/ vocal bleed-through from previously recorded
vocal track w/ ambient echo, next 2 meas.

**w/ echo, next 3 meas.

my, ___ my, ___ my, ___ my, ___   oh. ___

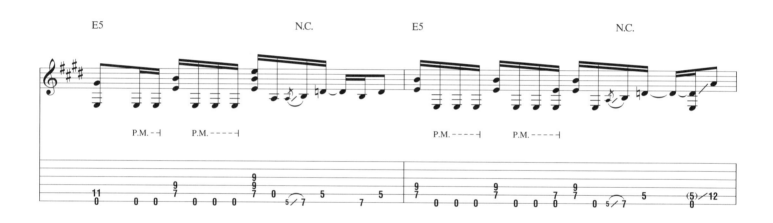

Shake ___ for me,   girl,   I wan-na be your back - door man. ___

Hey,   oh,   hey,   oh,

hey,   oh,   oo,

oh,

Gtr. 1: w/ Riff B (till fade)

oh,   oh,   oh,   oo, __ ma,   ma,   hey.

*w/ad lib. echo (till fade).

Keep   it   cool - in',   ba   -   by,

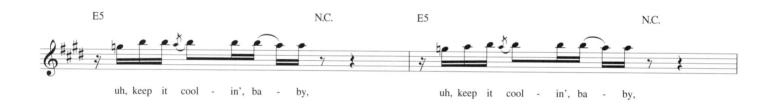

uh, keep   it   cool - in',   ba   -   by,   uh, keep   it   cool - in',   ba   -   by,

Begin fade

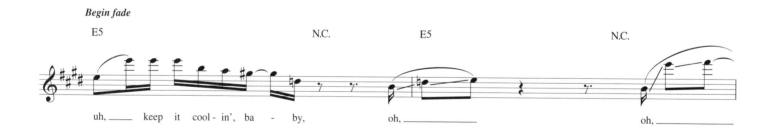

uh, __ keep   it   cool - in',   ba   -   by,   oh, _____   oh, _____

Fade out

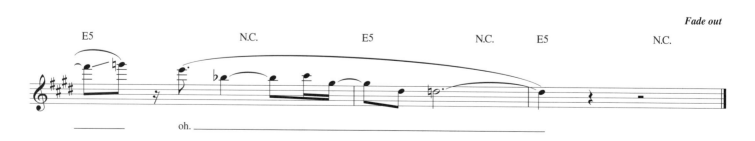

_____   oh. _____

from The Who - *Who's Next*

Won't Get Fooled Again

Words and Music by Peter Townshend

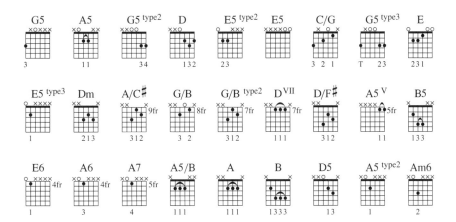

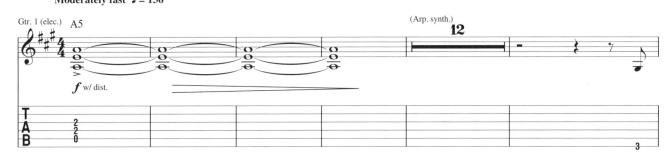

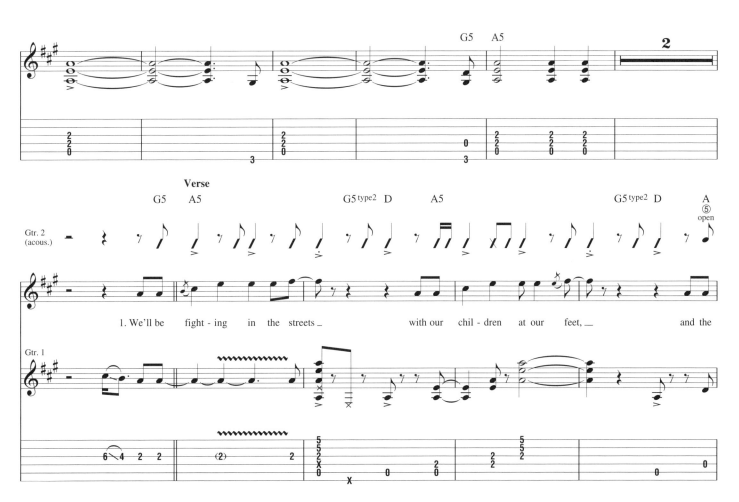

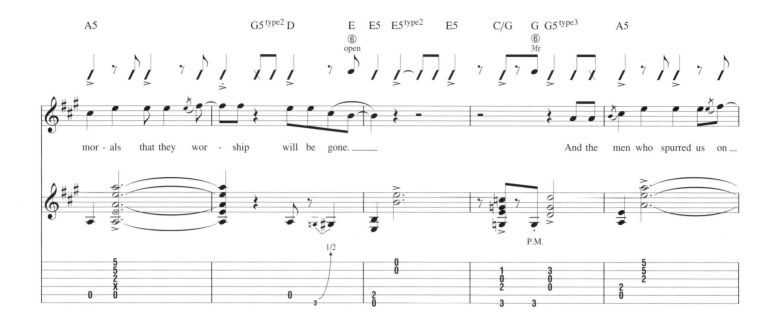

mor - als that they wor - ship will be gone. _____ And the men who spurred us on _

_ sit in judge - ment of all wrong, _ they de - cide and the shot - gun sings the song. _

Chorus

I'll tip my hat to the new con - sti - tu - tion, take a bow _ for the

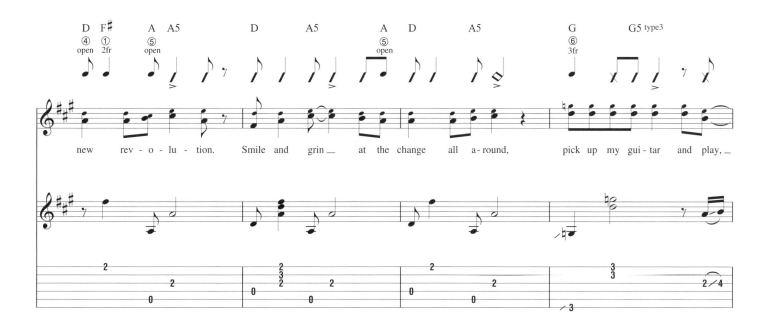

new rev-o-lu-tion. Smile and grin _ at the change all a-round, pick up my gui-tar and play, _

_ just like yes-ter-day, _ then I'll get on my knees and pray _

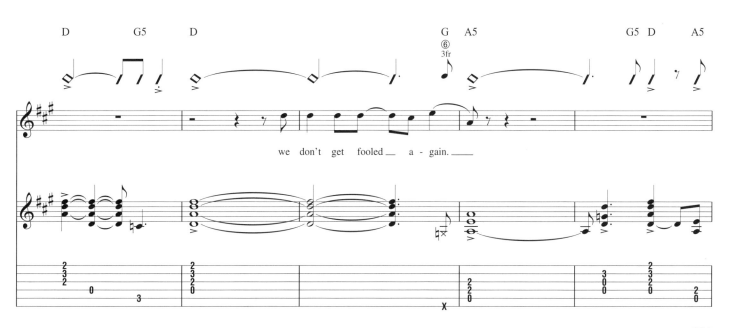

we don't get fooled _ a-gain. _

Chorus

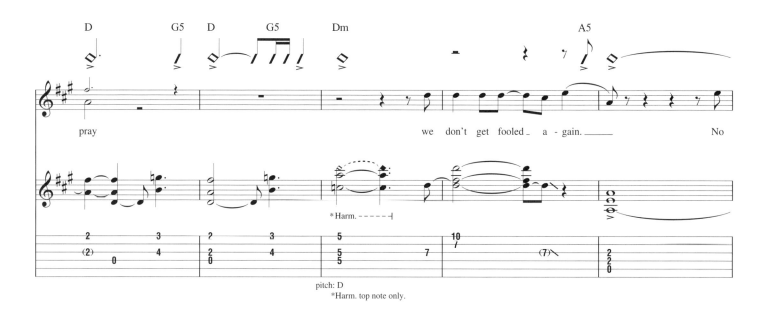

pray

we don't get fooled a - gain. _____ No

pitch: D
*Harm. top note only.

no!

** Occasionally strike⑤ open (next 16 meas.)
† Mute strings by releasing finger pressure
(next 16 meas.)

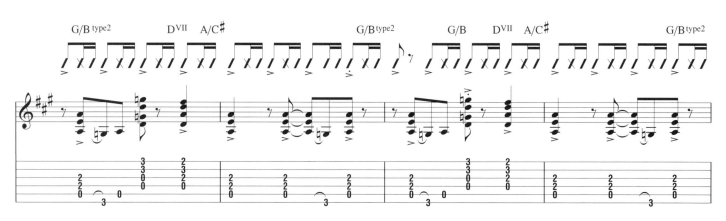

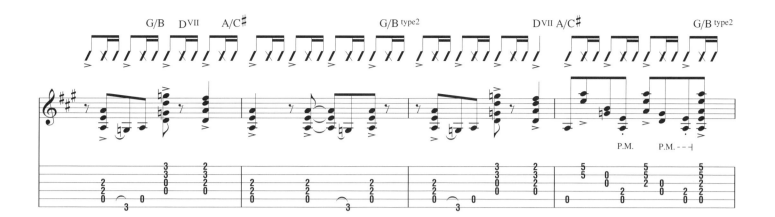

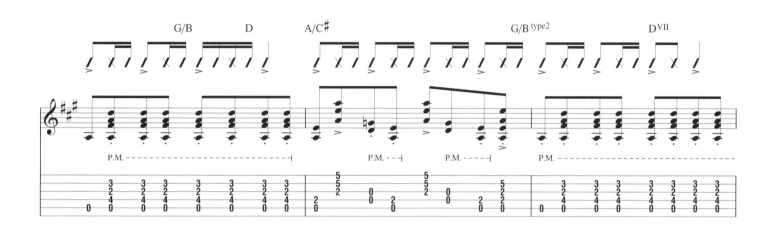

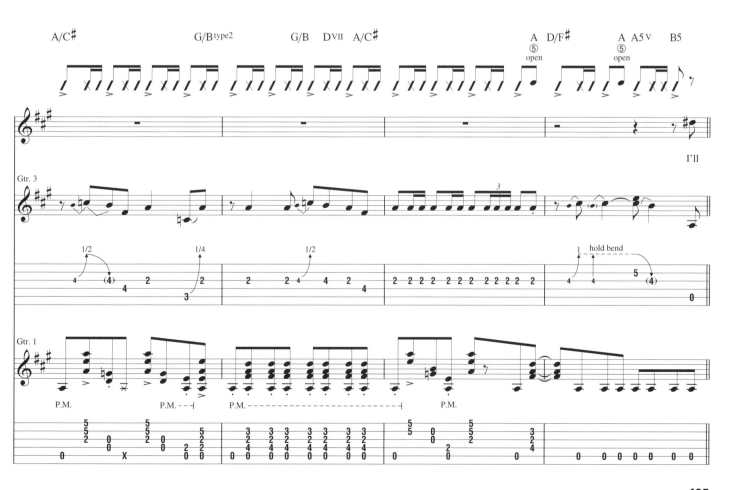

Bridge

move my-self and my fam-'ly a-side,_____ if we hap-pen to be left half_____ a-live.___ I'll

get all my pa-pers and smile___ at the sky, oh, I know___ that the hyp-no-tized nev-er lie.

Do ya?

slo - gans are re - placed __ by __ the by. _____ And the

part - ing on the left ___ is now part - ing on the right, __ and the

then I'll get on my knees and pray

we

don't get fooled _ a - gain. _____ Don't get fooled _ a - gain. _____ No, no!

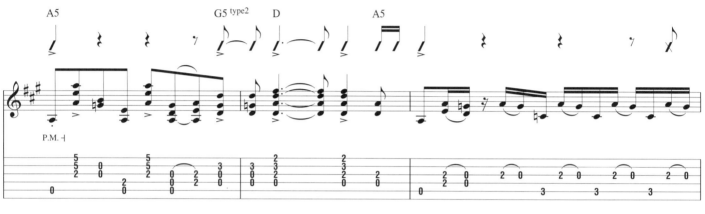

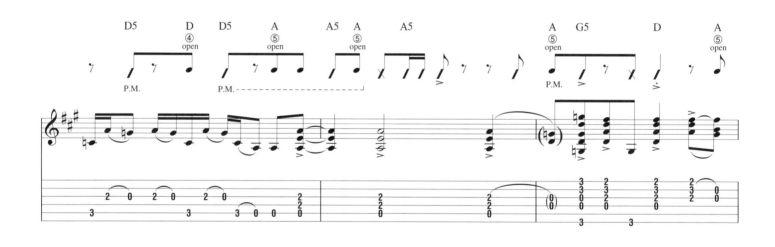

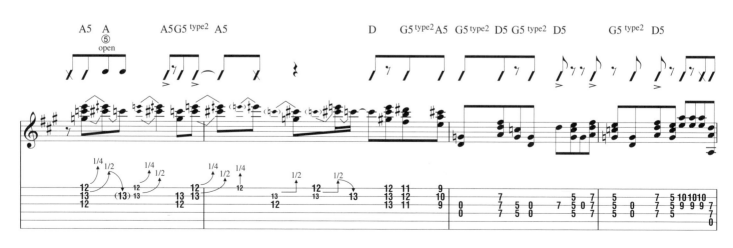

*Played ahead of the beat

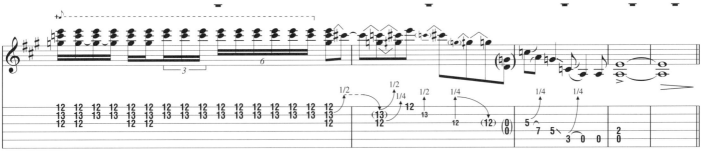

Interlude

(w/ Arp. synth.)

P.M. - - - - - - - - - - - - - - - -

†vib. w/ neck

†Vibrato achieved by applying force with right hand on gtr. body & left hand on neck.

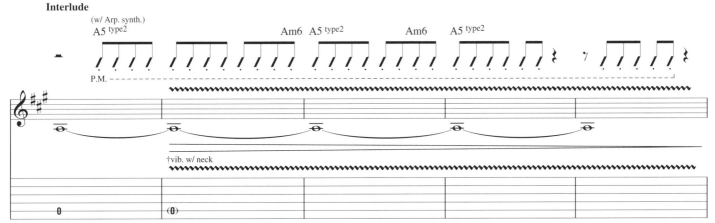

Gtrs. 1 & 2 tacet   (Arp. synth.)

Outro

Gtr. 2

Yeah! _____   Meet the new ___ boss.

Gtrs. 1 & 3

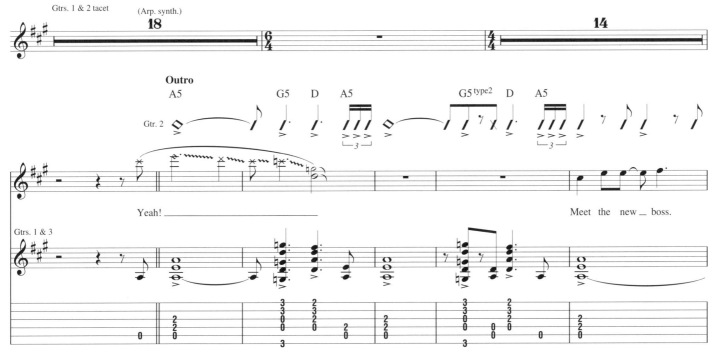

Same as the old boss.

(Townshend:) Hey! __

You Really Got Me

Words and Music by Ray Davies

Tune down 1/2 step:
(low to high) Eb-Ab-Db-Gb-Bb-Eb

Intro

Moderately fast ♩ = 140

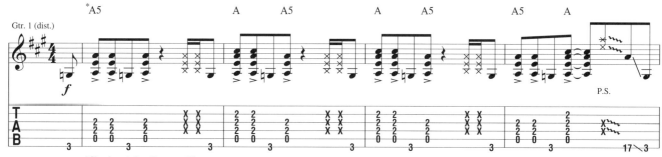

*Chord symbols reflect overall harmony.

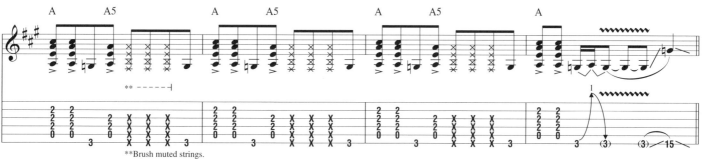

**Brush muted strings.
Allow random harmonics
to sound (between 2nd & 3rd frets).

Verse

A5

1. Girl, you real-ly got me now, — you got me so I don't know what I'm do-in'. —

slight P.M. P.M. P.M. rake

— Girl, you real-ly got me now, — you got me

semi-P.H. P.M. P.M. P.M.

Pitch: D E D B Bb A F# Fb E

*Harmonic located six-tenths the distance between 2nd & 3rd frets.

Guitar Solo

*Using a guitar with Les Paul style electronics, set lead vol. to 0 and rhythm vol. to 10. Strike the strings while the pickup selector switch is in the lead position, then flip the switch in the rhythm indicated to simulate the re-attack.

Interlude

Gtr. 1 tacet

Ah. ___ Ah. ___ Ah. ___ Ah. ___ Ah. ___
(Ah, ah, ah, ah. Ah, ah. Chu, chu, chu, chu, chu, ch, ch.)

Verse

w/ misc. bkgd. vocs., next 8 meas.

3. Girl, you real-ly got me now, you got me so I don't know what I'm do-in'. ___

___ Ah. Girl, you real-ly got me now, ___ you got me so I can't sleep at night! ___

Bkgd. voc.: w/ Voc. Fig. 1

Girl, you real-ly got me now, ___ you got me so I don't know where I'm go-in', ___

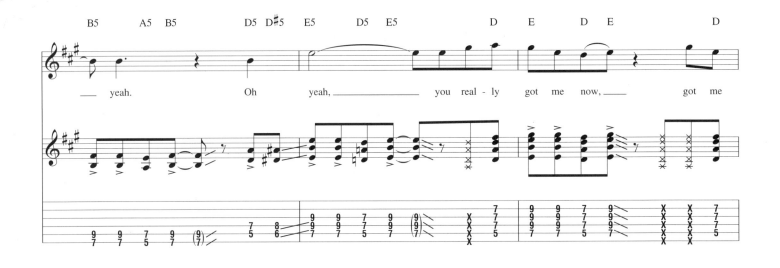

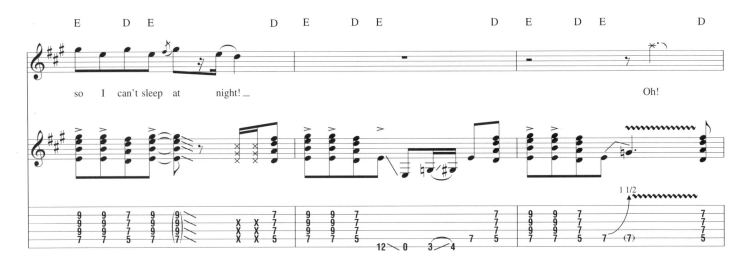

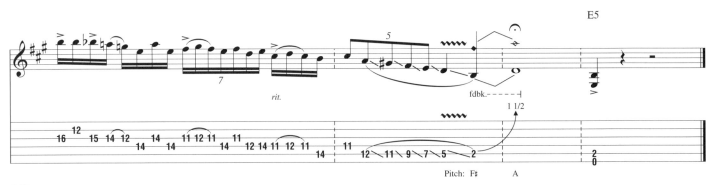

GUITAR NOTATION LEGEND

Guitar music can be notated three different ways: on a *musical staff*, in *tablature*, and in *rhythm slashes*.

RHYTHM SLASHES are written above the staff. Strum chords in the rhythm indicated. Use the chord diagrams found at the top of the first page of the transcription for the appropriate chord voicings. Round noteheads indicate single notes.

THE MUSICAL STAFF shows pitches and rhythms and is divided by bar lines into measures. Pitches are named after the first seven letters of the alphabet.

TABLATURE graphically represents the guitar fingerboard. Each horizontal line represents a string, and each number represents a fret.

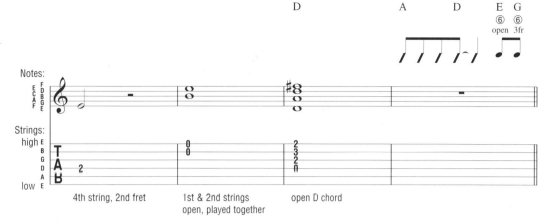

4th string, 2nd fret   1st & 2nd strings open, played together   open D chord

Definitions for Special Guitar Notation

HALF-STEP BEND: Strike the note and bend up 1/2 step.

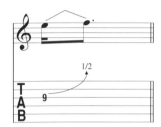

WHOLE-STEP BEND: Strike the note and bend up one step.

GRACE NOTE BEND: Strike the note and immediately bend up as indicated.

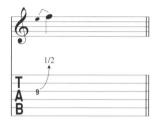

SLIGHT (MICROTONE) BEND: Strike the note and bend up 1/4 step.

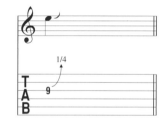

BEND AND RELEASE: Strike the note and bend up as indicated, then release back to the original note. Only the first note is struck.

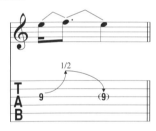

PRE-BEND: Bend the note as indicated, then strike it.

PRE-BEND AND RELEASE: Bend the note as indicated. Strike it and release the bend back to the original note.

UNISON BEND: Strike the two notes simultaneously and bend the lower note up to the pitch of the higher.

VIBRATO: The string is vibrated by rapidly bending and releasing the note with the fretting hand.

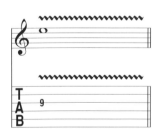

WIDE VIBRATO: The pitch is varied to a greater degree by vibrating with the fretting hand.

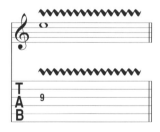

HAMMER-ON: Strike the first (lower) note with one finger, then sound the higher note (on the same string) with another finger by fretting it without picking.

PULL-OFF: Place both fingers on the notes to be sounded. Strike the first note and without picking, pull the finger off to sound the second (lower) note.

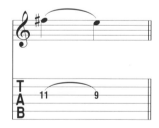

LEGATO SLIDE: Strike the first note and then slide the same fret-hand finger up or down to the second note. The second note is not struck.

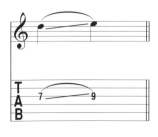

SHIFT SLIDE: Same as legato slide, except the second note is struck.

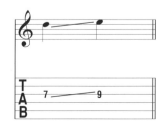

TRILL: Very rapidly alternate between the notes indicated by continuously hammering on and pulling off.

TAPPING: Hammer ("tap") the fret indicated with the pick-hand index or middle finger and pull off to the note fretted by the fret hand.

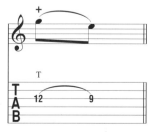

NATURAL HARMONIC: Strike the note while the fret-hand lightly touches the string directly over the fret indicated.

PINCH HARMONIC: The note is fretted normally and a harmonic is produced by adding the edge of the thumb or the tip of the index finger of the pick hand to the normal pick attack.

HARP HARMONIC: The note is fretted normally and a harmonic is produced by gently resting the pick hand's index finger directly above the indicated fret (in parentheses) while the pick hand's thumb or pick assists by plucking the appropriate string.

PICK SCRAPE: The edge of the pick is rubbed down (or up) the string, producing a scratchy sound.

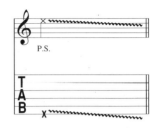

MUFFLED STRINGS: A percussive sound is produced by laying the fret hand across the string(s) without depressing, and striking them with the pick hand.

PALM MUTING: The note is partially muted by the pick hand lightly touching the string(s) just before the bridge.

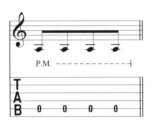

RAKE: Drag the pick across the strings indicated with a single motion.

TREMOLO PICKING: The note is picked as rapidly and continuously as possible.

ARPEGGIATE: Play the notes of the chord indicated by quickly rolling them from bottom to top.

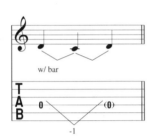

VIBRATO BAR DIVE AND RETURN: The pitch of the note or chord is dropped a specified number of steps (in rhythm), then returned to the original pitch.

VIBRATO BAR SCOOP: Depress the bar just before striking the note, then quickly release the bar.

VIBRATO BAR DIP: Strike the note and then immediately drop a specified number of steps, then release back to the original pitch.

Additional Musical Definitions

 (accent) • Accentuate note (play it louder).

 (accent) • Accentuate note with great intensity.

 (staccato) • Play the note short.

 • Downstroke

V • Upstroke

D.S. al Coda • Go back to the sign (𝄋), then play until the measure marked "*To Coda*," then skip to the section labelled "**Coda**."

D.C. al Fine • Go back to the beginning of the song and play until the measure marked "*Fine*" (end).

Rhy. Fig. • Label used to recall a recurring accompaniment pattern (usually chordal).

Riff • Label used to recall composed, melodic lines (usually single notes) which recur.

Fill • Label used to identify a brief melodic figure which is to be inserted into the arrangement.

Rhy. Fill • A chordal version of a Fill.

tacet • Instrument is silent (drops out).

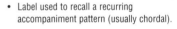 • Repeat measures between signs.

 • When a repeated section has different endings, play the first ending only the first time and the second ending only the second time.

NOTE: Tablature numbers in parentheses mean:
  1. The note is being sustained over a system (note in standard notation is tied), or
  2. The note is sustained, but a new articulation (such as a hammer-on, pull-off, slide or vibrato) begins, or
  3. The note is a barely audible "ghost" note (note in standard notation is also in parentheses).